● Collins

easy
Greek

HarperCollins Publishers
Westerhill Rd, Bishopbriggs, Glasgow, G64 2QT

www.harpercollins.co.uk

First published 2003
This edition published 2006

Reprint 10 9 8 7 6 5 4 3 2 1 0

ISBN 0 00 720837 5

A catalogue reference for this book is available from
The British Library

Consultant: Juliet A Quincey

Photography: Juliet A Quincey
Food Map: Heather Moore
Additional photography: Athens Metro (pp 27, 30, 31);
Artville (pp 93; 94 [tl]; 95 [br]; 96 [br]; 97 [tl, tr]; 98; 99 [tl];
100 [br]; 101 [br]; 102 [bl]; The Anthony Blake Photo Library
(pp 94 [tr]; 95 [tr]; 96 [tl]; 97 [bl]; 99 [br, bl]; 102 [tl, br];
103 [tl]; 104 [tl]).
Layout: The Printer's Devil, Glasgow
Layout & Origination: The Printer's Devil and
Davidson Pre-Press Graphics Ltd, Glasgow

Other titles in the Collins Easy Photo Phrase Book series:
French (0 00 720840 5)
German (0 00 720839 1)
Italian (0 00 720836 7)
Portuguese (0 00 720835 9)
Spanish (0 00 720833 2)
These titles are also published in a CD pack containing
a 60-minute CD and Easy Photo Phrase Book.

Printed in China by Imago

Contents

Useful Websites

Currency converters
www.xe.com
www.oanda.com

UK Passport Office
www.passport.gov.uk

Foreign Office travel advice
www.fco.gov.uk

Health advice
www.traveldoctor.co.uk
www.dh.gov.uk/PolicyAndGuidance/
  HealthAdviceForTravellers/fs/en

Pet advice
www.defra.gov.uk/animalh/
  quarantine/index.htm

Facts and figures
www.cia.gov/cia/publications/
  factbook/

Weather
www.bbc.co.uk/weather

Internet cafes
www.cybercafes.com

Hotels
www.hrs.com
www.greekhotels.gr

Hostels
www.hostels.com
www.europeanhostels.com

Campsites
www.greecetravel.com/campsites

Rail fares and tickets
www.raileurope.co.uk

Driving abroad
www.drivingabroad.co.uk

Skiing
www.goski.com

Ferries
www.greekferries.gr
www.ferries.gr

Railways
www.osenet.gr

Tourist info
www.willgoto.com
www.travelinfo.gr
www.greektravel.com
  (a personal view)

Greek cuisine
www.gourmed.gr

Greek Yellow Pages
www.xo.gr

Introduction

In the age of the euro, the internet and cash machines that offer a choice of languages, foreign travel might seem less of an adventure than it once was. But English is not the universal language yet, and there is much more to communication than knowing the right words for things. Once out of the airport you will not get far without some idea of the language, and also the way things are done in an unfamiliar culture. Things you might assume are the same everywhere, such as road signs and colour-coding, can turn out not to be. Red for trunk roads and skimmed milk, blue for motorways and full cream? Not everywhere! You may know the word for 'coffee' but what sort of coffee will you get? Will they understand what you mean when you say say you're a vegetarian? What times do the shops open, and which ticket gives you the best deal? *Collins Easy Photo Phrase Books* keep you up to speed with handy tips for each topic, and a wealth of pictures of signs and everyday objects to help you understand what you see around you. Even if your knowledge of the language is excellent, you may still find yourself on the back foot when trying to understand what's on offer in a restaurant, so the food and drink section features a comprehensive menu reader to make sure eating out is a pleasure.

The unique combination of practical information, photos and phrases found in this book provides the key to hassle-free travel. The colour-coding below shows how information is presented and how to access it as quickly as possible.

The food and drink section allows you to choose more easily from what is on offer, both for snacks and at restaurants.

The practical Dictionary means that you will never be stuck for words.

 General, practical information which will provide useful tips on getting the best out of your trip.

< keywords

δεξιά
dhekseea
on/to the right

αριστερά
areestera
on/to the left

these are words that are useful to know both when you see them written down or when you hear them spoken

key talk >

short, simple phrases that you can change and adapt to suit your own situation

excuse me!   can you help me?
seeghnomee   *boreete na me voeetheesete*
συγνώμη!   μπορείτε να με βοηθήσετε;

do you know where...?
kserete poo...
ξέρετε πού...;

The **Food Section** allows you to choose more easily from what is on offer both for snacks and at restaurants.

The practical **Dictionary** means that you will never be stuck for words.

Speaking Greek

In the pronunciation system in this book, Greek sounds are represented by spellings of the nearest possible sounds in English. When you read the pronunciation, sound the letters as if you were reading English (but make sure you also pronounce vowels at the end of a word). The vowels in **heavy type** show where the stress falls (in the Greek script it is marked with an accent).

The following notes should help:

	REMARKS	EXAMPLE	PRONOUNCED
gh	like French **r** at back of throat	γάλα	_gh_ala
dh	like **th** in this	δάχτυλο	_dh_akhteelo
th	like **th** in thin	θέατρο	_th_eatro
ks	like **x** in fox	ξένος	_ks_enos
r	slightly trilled **r**	ρόδα	_r_odha
kh	like **ch** in loch i.e. a rough **h**	χάνω	_kh_ano

Here are a few tricky letter combinations:

αι	met	**e**	γυναίκα	ghe_en_eka
αυ	c_af_é or h_av_e	**af** / **av**	αυτό / αύριο	_af_to / _av_reeo
ει	m_ee_t	**ee**	είκοσι	_ee_kosee
ευ	_ef_fect or _ev_ery	**ef** / **ev**	Δευτέρα / Ευρώπη	dh_ef_tera / _ev_ropee
γγ	ha_ng_	**ng**	Αγγλία	a_ng_leea
γκ	_g_et / ha_ng_	**g** / **ng**	γκάζι / άγκυρα	_g_azee / _a_ngkeera
ντ	ha_nd_ / _d_og	**nd** / **d**	αντίο / ντομάτα	a_nd_eeo / _d_omata
μπ	_b_ag	**b**	μπλούζα	_b_looza
οι	m_ee_t	**ee**	πλοίο	pl_ee_o
ου	m_oo_n	**oo**	ούζο	_oo_zo

The letters η, ι, υ, οι, and ει have the same sound **ee**. Also, αι and ε have the same sound **e** (as in m**e**t).

Vowel combinations to look out for are ευ and αυ. ευ is pronounced _ef_ or _ev_, and αυ _af_ or _av_. So ευρώ (euro) is pronounced _evro_ and αυτό (it, this) is pronounced _afto_.

Note also that the Greek question mark is a semi-colon – ;.

Everyday Talk

> There are two forms of address in Greek, formal and informal. Greek people will use the formal until they are on a first-name basis, so for the purposes of this book we will use the formal. The important thing for foreign visitors, though, is that they 'have a go' at Greek. You'll hear the greetings **ya sas** and **ya soo**. Both mean hello and bye (a bit like **ciao**), but **ya sas** is more formal.

yes	**no**	**ok/that's fine**
ne	*okhee*	*endaksee*
ναι	όχι	εντάξει

please	**thank you**	**thanks very much**
parakalo	*efkhareesto*	*efkhareesto polee*
παρακαλώ	ευχαριστώ	ευχαριστώ πολύ

don't mention it	**never mind**
parakalo	*dhen peerazee*
παρακαλώ	δεν πειράζει

hello	**hello** (informal)	**goodbye**
ya sas	*ya soo*	*andeeo*
γειά σας	γειά σου	αντίο

good morning/day	**good afternoon/evening**	**good night**
kaleemera	*kaleespera*	*kaleeneekhta*
καλημέρα	καλησπέρα	καληνύχτα

see you later	**sorry/excuse me!**	**I am sorry**
ta leme	*seeghnomee*	*leepame*
τα λέμε	συγνώμη!	λυπάμαι

I don't understand	**I don't know**
dhen katalaveno	*dhen ksero*
δεν καταλαβαίνω	δεν ξέρω

Addressing people

When addressing someone for the first time, or attracting attention, use **Κύριε** *keeree-e* (Mr), **Κυρία** *keereea* (Mrs/Ms) or **Δεσποινίς** *dhespeenees* (Miss). These titles may be used without a name, like French *Monsieur* and *Madame*. It is also quite common to use them with the person's first name.

welcome	(reply to this)
kalos eerthate/kalos oreesate	*kalos sas vreekame*
καλώς ήρθατε/καλώς ορίσατε	καλώς σάς βρήκαμε

how are you?	**fine, thanks**	**and you?**
pos eeste	*polee kala efkhareesto*	*esees*
πώς είστε;	πολύ καλά ευχαριστώ	εσείς;

*Asking for something in a shop or bar, you would ask for what you want, adding **parakalo**.*

keywords keywords keywords

1	ένα ena
2	δύο dheeo
3	τρία treea
4	τέσσερα tesera
5	πέντε pende
6	έξι eksee
7	επτά epta
8	οκτώ okhto
9	εννέα ene-a
10	δέκα dheka

a...
ena... (o words)
ένα...

meea... (η words)
μία...

ena... (το words)
ένα...

an iced coffee please
ena frape parakalo
ένα φραπέ παρακαλώ

a beer please
meea beera parakalo
μία μπύρα παρακαλώ

a tea please
ena tsaee parakalo
ένα τσάι παρακαλώ

the menu please
ton katalogho parakalo
τον κατάλογο παρακαλώ

the bill please
to logharyasmo parakalo
το λογαριασμό παρακαλώ

my...
...moo
...μου

my passport
to dheeavateereeo moo
το διαβατήριό μου

my room
to dhomateeo moo
το δαμάτιο μου

my key
to kledhee moo
το κλειδί μου

my suitcase
ee valeetsa moo
το βαλίτσα μου

To catch someone's attention

The easiest way to catch someone's attention is with **συγνώμη!** *seeghnomee*. Note that the word no in Greek, **όχι** *okhee*, is often accompanied by an upward tilting of the face, or slight raising of the eyebrows and a click of the tongue. You may think that this is a nod for yes, rather than a no!

excuse me!
seeghnomee
συγνώμη!

do you know where...?
kserete poo...
ξέρετε πού...;

can you help me?
boreete na me voeetheesete
μπορείτε να με βοηθήσετε;

By combining key words and phrases you can build up your language and adapt the phrases to suit your own situation.

ekhete... **do you have...?**	**do you have a map?** *ekhete ena khartee* έχετε ένα χάρτη;	**do you have a room?** *ekhete ena dhomateeo* έχετε ένα δωμάτιο;
poso kanee **how much is it?**	**how much is the cheese?** *poso kanee to teeree* πόσο κάνει το τυρί;	**how much is the ticket?** *poso kanee to eeseeteereeo* πόσο κάνει το εισιτήριο;
tha eethela... **I'd like...**	**I'd like a slice of gateau** *tha eethela meea pasta* θα ήθελα μία πάστα	**I'd like an ice cream** *tha eethela ena paghoto* θα ήθελα ένα παγωτό
khreeazome... **I need...**	**I need a taxi** *khreeazome ena taksee* χρειάζομαι ένα ταξί	**I need a receipt** *khreeazome meea apodheeksee* χρειάζομαι μία απόδειξη
pote **when?**	**when does it open?** *pote aneeghee* πότε ανοίγει;	**when does it close?** *pote kleenee* πότε κλείνει;
	when does it leave? *pote fevyee* πότε φεύγει;	**when does it arrive?** *pote ftanee* πότε φτάνει;
poo **where?**	**where is the bank?** *poo eene ee trapeza* πού είναι η τράπεζα;	**where is the hotel?** *poo eene to ksenodhokheeo* πού είναι το ξενοδοχείο;
ekhee... **is there...?**	**is there a market?** *ekhee la-eekee aghora* έχει λαϊκή αγορά	**where is there a market?** *poo ekhee la-eekee aghora* πού έχει λαϊκή αγορά;
dhen ekhee... **there is no...**	**there is no bread** *dhen ekhee psomee* δεν έχει ψωμί	**there is no hot water** *dhen ekhee zesto nero* δεν έχει ζεστό νερό
boro na... **can I...?**	**can I smoke?** *boro na kapneeso* μπορώ να καπνίσω;	
	can I hire a car? *boro na neekyaso ena aftokeeneeto* μπορώ να νοικιάσω ένα αυτοκίνητο;	
	where can I buy bread? *poo boro na aghoraso psomee* πού μπορώ να αγοράσω ψωμί;	
eene... **is it...?**	**is it near?** *eene konda* είναι κοντά;	**is it far?** *eene makreea* είναι μακριά;

These are a selection of small but very useful words.

keywords keywords keywords keywords keywords keywords

μεγάλο
meghalo
big

μικρό
meekro
little

λίγο   πολύ
leegho   polee
a little   a lot

αρκετά
arketa
enough

κοντά   μακριά
konda   makreea
near   far

κοντινότερο
kondeenotero
nearest

πολύ ακριβό
polee akreevo
too expensive

και
ke
and

με   χωρίς
me   khorees
with   without

... μου
... moo
my...

αυτό   εκείνο
afto   ekeeno
this one   that one

αμέσως
amesos
straight away

αργότερα
arghotera
later

a large car
ena meghalo aftokeeneeto
ένα μεγάλο αυτοκίνητο

a small beer
meea meekree beera
μία μικρή μπίρα

a little please
leegho parakalo
λίγο παρακαλώ

a lot please
polee parakalo
πολύ παρακαλώ

that's enough thanks
arketa efkhareesto
αρκετά ευχαριστώ

where is the nearest chemist?
poo eene to kondeenotero farmakeeo
πού είναι το κοντινότερο φαρμακείο;

it is too expensive
eene polee akreevo
είναι πολύ ακριβό

it is too small
eene polee meekro
είναι πολύ μικρό

a tea and an iced coffee
ένα τσάι και ένα φραπέ
ena tsaee ke ena frappé

with milk
me ghala
με γάλα

with ice
me paghakeea
με παγάκια

without sugar
khorees zakharee
χωρίς ζάχαρη

without ice
khorees paghakeea
χωρίς παγάκια

for me   for her
για μένα   γι' αυτήν
ya mena   yafteen

for him   for us
γι' αυτόν   για μας
yafton   ya mas

my passport
to dheeavateereeo moo
το διαβατήριό μου

my key
to kleedhee moo
το κλειδί μου

I'd like this one
tha eethela afto
θα ήθελα αυτό

I'd like that one
tha eethela ekeeno
θα ήθελα εκείνο

I need a taxi straight away
khreeazome taksee amesos
χρειάζομαι ταξί αμέσως

is it safe?
eene asfales
είναι ασφαλές;

I'll phone back later
tha ksanaparo arghotera
θα ξαναπάρω αργότερα

It is always good to be able to say a few words about yourself to break the ice, even if you won't be able to tell your life story.

what's your name?
pos se lene
πώς σε λένε;

my name is...
me lene...
με λένε...

I'm from England
eeme apo teen angleea
είμαι από την Αγγλία

I'm from America
eeme apo teen amereekee
είμαι από την Αμερική

where do you live?
poo menees
πού μένεις;

where do you live? (plural)
poo menete
πού μένετε;

I'm single
eeme elefther-os(-ee)
είμαι ελεύθερος(-η)

I'm married
eeme pandremen-os(-ee)
είμαι παντρεμένος(-η)

I'm divorced
eeme khoreesmen-os(-ee)
είμαι χωρισμένος(-η)

I have...
ekho...
έχω...

a boyfriend
ena feelo
ένα φίλο

a girlfriend
meea feelee
μία φιλη

I have ... children
ekho ... pedheea
έχω ... παιδιά

I have no children
dhen ekho pedheea
δεν έχω παιδιά

I'm here on holiday
vreeskome edho ya dheeakopes
βρίσκομαι εδώ για διακοπές

I'm here for work
vreeskome edho ya dhooleea
βρίσκομαι εδώ για δουλειά

where do you live?
poo menees
πού μένεις;

I live in Glasgow
zo stee ghlaskovee
ζω στη Γλασκώβη

you have a beautiful home
ekhete oreo speetee
έχετε ωραίο σπίτι

the meal was delicious
to fagheeto eetan nosteemotato
το φαγητο ήταν νοστιμότατο

this is a gift for you
eene ena dhoro ya sas
είναι ένα δώρο για σας

pleased to meet you
khareeka ya tee ghnoreemeea
χάρηκα για τη γνωριμία

this is my husband
apo dho o seezeeghos moo
από 'δω ο σύζυγός μου

this is my wife
apo dho ee seezeeghos moo
από 'δω η σύζυγός μου

thanks for your hospitality
efkhareesto ya teen feelokseneea
ευχαριστώ για την φιλοξενία

I've enjoyed myself very much
perasa polee oraya
πέρασα πολύ ωραία

what is your address?
pya eene ee dheeeftheensee sas
ποιά είναι η διεύθυνσή σας;

i *Although problems are not something anyone wants, you might come across the odd difficulty, and it is best to be armed with a few phrases to cope with the situation.*

excuse me!
seeghn*o*mee
συγνώμη!

can you help me?
bor*ee*te na me voeeth*ee*sete
μπορείτε να με βοηθήσετε;

I don't speak Greek
dhen meela*o* eleen*ee*ka
δεν μιλάω Ελληνικά

do you speak English?
meel*a*te angleek*a*
μιλάτε Αγγλικά;

I'm lost
ekho khath*ee*
έχω χαθεί

how do I get to...?
pos bor*o* na pao sto/st*ee*...
πώς μπορώ να πάω στο/στη...;

I've lost...
ekhasa...
έχασα...

my purse
to portof*o*lee moo
το πορτοφόλι μου

my keys
ta kleedhya moo
τα κλειδιά μου

I've left my bag in...
ksekhasa teen tsanda moo...
ξέχασα την τσάντα μου...

on the bus
sto leofor*ee*o
στο λεωφορείο

on the boat
sto pl*ee*o
στο πλοίο

I've missed...
ekhasa...
έχασα...

my flight
teen pt*ee*see moo
την πτήση μου

my connection
teen andap*o*kreesee moo
την ανταπόκριση

I'm late
ekho argh*ee*see
έχω αργήσει

I need to get to...
pr*e*pee na ftaso sto...
πρέπει να φτάσω στο...

I have no money
dhen *e*kho khr*ee*mata
δεν έχω χρήματα

my luggage hasn't arrived
ee aposkeves moo dhen eftasan
οι αποσκευές μου δεν έφτασαν

this is my address
aft*ee* *ee*ne ee dhee*ee*ftheensee moo
αυτή είναι η διεύθυνση μου

I'm sorry
leepame
λυπάμαι

I didn't know
dhen *ee*ksera
δεν ήξερα

this is broken
espase aft*o*
έσπασε αυτό

where can I get this repaired?
poo tha moo to epeeskevas*oon*
πού θα μου το επισκευάσουν;

someone's stolen my...
kap*ee*os moo eklepse...
κάποιος μου έκλεψε...

handbag
teen tsanda
την τσάντα

traveller's cheques
tees takseedheeot*ee*kes epeetagh*e*s
τις ταξιδιωτικές επιταγές

leave me alone!
af*ee*ste me *ee*seekho
αφήστε με ήσυχο!

go away!
f*ee*yete
φύγετε!

Greeks like to receive good service and quality. They will complain when things are not as they ought to be.

there is no...
dhen ekhee...
δεν έχει...

there is no toilet paper
dhen ekhee khartee tooaletas
δεν έχει χαρτί τουαλέτας

there is no hot water
dhen ekhee zesto nero
δεν έχει ζεστό νερό

there is no bread
dhen ekhee psomee
δεν έχει ψωμί

it is dirty
eene vromeeko
είναι βρώμικο

the bath is dirty
to banyo eene vromeeko
το μπάνιο είναι βρώμικο

it is broken
khalase
χάλασε

can you repair it?
boreete na to epeedheeorthosete
μπορείτε να το επιδιορθώσετε;

the shower doesn't work
to doos dhen dhoolevee
το ντους δεν δουλεύει

the light	**the telephone**	**...doesn't work**
to fos	*to teelefono*	*...dhen dhoolevee*
το φως	το τηλέφωνο	...δεν δουλεύει

the toilet	**the heating**	**...doesn't work**
ee tooaleta	*ee thermansee*	*...dhen dhoolevee*
η τουαλέτα	η θέρμανση	...δεν δουλεύει

it is too noisy
ekhee polee thoreevo
έχει πολύ θόρυβο

I didn't order this
dhen zeeteesa afto
δεν ζήτησα αυτό

I want to complain
thelo na kano parapona
θέλω να κάνω παράπονα

I want a refund
thelo ta lefta moo peeso
θέλω τα λεφτά μου πίσω

we've been waiting for a long time
pereemenoome polee ora
περιμένουμε πολή ώρα

we're in a hurry
eemaste veeasteekee
είμαστε βιαστικοί

it's very expensive
eene polee akreevo
είναι πολύ ακριβό

where is the manager?
poo eene o dheeeftheendees
πού είναι ο διευθυντής;

there is a mistake
egheene lathos
έγινε λάθος

Everyday Greece

 The next four pages should give you an idea of the type of things you will come across in Greece.

entrance *ee*sodhos

ΕΞΟΔΟΣ

exit *e*ksodhos

ΕΛΞΑΤΕ

pull *e*lksate

ΩΘΗΣΑΤΕ

push ot*hee*sate

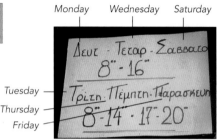

Monday   Wednesday   Saturday

Tuesday —
Thursday —
Friday —

Shops generally open in the morning (8–9am until 1–2pm) and again in the evening (approx 5–8pm). They close in the afternoon and all day Sunday. However, in busy tourist areas they usually open all day every day.

 The euro symbol. Greece is in the euro zone.

kiosk per*ee*ptero
These kiosks sell all kinds of things including maps, postcards, stamps, cigarettes, snacks and drinks. They often have a payphone and will give directions.

Tickets on sale for the lottery, which is drawn twice a week.

talking	**do you have...?**	**stamps**	**phonecards**
	ekhete...	*ghramatoseema*	*teelekartes*
	έχετε...;	γραμματόσημα	τηλεκάρτες
	where can I buy...?	**bread**	**tickets**
	poo boro na aghoraso...	*psomee*	*eeseeteereea*
	πού μπορώ να αγοράσω...;	ψωμί	εισιτήρια

welcome

Greek people may say this (*kalos eelthate*) to you. They like you to feel welcome in their country, and appreciate it if you try to speak the language, however tentatively.

ΔΩΜΑΤΙΑ

rooms *dhomateea*

All over Greece you can find rooms to rent, usually with car-parking space. If there are no signs, just ask.

open *aneekto*

closed *kleesto*

The Greek alphabet can seem daunting. But if you learn it, the language will come alive.

Greece is full of friendly little cafe-bars. Greeks are generally welcoming towards foreigners, although in Athens people are usually less friendly than elsewhere, and can seem rude.

$\delta \Delta = d$
$\eta H = e$
$\lambda \Lambda = l$
$\mu M = m$
$\nu N = n$
$\xi \Xi = x$
$\pi \Pi = p$
$\rho P = r$

Capital letters are written differently from lower case letters. These are ones that might fool you.

TAMEIO

pay here/cash desk *tameeo*

Greek post boxes are yellow and it is usually quite easy to find one. Red boxes are for express post around Athens. Times of collections are sometimes on the box. **EΛTA** is the Greek postal company.

---

excuse me!
seeghnomee
συγνώμη!

can you show me?
boreete na moo dheeksete
μπορείτε να μου δείξετε;

how does this work?
pos dhoolevee afto
πώς δουλεύει αυτό;

what does this mean?
tee seemenee afto
τι σημαίνει αυτό;

talking

Feel free to ask for all kinds of information, about the local area and Greece in general.

information

out of order

British & US papers are sold in cities and tourist areas in the summer.

closed *happy holidays!*

danger *keendheenos*

no smoking

A service charge is generally included in bills and tipping is a matter of choice. Some Greeks tip, some don't, so there is no obligation. It's entirely up to you.

can I smoke here?
boro na kapneeso edho
μπορώ να καπνίσω εδώ;

I don't smoke
dhen kapneezo
δεν καπνίζω

an ashtray please
ena tassakee parakalo
ένα τασάκι παρακαλώ

do you mind if I smoke?
sas peerazee na kapneeso
σας πειράζει να καπνίσω;

please don't smoke
parakalo mee kapneezete
παρακαλώ μην καπνίζετε

a non-smoking table please
ena trapezee ya mee kapneestes parakalo
ένα τραπέζι για μή καπνιστές παρακαλώ

There are a few public toilets in Greece, but not many. There may be a small charge. Otherwise look for toilets in shopping centres, department stores and petrol stations. Bars, snack bars etc will let you use the toilet but of course it's polite to buy a drink first – cans of soda or small bottles of water are cheap! It is wise to carry tissues at all times. A word about Greek plumbing: because of the sewerage system, all (yes, **all**) toilet paper **must** be deposited in the bin beside the toilet, not thrown into the toilet bowl. This applies wherever you are in Greece. It may seem strange, but please abide by this rule, otherwise the drains get blocked and some unfortunate person has the task of removing all the toilet paper from the pipes.

gents andhron

ladies yeenekon

PLEASE DO NOT THROW PAPER OR OTHER OBJECTS INTO THE TOILET BOWL.

ΤΟΥΑΛΕΤΕΣ

toilets tooaletes

hot zesto   **cold** kreeo

Watch out as sometimes you find that someone has swapped the tap colours round and you get hot water from the cold tap!

Greek toilets have very narrow plumbing and you must put toilet paper in the wastebins provided, rather than in the toilet.

excuse me! where is the toilet?
seeghnomee! poo eene ee tooaleta
συγνώμη! πού είναι η τουαλέτα;

may I use the toilet?
boro na pao steen tooaleta
μπορώ να πάω στην τουαλέτα;

do you have toilets for the disabled?
ekhete tooaletes ya anapeeroos
έχετε τουαλέτες για ανάπηρους;

the toilet doesn't work
ee tooaleta dhen leetoorghee
η τουαλέτα δεν λειτουργεί

do I need a key?
khreeazome kleedhee
χρειάζομαι κλειδί;

talking talking

Asking the Way

Tourist offices usually have free maps, in addition to brochures and leaflets about local attractions, trips etc. They can also help you with accommodation, transport and general information. You can buy all kinds of different maps at bookshops, newsagents and at traditional Greek kiosks (pereeptera). Pereeptera can be seen on many street corners. They sell a multitude of things and often have a pay phone, too.

office of tourism   Syntagma Square

tourist information office

Local maps are often available free from Tourist offices. You can also buy them cheaply at newsagent's or kiosks.

talking talking

excuse me!	**I'm looking**	**for...**
seeghnomee	psakhno ya	to (with o and το words)/tee (with η words)...
συγνώμη!	ψάχνω για	το/τη...

I'm looking for the station
psakhno ya to stathmo
ψάχνω για το το σταθμό

do you know where...? — **do you know where the tourist office is?**
kserete poo eene... — kserete poo eene to ghrafeeo tooreesmoo
ξέρετε πού είναι...; — ξέρετε πού είναι το γραφείο τουρισμού;

how do I get? — **to...**
pos boro na pao — sto (with o and το words)/stee (with η words)...
πώς μπορώ να πάω; — στο/στη...

where is...? — **where is the hotel?**
poo eene... — poo eene to ksenodhokheeo
πού είναι...; — πού είναι το ξενοδοχείο;

is it far? — **where is the nearest...?**
eene makreea — poo eene to kondeenotero...
είναι μακριά; — πού είναι το κοντινότερο...;

Brown signs show the way to local places of interest. Plaka is the area beneath the Acropolis which is full of lively bars, shops and restaurants.

to the Holy Church of Saint Kharalambos

Sites of historical interest often have English translations.

ΟΔΟΣ *odhos* road, street

ΑΠΟ *apo* from (8–2)

left *areestera*   right *dhekseea*

δεξιά
dhekhseea
to the right

αριστερά
areestera
to the left

ευθεία μπροστα
eftheea brosta
straight ahead

δρόμος
dhromos
road

πρώτο δρόμο
δεξιά
*proto dhromo
dhekseea*
first on right

δεύτερο δρόμο
αριστερά
*dheftero dhromo
areestera*
second on left

πλατεία
plateea
square

φανάρια
fanareea
traffic lights

δίπλα στο
dheepla sto
next to

κοντά στο
konda sto
near to

απέναντι
apenandee
opposite

από δω   από κει
apodo   apokee
this way   that way

πήγαινε
peeghene
go

στρίψε
streepse
turn

keywords keywords keywords keywords keywords

Banks & Money

i

Banking hours are usually 8am till 2pm Monday–Thursday and 8am till 1pm on Friday, but check opening-hours signs just to make sure. You can change cash and travellers' cheques at banks, travel agencies and at some hotels, but it's a good idea to check out the best exchange rate and ask about the commission before deciding where to change your money. It's also very easy to find a 24-hour ATM (cash machine). ATMs accept Switch, Maestro, Cirrus and most credit cards.

Prices are in euros.

TIMH: 13, 60 EYPΩ

price *teemee*   **euro** *evro*

These are two of the major banks in Greece. The Greek word for bank is τράπεζα *trapeza*.

You will find 24-hour cash machines at many banks and in tourist areas, with instructions in English, French, German and Italian.

24-hour indoor cash machine; swipe your card to get in.

Cash machine interface is as you would find at home.

Travel agents as well as banks offer exchange services; signs for these are usually in English.

Notes: 5, 10, 20, 50, 100, 200, 500

Coins: 2 euro, 1 euro, 50 cent, 20 cent, 10 cent, 5 cent, 2 cent, 1 cent

Greece's currency is the euro, ευρώ (*evro*), which breaks down into 100 euro cents. Euro notes are the same across Europe. The coins are officially cents, but Greek people call them λεπτά (*lepta*) The reverse of the coins carry different designs in each European member country.

where can I change money?
poo boro na alakso khreemata
πού μπορώ να αλλάξω χρήματα;

where is there a bank?
poo eene meea trapeza
πού είναι μία τράπεζα;

where is there a bureau de change?
poo eene ena enalakteereeo seenalaghmatos
πού είναι ένα εναλλακτήριο συναλλάγματος;

when does the bank open?
pote aneeghee ee trapeza
πότε ανοίγει η τράπεζα;

when does the bank close?
pote kleenee ee trapeza
πότε κλείνει η τράπεζα;

where is there a cash dispenser?
poo ekhee ena ay tee em
πού έχει ένα ay tee em;

I want to cash these traveller's cheques
tha eethela na alakso afta ta takseedhyoteeka tsek
θα ήθελα να αλλάξω αυτά τα ταξιδιωτικά τσεκ

When is...?

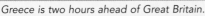

Greece is two hours ahead of Great Britain.
Π.μ. *means am* (**προ μεσημβρίας** *pro meseemvreeas – before midday*).
Μ.μ. *means pm* (**μετά μεσημβρίας** *meta meseemvreeas after midday*).

keywords keywords keywords

		at ...
πρωί proee **morning**	13:00	*stees dhekatreea* στις δεκατρία
απόγευμα apoyevma **afternoon**	14:00	*stees dhekatesera* στις δεκατέσσερα
απόψε apopse **this evening**	15:00	*stees dhekapende* στις δεκαπέντε
σήμερα seemera **today**	16:00	*stees dhekaeksee* στις δεκαέξι
χθές khthes **yesterday**	17:00	*stees dhekaefta* στις δεκαεφτά
αύριο avreeo **tomorrow**	18:00	*stees dhekaokto* στις δεκαοκτώ
τώρα tora **now**	19:00	*stees dhekaenea* στις δεκαεννέα
τότε tote **then**	20:00	*stees eekosee* στις είκοσι
αργότερα arghotera **later**	21:00	*stees eekosee ena* στις είκοσι ένα
	22:00	*stees eekosee dheeo* στις είκοσι δύο
	23:00	*stees eekosee treea* στις είκοσι τρία
	24:00	*stees eekosee tesera* στις είκοσι τέσσερα

talking

when is the next...?	train	bus	boat	to...?
pote eene to epomeno...	*treno*	*leoforeeo*	*pleeo*	*ya...*
πότε είναι το επόμενο...;	τραίνο	λεωφορείο	πλοίο	για...;

when does it open?	when does it close?
pote aneeghee	*pote kleenee*
πότε ανοίγει;	πότε κλείνει;

what time is...?	breakfast	dinner
tee ora serveerete...	*to proeeno*	*to vradheeno*
τι ώρα σερβίρεται...;	το πρωινό	το βραδυνό

when does it leave?	when does it arrive?
pote fevyee	*pote ftanee*
πότε φεύγει;	πότε φτάνει;

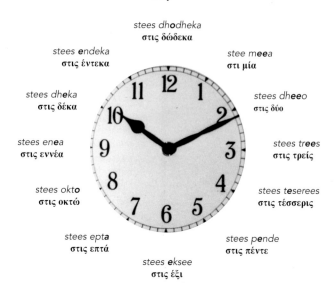

at ...
stees ...
στις

stees dh**o**dheka
στις δώδεκα

stees **e**ndeka
στις έντεκα

stee m**ee**a
στι μία

stees dh**e**ka
στις δέκα

stees dh**ee**o
στις δύο

stees en**e**a
στις εννέα

stees trees
στις τρείς

stees okt**o**
στις οκτώ

stees tes**e**rees
στις τέσσερις

stees ept**a**
στις επτά

stees p**e**nde
στις πέντε

stees **e**ksee
στις έξι

at 25 to...	at ... thirty	at a quarter past...
stees ... para tree**a**nta pente	stees ... ke mee**se**e	stees ... ke tet**a**rto
στις ... παρά τριάντα πέντε	στις ... και μισή	στις ... και τέταρτο

at midnight	at midday
ta mesan**ee**khta	to mese**e**meree
τα μεσάνυχτα	το μεσημέρι

what time is it please?	it's 9 o'clock
tee **o**ra **ee**ne parakal**o**	**ee**ne en**e**a ee **o**ra
τι ώρα είναι, παρακαλώ;	είναι εννέα η ώρα

in an hour's time	in a while	two hours ago
se m**ee**a **o**ra	se l**ee**gho	preen ap**o** dh**ee**o **o**res
σε μία ώρα	σε λίγο	πριν από δύο ώρες

what's the date today?	which month?
tee eemeromeen**ee**a **e**khoome s**ee**mera	pyos m**ee**nas
τι ημερομηνία έχουμε σήμερα;	ποιός μήνας;

it's the 5th of August 2006
eene ee p**e**mtee avgh**oo**stoo dh**ee**o kheelee**a**dhes **e**ksee
είναι η 5η Αυγούστου 2006

talking

Timetables

i *Key words to look out for are* **καθημερινές** *(katheemereenes)*
meaning weekday (i.e. Monday–Saturday) and **Κυριακές και γιορτές**
(keereeyakes ke yortes) meaning Sundays and public holidays. Timetables
vary according to whether they are **θερινές** *(thereenes – summer) or*
χειμερινές *(kheemereenes – winter).*

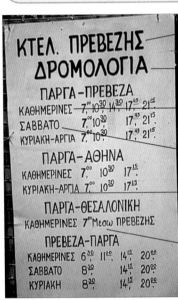

Timetable for long-distance coaches to
Preveza, Athens and Thessalonika.

ΚΤΕΛ. *(KTEL)*
Greek national
bus/coach service

ΔΡΟΜΟΛΟΓΙΑ
services
dromologheea

ΚΑΘΗΜΕΡΙΝΕΣ
weekdays
katheemereeenes

ΣΑΒΒΑΤΟ
Saturday
savato

ΚΥΡΙΑΚΗ-ΑΡΓΙΑ
Sunday-holiday
*keereeakee-
argheea*

Μέσω *via*
meso

Δευτέρα
dheftera
Monday

Τρίτη
treetee
Tuesday

Τετάρτη
tetartee
Wednesday

Πέμπτη
pemptee
Thursday

Παρασκευή
paraskevee
Friday

Σάββατο
savato
Saturday

Κυριακή
keereeakee
Sunday

In Greek days
of the week
begin with a
capital letter,
as do months
of the year.
Signs are
often written
in capital
letters.

09.00 π.μ.
9am

13.00 μ.μ.
1pm

today

---

talk

have you a timetable?
ekhete to orareeo
έχετε το ωράριο;

when does it leave?
pote fevyee
πότε φεύγει;

when does it arrive?
pote ftanee
πότε φτάνει;

Timetables, especially in tourist areas, will often have English translations alongside the Greek.

ΑΦΙΞΕΙΣ

arrivals afeeksees

ΑΝΑΧΩΡΗΣΕΙΣ

departures anakhoreesees

time ora

weekdays   *Saturdays*   — *Sundays*

Bus station timetable board showing local and longer-distance routes.

Tickets

In Athens, tickets for the Metro, bus, trolley-bus and trains must be validated. Keep your ticket till the end of your journey. On the Metro, buy your ticket (at the desk or from a machine) and validate it as you walk past the validating machines. On the buses you will see the validating machines as you get on. Other cities have a similar ticketing system to Athens, although Athens alone has a Metro. In the rural areas, buy a ticket and keep it throughout the journey.

You can buy a range of tickets for the Athens metro. This is a single-journey ticket.

Athens local bus ticket

24-hour unlimited travel on bus, trolley or metro.

note the Greek for euro

Another type of Athens local bus ticket.

Inter-city train ticket
All information is printed in English as well as in Greek.

You have to validate any ticket
you buy for public transport in a
validating machine. These are found
at the entrance of buses, train platforms
and metro stations, as shown here.
Simply insert your ticket in the slot
for punching.

cinema ticket
booth

price of ticket

price for students

ticket prices

Most signs will have translations. The word for ticket
is *eeseeteereeo* and the plural is *eeseeteereea*.

keywords

εισιτήριο
eeseeteereeo
ticket

απλό
aplo
single

με επιστροφή
me epeestro-fee
return

ημερήσιο
εισιτήριο
*eemereeseeo
eeseeteereeo*
all day ticket

εισιτήριο
διαρκείας
*eeseeteereeo
deearkheeas*
season ticket

ταξιδιωτικό
πάσο
*takseedheeot
eeko paso*
travel pass

ολόκληρο
olokleero
adult

παιδικό
pedeeko
child

οικογενειακό
eekoyenee-ako
family

φοιτητικό
feeteeteeko
student

ηλικιωμένων
eelee-keeomenon
over 60

αναπηρικό
anapeereeko
disabled

Public Transport

Buses and trains are reasonably priced and reliable. There are good bus services within cities and regular long-distance coaches catering for people in towns and in country villages. Tickets are bought from a ticket office or on the bus in rural areas. Because Greece is so mountainous, the railway system is more limited. There is a line from Athens to Thessalonika and from Thessalonika across to the Turkish border. There is also a line from Athens to Patras and around the Peloponnese, which is very scenic. You buy tickets at the stations.

bus station

A bus-stop in Athens showing where this Averof IKA stop is on the bus-route.

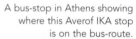

Bus stop with route numbers.

ticket office

bus stop *stasee*

In Athens you can catch trolley-buses like this, or city buses or the Metro.

You can buy bus and trolley-bus tickets here.

ΚΑΡΤΕΣ = *cards*
ΚΑΙ = *and*
ΕΙΣΙΤΗΡΙΑ = *tickets*

where is the bus to the centre?
poo eene to leforeeo ya to kendro
πού είναι το λεωφορείο για το κέντρο;

which bus goes to Pireus?
pyo leforeeo pa-ee ston peeraya
ποιο λεωφορείο πάει στον Πειραιά;

to the station
sto stathmo
στο σταθμό

to the museum
sto mooseeo
στο μουσείο

to the Acropolis
steen akropolee
στην Ακρόπολη

to Plaka
steen plaka
στην Πλάκα

where is this bus going to?
poo pa-ee afto to leforeeo
πού πάει αυτό το λεωφορείο;

where is the bus station?
poo eene o stathmos leforeeon
πού είναι ο σταθμός λεωφορείων;

where is the bus stop?
poo eene ee stasee too leforeeoo
πού είναι η στάση του λεωφορείου;

talking talking talking

The new Metro in Athens is very impressive. It is built in pink and grey marble and contains many exhibits of archaeological discoveries made during construction. Security is high there: there is no smoking, no eating/drinking and most definitely no graffiti. It opens at 5.30am and closes at midnight. A ticket is valid for one single journey of any length.You can also get a ticket valid for 24 hours (as many trips as you want) The 24 hour ticket is also valid for use on the buses, trolley-buses and trains in the same period of time.

Metro symbol with station name and network map below.

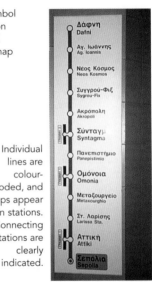

Individual lines are colour-coded, and maps appear in stations. Connecting stations are clearly indicated.

Προς Δάφνη To Dafni

Overhead direction indicator in station.

Athens' Metro system is modern.

ticket office

Έκδοση Εισιτηρίων
Tickets Issue

Automatic ticket machines in the Athens Metro are easy to use and are multilingual.

In the Metro you must validate your ticket in one of these machines and then keep it during your journey.

where is the nearest metro station?
poo eene o kondeenoteros stathmos too metro
πού είναι ο κοντινότερος σταθμός του μετρό;

one ticket
ena eeseeteereeo
ένα εισιτήριο

4 tickets please
tessera eeseeteereea parakalo
τέσσερα εισιτήρια παρακαλώ

have you a map of the metro?
ekhete khartee ya to metro
έχετε χάρτη για το μετρό;

I want to go to...
thelo na pao sto/stee...
θέλω να πάω στο/στη...

can I go by underground?
boro na pao me to metro
μπορώ να πάω με το μετρό;

do I have to change?
prepee nalakso ghramee
πρέπει ν'αλλάξω γραμμή;

where?
poo
πού;

which line do I take?
pya ghrammee prepee na paro
ποια γραμμή πρέπει να πάρω;

excuse me!
me seeghkhoreete
με συγχωρείτε!

I'm getting off
kateveno
κατεβαίνω

talking talking talking talking talking

i Because Greece is so mountainous the train service is quite limited, but inexpensive. Trains tend to be rather slow and do not go to more remote areas or many places of archaeological interest. The initials of the Greek National Railway are **ΟΣΕ** and you can visit their website for details of trains and timetables on **www.ose.gr**. Tickets can be bought at railway stations and travel agents. However, you must remember (as with all other forms of public transport) to validate your ticket at the validating machines in the station before you begin your journey.

ΕΙΣΙΤΗΡΙΑ ΕΣΩΤΕΡΙΚΟΥ
ΠΛΗΝ ΑΜΑΞ/ΧΙΩΝ INTERCITY

Tickets within greece except intercity tickets.

ΑΘΗΝΑΙ
ATHINE

Athens station

waiting room

talking talking talking

a single to...
ena aplo eeseeteereeo ya...
ένα απλό εισιτήριο για...

2 singles to...
dheeo apla eeseeteereea ya...
δύο απλά εισιτήρια για...

a return to...
ena eeseeteereeo me epeestrofee ya...
ένα εισιτήριο με επιστροφή για...

2 returns to...
dheeo eeseeteereea me epeestrofee ya...
δύο εισιτήρια με επιστροφή για...

a child's ticket to...
ena pedheeko eeseeteereeo ya...
ένα παιδικό εισητήριο για...

he/she is ... years old
eene ... khronon
είναι ... χρονών

I want to book 2 seats
thelo na kleeso dheeo thesees
θέλω να κλείσω δύο θέσεις

economy class
tooreesteekee thesee
τουριστική θέση

smoking
kapneezontes
καπνίζοντες

non smoking
mee kapneezontes
μη καπνίζοντες

is there a supplement to pay?
eeparkhee epeepleon epeevareensee
υπάρχει επιπλέον επιβάρυνση;

Arrivals and departures board in the station.
In major stations, information is displayed in
both Greek and English, alternating continually.

Automatic
ticket
machine in
the railway
station.
Instructions
are available
in English
as well as
Greek.

Overhead departure board on platform.

απλό
aplo
single

μετ επιστροφής
met epeestrofees
return

κράτηση
krateesee
reservation

επιτρέπεται το
κάπνισμα
*epeetrepete to
kapneesma*
**smoking is
allowed**

απαγορεύεται το
κάπνισμα
*apagorevete to
kapneesma*
non-smoking

γραφείο εισιτηρίων
*grafeeo
eesseeteereeon*
ticket office

γραφείο αποσκευών
grafeeo aposkevon
left luggage

βαγόνι
vagonee
carriage

πλατφόρμα
platforma
platform

which platform does it leave from?
apo pya platforma fevyee
από ποια πλατφόρμα φεύγει;

is this seat free?
eene ee thesee elevtheree
είναι η θέση ελεύθερη;

is this the train for...?
afto eene to treno ya...
αυτό είναι το τρένο για...;

this is my seat
aftee eene ee thesee moo
αυτή είναι η θέση μου

talking

Taxi

Taxis abound in Greece. Each town has its own colour for taxis. Taxis in Athens are yellow. It is easy to flag them down in cities, as the local people do. You can also ask at a kiosk for the phone number of a taxi firm, or ask your hotel to call a taxi for you. Tipping is not all that common in Greece but small tips are always gratefully received.

You can ring for a taxi, wait at a stand or flag one down in the street.

Taxis are quite cheap, but you should still ask the price beforehand. The grey taxis are for long-distance journeys, i.e. town to town.

A taxi stand and phone in a small town.

All taxis have meters.

where can I get a taxi?
poo boro na vro taksee
πού μπορώ να βρω ταξί;

please take me to this address
se afteen teen dheeevtheensee parakalo
σε αυτήν την διεύθυνση, παρακαλώ

how much will it cost?
poso kosteezee
πόσο κοστίζει;

how much is to the centre?
poso kosteezee ya to kentro
πόσο κοστίζει για το κέντρο;

can I have a receipt?
boreete na moo dhosete apodheeksee
μπορείτε να μου δώσετε απόδειξη;

to the airport
sto aerodhromeeo
στο αεροδρόμιο

it's too much
eene polee akreeva
είναι πολύ ακριβά

please order me a taxi
parakalo kaleste ena taksee
παρακαλώ καλέστε ένα ταξί

keep the change
krateeste ta resta
κρατήστε τα ρέστα

You will find all the major car-hire companies in Greece, plus various local ones. You can also book a car from abroad, before your trip, and the car should be waiting for you at the airport – usually a cheap, easy option. Within Greece, restrictions vary. You HAVE to have held a driving licence for at least one year, but the minimum age differs between companies from 21–25. Some companies charge supplements for young drivers. A few local companies will let you rent a car at age 20.

I want to hire a car
thelo na neekyaso ena aftokeeneeto
θέλω να νοικιάσω ένα αυτοκίνητο

for one day
ya meea mera
για μία μέρα

for ... days
ya ... meres
για ... μέρες

I prefer a...
proteemo ena...
προτιμώ ένα ...

large
meghalo
μεγάλο

small
meekro
μικρό

car
aftokeeneeto
αυτοκίνητο

how much is it...?
poso kanee...
πόσο κάνει...;

per day
tee mera
τη μέρα

per week
teen evdhomadha
την εβδομάδα

how much is the deposit?
posee eene ee prokatavolee
πόση είναι η προκαταβολή;

is there a charge per kilometre?
yeenete khreosee ana kheeleeometro
γίνεται χρέωση ανά χιλιόμετρο;

how much?
poso kanee
πόσο κάνει;

what is included in the insurance?
tee pereelamvanete steen asfaleea
τι περιλαμβάνεται στην ασφάλεια;

I want to take out additional insurance
thelo na paro prosthetee asfaleea
θέλω να πάρω πρόσθετη ασφάλεια

what do I do if I break down?
tee tha kano se pereeptosee vlavees
τι θα κάνω σε περίπτωση βλάβης;

where are the documents?
poo eene ee adheea keekloforeeas ke ee asfalya
πού είναι η άδεια κυκλοφορίας και η ασφάλεια;

talking talking talking talking talking

Driving

The minimum age for driving in Greece is 18. Greek people generally drive carefully and the roads are good. Watch out when driving in Athens, though, as it can get quite chaotic. Take care at all times, especially on zebra crossings, as you will occasionally come across impatient drivers and people who overtake dangerously. Cars do not often stop for pedestrians – the zebra crossing is really just an accepted crossing point for pedestrians once the road is clear. There are many excellent new highways in Greece, linking major towns and cities. In Greece's mountainous areas, you will find twisting roads with hairpin bends but there won't usually be a lot of traffic about. Even the remotest roads nowadays have tarmac but you might still find the odd dirt track, linking tiny villages. If you take your own car to Greece, a Green Card may or may not be necessary – ask your Insurance Company to explain this in full. Keep your driving licence, car documents and passport with you at all times. Police often set up speed checks, especially where there is a small village along an otherwise deserted highway – so watch your speed! Seatbelts and motorbike helmets are compulsory and fines are issued. Occasionally you may see three people on one motorbike without a helmet in sight, but don't let this deceive you, fines are hefty for these offences!

Speed restrictions

built up area	50 km/h
(motorcycles)	40 km/h
main roads	90 km/h
(motorcycles)	70 km/h
motorway	120 km/h
(motorcycles)	90 km/h

Speed restrictions vary for cars and motorcycles. It is compulsory to wear seatbelts.

Each county has its own set of designated letters, 'ATE' is Athens. Only letters recognizable throughout Europe are used on numberplates.

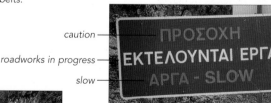

caution — ΠΡΟΣΟΧΗ
roadworks in progress — ΕΚΤΕΛΟΥΝΤΑΙ ΕΡΓΑ
slow — ΑΡΓΑ - SLOW

Greek main roads are all 'E' roads (European routes) and are marked in green.

— caution
— in progress
— roadworks
— speed 10 kph

Toll-free main roads are signed in blue, while you pay a toll on the motorways.

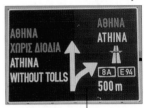

motorway *(aftokeeneetodhromos)*
Signs are green in Greece.
A = motorway   E = European route

Beaches are well signposted.

No motorbikes allowed at night. Note that it is compulsory to wear a crash helmet.

— **Από** *apo* from
— **Έως** *eos* till
Π.μ. = am
Μ.μ. = pm

Signpost indicating Vrahos tunnel.

north voras
west dheesee
east anatolee
south notos

A diagonal red line shows that you are leaving a town or village.

No overtaking: uneven surface.

Caution: road narrows: no overtaking.

A high-wind sign.

road narrows

danger

Restricted access times for heavy vehicles.

from 10am to 11pm

ΑΠΟ 10:00
ΕΩΣ 23:00

---

we're going to...
peeghenoome sto...
πηγαίνουμε στο...

what is the best route?
pya eene ee kaleeteree dheeadhromee
ποια είναι η καλύτερη διαδρομή;

how do I get to the motorway?
pos tha pao steen ethneekee
πως θα πάω στην εθνική;

which junction is it for...?
se pya dheeastavrosee eene...
σε ποια διασταύρωση είναι...;

when is the best time to drive?
pya eene ee kaleeteree ora ya odheegheesee
ποια είναι η καλύτερη ώρα για οδήγηση;

is the road good?
eene kalos o dhromos
είναι καλός ο δρόμος;

talking

When driving on the motorway you pay a toll. Toll-stations are well signed and easy to deal with. Rates are quite low and you pay a fixed rate per section, e.g Patras to Corinth. You pay at the start of the motorway and should keep your ticket in case they check it on leaving. Keep your eye on the speed limit and watch out for occasional impatient overtaking.

Signs give you lane directions as you approach the motorway toll-booths. Stay in cash-only lanes.

toll booth

Keep your toll receipt until you get off the motorway.

If you break down

For roadside help, dial 104. The Automobile and Touring Club of Greece provides 24-hour information to foreign tourists on 174.

can you help me?
boreete na me voeetheesete
μπορείτε να με βοηθήσετε;

I'm on my own *(female)*
eeme monee moo
είμαι μόνη μου

the car is...
to aftokeeneeto eene...
το αυτοκίνητο είναι...

registration number...
o areethmos keekloforeeas...
ο αριθμός κυκλοφορίας...

my car has broken down
to aftokeeneeto moo khalase
το αυτοκίνητό μου χάλασε

I have children in the car
ekho pedya sto aftokeeneeto
έχω παιδιά στο αυτοκίνητο

a blue Fiat
ena ble Fiat
ένα μπλε Fiat

You can park by the roadside in small towns. In bigger places there will be various restrictions. A tow-away sign makes the situation fairly obvious, but other signs may be less easy to be sure about. If in doubt, ask before parking, as fines are high. The safest place to park in a big town is a 'parking' where you pay a fixed amount for a fixed length of time. In Athens you can leave your car long-term in a technologically operated 'robot' car-park, where it will be completely safe. Parking meters are very rarely seen.

no parking

prohibited   *KTEL (bus) station*

entrance

parking 50m right

ΔΕΧΟΜΕΘΑ = receiving
ΑΥΤΟΚΙΝΗΤΑ = cars
ΔΙΑΝΥΚΤΕΡΕΥΕΙ = open all night

underground parking (private)

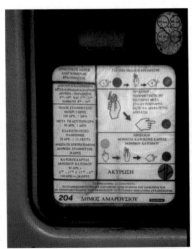

There are not many pay-and-display parking meters in Greece, and you will probably find them only in Athens. Instructions for use are the same as the meters in the UK.

talking

can I park here?
boro na parkaro edho
μπορώ να παρκάρω εδώ;

where is the best place to park?
poo eene kaleetera na parkaro
πού είναι καλύτερα να παρκάρω;

how long can I park here?
ya posee ora boro na parkaro edho
για πόση ώρα μπορώ να παρκάρω εδώ;

do I need a parking ticket?
khreeazome karta stathmefsees
χρειάζομαι κάρτα στάθμευσης;

is there a car park?
eeparkhee kapyo parking
υπάρχει κάποιο πάρκινγκ;

Petrol is relatively cheap and diesel even less. Opening hours of petrol stations vary, but they are plentiful and many open all day and into the evening. The attendant will fill your tank – there is no self-service. Filling stations also have air, oil, water and sometimes a carwash and vacuum cleaner, and some will mend punctures.

Πλυντήριο = car wash

Λιπαντήριο = lubrication

air *aeras*   water *nero*

Petrol pumps are generally labelled in English.

auto car wash

change of oil free of charge

is there a petrol station near here?
eeparkhee venzeenadheeko edho konda
υπάρχει βενζινάδικο εδώ κοντά;

fill it up, please
yemeeste to parakalo
γεμίστε το, παρακαλώ

unleaded
amoleevdhee
αμόλυβδη

20 euros worth of unleaded petrol
eekosee evro amoleevdhee venzeenee
είκοσι ευρώ αμόλυβδη βενζίνη

talking

> You can find all the main dealerships in the major towns. There are also lots of smaller garages and auto-electricians. It's a good idea to ask the price of the repair first, as in any country. If you break down, there are a number of companies you can call, two of which are ELPA (tel 104) and Express Service (tel 154). Check their rates before you ask them to come out.

tel 154

Express Service and ELPA are breakdown services like the AA. Non-members can also phone for help but will pay a supplement.

tyres   accessories

I've broken down
khalase to aftokeeneeto moo
χάλασε το αυτοκίνητό μου

where is the nearest garage? *(for repairs)*
poo eene to pyo kondeeno garaz
πού είναι το πιο κοντινό γκαράζ;

is it serious?
eene sovaro
είναι σοβαρό;

the ... doesn't work properly
o/ee/to ... dhen dhoolevee kala
ο/η/το ... δεν δουλεύει καλά

the ... don't work properly
ee/ta ... dhen dhoolevoon kala
οι/τα ... δεν δουλεύουν καλά

I don't have a spare tyre
dhen ekho rezerva
δεν έχω ρεζέρβα

have you the parts?
ekhete ta andalakteeka
έχετε τα ανταλλακτικά;

could you please help me to change the tyre
boreete na me voeetheesete na alakso lasteekho
μπορείτε να με βοηθήσετε να αλλάξω λάστιχο;

when will it be ready?
pote tha eene eteemo
πότε θα είναι έτοιμο;

how much will it cost?
poso tha kosteesee
πόσο θα κοστίσει;

the car won't start
ee meekhanee dhen ksekeena
η μηχανή δεν ξεκινά

the battery is flat
ee batareea eene adheea
η μπαταρία είναι άδεια

the engine is overheating
afksanete ee thermokraseea tees mekhanees
αυξάνεται η θερμοκρασία της μηχανής

I have a flat tyre
me epyase lasteekho
με έπιασε λάστιχο

can you replace the windscreen?
boreete na ftyaksete to parbreez
μπορείτε να φτιάξετε το παρμπρίζ;

Toll prices for different vehicles.

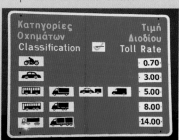

centre *kendro*

ΚΕΝΤΡΟ

left *areestera*

αριστερά

right *dhekseea*

δεξιά

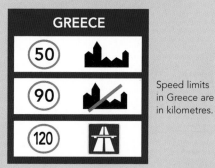

Speed limits in Greece are in kilometres.

Athens City

Many signs will have the Greek spelling and a transcription in the western alphabet.

head lights on
Ανάψτε τα φώτα

Parking with a ticket.

me karta

ME = with

No parking on odd months (Jan, March, May, etc).

No parking on even months (Feb, April, June, etc).

MH = *no*

no parking
mee parkarete

Shopping

> When you go into a shop, especially a small one, it is polite to say kaleemera or ya sas to the shopkeeper (even tee kanete if you're feeling really daring!) before asking/looking for what you want, as Greece is a much more 'personal' part of the world than more northernly countries. Our impersonal approach can sometimes seem rude! Shops generally open in the morning (8–9am until 1–2pm) and again in the evening (approx 5–8pm). They close in the afternoon and all day on Sundays. However, in busy tourist areas they usually open all day every day (including Sunday) during the summer.

bakery

Bread is baked freshly every day at the baker's shop. For a big loaf, ask for **ένα κιλό** *ena keelo* (a kilo loaf). For a small loaf ask for **μισόκιλο** *meesokeelo* (a half kilo loaf). For a round sandwich bun ask for **ένα ψώμακι** *ena psomakee*. Many bakers sell sandwiches. **ΑΡΤΟΣ** is the ancient Greek for bread (used in shop signs only).

butcher's   since 1942

φούρνος
foornos
baker's

κρεοπωλείο
krayopoleeo
butcher's

ιχθυοπωλείο
eekhtheeopoleeo
fish shop

παντοπωλείο
pandopoleeo
grocer's

μανάβικο
manaveeko
greengrocer's

καπνοπωλείο
kapnopoleeo
tobacconist's

ζαχαροπλαστείο
zakharoplasteeo
cake shop

keywords keywords keywords

bookshop

book shop
photocopies
cigarettes
phonecards

optician   contact lenses

In Greece, especially in big towns and cities, you will find well-stocked supermarkets and hypermarkets. There are both national and international chains. Some will open all day, others will open in the morning and evening only, depending on the size of the supermarket, time of year, etc. All kinds of food and drink are available in supermarkets and mini-markets. In most cases, though, fresh bread is best bought at the baker's.

One of the large Greek supermarket chains.

Co-operative supermarkets, like this one, tend to be cheaper.

Special offers at the supermarket.

TIMH *teemee* = *price*

co-op

where can I buy...?	**matches**	**bread**	**water**
poo boro na aghoraso...	*speerta*	*psomee*	*nero*
πού μπορώ να αγοράσω...;	σπίρτα	ψωμί	νερό
do you have...?	**milk**	**bread rolls**	
ekhete...	*ghala*	*psomakeea*	
έχετε...;	γάλα	ψωμάκια	
how much does it cost?	**I'd like a good wine**		
poso kosteezee	*tha eethela ena kalo krasee*		
πόσο κοστίζει;	θα ήθελα ένα καλό κρασί		
I'm looking for a present	**can I pay with this card?**		
psakhno ya ena dhoro	*boro na pleeroso me aftee teen karta*		
ψάχνω για ένα δώρο	μπορώ να πληρώσω με αυτή την κάρτα;		
is there a market?	**which day?**		
ekhee laeekee aghora	*pya mera*		
έχει λαϊκή αγορά;	ποια μέρα;		

talking talking talking

Quantities are expressed in kilos and grams. One kilo (keelo) is roughly equivalent to 2lb; half a kilo (meeso keelo) is equivalent to 1lb. If you want roughly a quarter ($\frac{1}{4}$lb) of something, ask for 100 grams (ekato ghramareea). If you want to ask for ham, cheese, salami, etc in slices, ask for fetes. 10 slices is dheka fetes. Many towns have a weekly market which is great for fresh, local produce. It's best to go good and early. As well as food, markets sell clothes, shoes and all kinds of household items. It's a lot of fun, too!

Fruit and vegetables are generally sold by the kilo, although larger items, such as melons, are sold individually. Small supermarkets/mini-markets may well have no fish/meat or fruit/vegetables, so you have to get these from the fishmonger/butcher or greengrocer.

Butcher's stall in the market.
ΜΟΣΧΑΡΙ *(moskharee) beef*
ΚΥΜΑΣ *(keemas) mince*
ΧΟΙΡΙΝΟ *(kheereeno) pork*
ΜΠΡΙΖΟΛΑ *(breezola) chop*

milk

green:
Άπαχο
(apakho) =
skimmed

red: **Πλήρες** *(pleeres)*
= full-cream

Λιπαρά *(leepara) = fat*

blue:
Ημίπαχο
(eemeepakho)
= semi-
skimmed

The colour-coding of milk **γάλα** *(ghala)* cartons varies from one company to another.

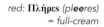

this one
afto
αντό

that one
ekeeno
εκείνο

a piece of cheese
ena komatee teeree
ένα κομμάτι τυρί

a little more
leegho akoma
λίγο ακόμα

a little less
leeghotero
λιγότερο

10 slices of ham
deka fetes zambon
δέκα φέτας ζαμπόν

a litre of milk
ena leetro ghala
ένα λίτρο γάλα

bottled water
ena emfeealomeno nero
ένα εμφιαλωμένο νερό

fizzy   still
aeryookho   *aplo*
αεριούχο   απλό

a tin of tomatoes
ena kootee domates
ένα κουτί ντομάτες

a kilo of potatoes
ena keelo patates
ένα κιλό πατάτες

half a kilo of grapes
meeso keelo stafeeleea
μισό κιλό φασολάκια

3 peaches
trees rodhakeena
τρεις ροδάκινα

250g of olives
ena tetarto keelo elyes
ένα τέταρτο κιλό ελιές

pasta

MAKAPONIA
Slim Line

1 Θερμίδα ανά 1 γραμ. βρασμένου ζυμαρικού

1 calorie per 1 gram

boiled pasta

energy — **ΕΝΕΡΓΕΙΑ**
proteins — **ΠΡΩΤΕΪΝΕΣ**
carbo- — **ΥΔΑΤΑΝΘΡΑΚΕΣ**
hydrates
ΛΙΠΑΡΑ:
fats
    ΚΟΡΕΣΜΕΝΑ
    ΜΟΝΟΑΚΟΡΕΣΤΑ
    ΠΟΛΥΑΚΟΡΕΣΤΑ
    ΧΟΛΗΣΤΕΡΟΛΗ
iron — **ΣΙΔΗΡΟΣ Fe**
magnesium — **ΜΑΓΝΗΣΙΟ Mg**
potassium — **ΚΑΛΛΙΟ   K**

saturated
monounsaturated
polyunsaturated
cholesterol

eat before

ΗΜ. ΛΗΞΗΣ
6-5-06

ΠΑΙΔΙΚΑ ΜΠΙΣΚΟΤΑ,
ΜΕ ΒΙΤΑΜΙΝΕΣ,
ΣΙΔΗΡΟ ΚΑΙ
ΑΣΒΕΣΤΙΟ.

children's biscuits, with
vitamins, iron and calcium

Sweets – χωρίς ζάχαρη
(khorees zakharee)
without sugar

ΚΑΡΑΜΕΛΛΕΣ **LIHN** ΧΩΡΙΣ ΖΑΧΑΡΗ (ΜΕ ΣΟΡΒΙΤΗ)
ΜΕ ΑΡΩΜΑ ΦΡΟΥΤΟΥ

Here is a list of basic foodstuffs you might need.

Everyday Foods

biscuits τα μπισκότα *beeskota*
bread το ψωμί *psomee*
bread rolls τα ψωμάκια *psomakeea*
butter το βούτυρο *vooteero*
cereal τα δημητριακά *dheemeetreeaka*
cheese το τυρί *teeree*
cheese pie η τυρόπιτα *teeropeeta*
chicken το κοτόπουλο *kotopoolo*
chips οι πατάτες τηγανητές *patates teeghaneetes*
chocolate η σοκολάτα *sokolata*
coffee *(instant)* το Νεσκαφέ *Nescafe*®
cream η κρέμα *krema*
crisps τα πατατάκια *patatakeea*
eggs τα αβγά *avgha*
fish το ψάρι *psaree*
flour το αλεύρι *alevree*
ham το ζαμπόν *zambon*
herbal tea το τσάι από βότανα *tsaee apo votana*
honey το μέλι *melee*
jam η μαρμελάδα *marmeladha*
juice ο χυμός *kheemos*
lamb το αρνάκι *arnakee*
marmalade η μαρμελάδα πορτοκάλι *marmeladha portokalee*
meat balls οι κεφτέδες *keftedhes*
milk το γάλα *ghala*
mustard η μουστάρδα *moostardha*

olive oil το ελαιόλαδο *eleoladho*
orange juice ο χυμός πορτοκάλι *kheemos portokalee*
pasta τα ζυμαρικά *zeemareeka*
pepper το πιπέρι *peeperee*
pork το χοιρινό *kheereeno*
rice το ρύζι *reezee*
salt το αλάτι *alatee*
spinach pie η σπανακόπιτα *spanakopeeta*
sugar η ζάχαρη *zakharee*
tea το τσάι *tsaee*
tomatoes *(tin)* οι ντομάτες κονσέρβα *domates konserva*
tuna ο τόνος *tonos*
vegetable oil το φυτικό λάδι *feeteeko ladhee*
vinegar το ξύδι *kseedhee*
yoghurt το γιαούρτι *yaoortee*

Fruit

apples τα μήλα *meela*
apricots το βερύκοκκα *vereekoka*
bananas οι μπανάνες *bananes*
cherries τα κεράσια *keraseea*
figs τα σύκα *seeka*
grapefruit το γκρέιπφρουτ
  greipfroot
grapes τα σταφύλια *stafeeleea*
lemon το λεμόνι *lemonee*
melon το πεπόνι *peponee*
nectarines τα νεκταρίνια
  nektareeneea
oranges τα πορτοκάλια *portokaleea*
peaches τα ροδάκινα *rodhakeena*
pears τα αχλάδια *akhladheea*
pineapple ο ανανάς *o ananas*
plums τα δαμάσκηνα *dhamaskeena*
strawberries οι φράουλες *fraooles*
watermelon το καρπούζι *karpoozee*

Vegetables

asparagus τα σπαράγγια
  sparangeea
aubergine η μελιτζάνα *meleetzana*
basil ο βασιλικός *vaseeleekos*

bean *(haricot)* το φασόλι *fasolee*
  (broad) το κουκί *kookee*
cabbage το λάχανο *lakhano*
carrots τα καρότα *karota*
cauliflower το κουνουπίδι
  koonoopeedhee
celery το σέλινο *seleeno*
chickpeas τα ρεβίθια *reveetheea*
courgettes τα κολοκυθάκια
  kolokeethakeea
cucumber το αγγούρι *angooree*
eggplant η μελιτζάνα *meleetzana*
garlic το σκόρδο *skordho*
green beans τα φασολάκια
  fasolakeea
lettuce το μαρούλι *maroolee*
mushrooms τα μανιτάρια
  maneetareea
olives οι ελιές *elyes*
onions τα κρεμμύδια *kremeedheea*
parsley ο μαϊντανός *maeendanos*
peas ο αρακάς *arakas*
peppers οι πιπεριές *peeperee-es*
potatoes οι πατάτες *patates*
spinach το σπανάκι *spanakee*
tomatoes οι ντομάτες *domates*
zucchini τα κολοκυθάκια
  kolokeethakeea

In the cities there are many high-quality department stores. One of the most popular of these is the 'Hondos Centre' which has branches throughout Greece.

shoe shop

The word for shoes is **παπούτσια** (pap**oo**tseea) and for sandals **σανδάλια** (sand**a**leea).

4th floor *orofos*

sale

Móvo — **only**
mono
1.230 €
το άτομο — **per person**
to atoma

Δώρο! — **free gift**
doro

The rural answer to the department store! In the country areas and smaller villages you will sometimes find vans like this selling clothes, food, linen, chairs and tables, even baby chicks. They have amegaphone to advertise their wares.

keywords keywords keywords keywords

πολυκατάστημα
poleekatasteema
department store

υπόγειο
eepoyo
basement

ισόγειο
eesoyo
ground floor

πρώτος όροφος
protos orofos
1st floor

κατάστημα
katasteema
department

ηλεκτρικά είδη
eelektreeka eedee
electrical goods

κοσμήματα
kosmeemata
jewellery

γυναικεία
yeenekeea
ladies'

ανδρικά
andreeka
men's

παιδικά
pedeeka
children's

where can I find...?
poo na vro...
πού να βρω...;

batteries for this
batareees yafto
μπαταρίες γι' αυτό

toys
peghneedhya
παιγνίδια

shoes
papootseea
παπούτσια

talking

Women's clothes sizes

UK/Australia	8	10	12	14	16	18	20	22
Europe	36	38	40	42	44	46	48	50
US/Canada	6	8	10	12	14	16	18	20

Men's clothes sizes (suits)

UK/US/Canada	36	38	40	42	44	46
Europe	46	48	50	52	54	56
Australia	92	97	102	107	112	117

Shoes

UK/Australia	2	3	4	5	6	7	8	9	10	11
Europe	35	36	37	38	39	41	42	43	45	46
US/Canada women	4	5	6	7	8	9	10	11	12	-
US/Canada men	3	4	5	6	7	8	9	10	11	12

Children's Shoes

UK/US/Canada	0	1	2	3	4	5	6	7	8	9	10	11
Europe	15	17	18	19	20	22	23	24	26	27	28	29

talking talking

can I try this on?
boro na to dhokeemaso
μπορώ να το δοκιμάσω;

it's too big for me
moo eene meghalo
μου είναι μεγάλο

it's too small for me
moo eene polee steno
μου είναι πολύ στενό

it's too expensive
eene polee akreevo
είναι πολύ ακριβό

I'll take this one
tha to paro
θα το πάρω

I take a size...
foro ... noomero
φορώ ... νούμερο

where are the changing rooms?
poo eene ta dhokeemasteereea
πού είναι τα δοκιμαστήρια;

have you a smaller one?
ekhete meekrotero noomero
έχετε μικρότερο νούμερο;

have you a larger one?
ekhete meghaleetero noomero
έχετε μεγαλύτερο νούμερο;

do you have this in my size?
ekhete afto sto noomero moo
έχετε αυτό στο νούμερό μου;

can you give me a discount?
tha moo kanete kaleeteree teemee
θα μου κάνετε καλύτερη τιμή;

I like it
moo aresee
μου αρέσει

I don't like it
dhen moo aresee
δεν μου αρέσει

Post Offices open in the morning, from 8–9am until 1–2pm, according to the location. They do not open in the afternoon or on Saturdays, with the exception of the main Post Office in Syntagma Square in Athens, which opens on Saturdays and Sundays in summer. Stamps can also be bought at kiosks (per**ee**ptero) and at shops selling postcards.

Post Offices may be signposted.

Red postboxes are for express mail in the Athens area. Yellow boxes are for general post, and often detail collection times.

Opening hours are sometimes printed in English. Post offices usually open only in the morning.

where is the post office?
poo **ee**ne to takheedhrom**ee**o
πού είναι το ταχυδρομείο;

do you sell stamps?
ekhete ghrammat**o**seema
έχετε γραμματόσημα;

where can I buy stamps?
poo bor**o** na aghor**a**so ghramat**o**seema
πού μπορώ να αγοράσω γραμματόσημα;

10 stamps dheka ghramat**o**seema δέκα γραμματόσημα	**for postcards** ya kartes για κάρτες	**urgent mail** epeeghon επείγον
to Britain ya angl**ee**a για Αγγλία	**to America** ya amer**ee**kee για Αμερική amer**ee**kee	

I want to send this letter registered post
thelo na st**ee**lo afto to ghrama seest**ee**meno
θέλω να στείλω αυτό το γράμμα συστημένο

how much is it to send this parcel?
p**o**so kost**ee**zee na st**ee**lo aft**o** to pak**e**to
πόσο κοστίζει να στείλω αυτό το πακέτο;

by air
aeroporeek**o**s
αεροπορικώς

talking talking

Many photographers develop and print in their shops.

Pay attention to prohibitions: photography is not allowed in some areas and laws may be strictly enforced.

Photo booths can be found in airports, some railway stations and larger shopping centres.

where can I buy...?   **film**   **tapes for a camcorder?**
poo boro na aghoraso...   *film*   *kasetes ya videocamera*
πού μπορώ να αγοράσω...;   φιλμ   κασέτες για βιντεοκάμερα;

a colour film   **24**   **36**
ena enkhromo film   *eekoseetesaree*   *treeantaeksaree*
ένα έγχρωμο φιλμ   εικοσιτεσσάρι   τριανταεξάρι

have you batteries for this camcorder?
ekhete batareees yaftee tee videocamera
έχετε μπαταρίες γι'αυτή τη βιντεοκάμερα;

is it OK to take pictures here?
peerazee an traveekso fotoghrafeees edho
πειράζει αν τραβήξω φωτογραφίες εδώ;

would you take a picture of us, please?
boreete na mas traveeksete meea fotoghrafeea parakalo
μπορείτε να μας τραβήξετε μία φωτογραφία, παρακαλώ;

Phones

Payphones abound in Greece – just look for the blue sign. The instructions are easy to follow. Cards are easier to use than coins – ask for teelekarta. The cheapest of these cost 4 euros. You can get cards from supermarkets, kiosks, newsagents and Post Offices. To phone direct from a hotel phone will cost you a lot more than if you use a phonecard. Some kiosks have a small payphone on the counter – the card goes in at the side. The telephone offices (OTE) have cardphones too, and it may be possible to have someone call you back on a phone in the OTE office.

Public phones take coins and cards.

A Greek pay-phone Pictograms show you how to use the phone. The easiest way to phone is by using a phonecard, available at kiosks, newsagents and some supermarkets.

do you have phonecards?
ekhete teeleekartes
έχετε τηλεκάρτες

a phonecard
meea teelekarta
μία τηλεκάρτα

Mr Antoniou please
ton keereeo andoneeoo parakalo
τον κύριο Αντωνίου, παρακαλώ

extension ... please
esotereeko ... parakalo
εσωτερικό ... παρακαλώ

can I speak to...?
boro na meeleeso ston/steen...
μπορώ να μιλήσω στον/στην...;

this is Caroline
eeme ee caroline
είμαι η caroline

can I have an outside line
boro na ekho meea eksotereekee ghrammee
μπορώ να έχω μία εξωτερική γραμμή

what is your phone number?
pyos eene o areethmos too teelefonoo soo
ποιός είναι ο αριθμός του τηλεφώνου σου;

my phone number is...
o areethmos too teelefonoo moo eene...
ο αριθμός του τηλεφώνου μου είναι...

talking talking

keywords keywords keywords

τηλέφωνο
teelefono
phone

τηλεκάρτα
teelekarta
phonecard

κινητό (τηλέφωνο)
keeneeto (teelefono)
mobile

κωδικός
kodeekos
code

κατάλογος
kataloghos
phone book

χρυσός οδηγός
khreesos odeeghos
yellow pages

πληροφορίες
καταλόγου
*pleeroforee-es
kataloghoo*
directory enquiries

Look for this sign if you need a phone-box.
OTE is the Greek phone company.

OTE phonecard. The cards are economical
and easy to use.

yellow pages

International dialling codes
UK 00 44
USA & Canada 00 1
Australia 00 61
Greece 00 30

τηλ: — *abbreviation for tel:*

Κιν. 6946793055 — κιν = κινητό *mobile phone*

talking

I'll call later
tha paro arghotera
θα πάρω αργότερα

I'll call back tomorrow
tha ksanaparo avreeo
θα ξαναπάρω αύριο

do you have a mobile?
ekhete keeneeto
έχετε κινητό;

what is the number?
pyo eene to noomero
ποιο είναι το νούμερο;

my mobile number is...
o areethmos too keeneetoo moo (teelefonoo) eene...
ο αριθμός του κινητού μου (τηλεφώνου) είναι...

E-mail, Internet, Fax

*It is usually easy to find an Internet cafe to check your e-mail messages etc. National and local tourist information can be accessed via the Internet. Greek web-sites end in **.gr**. Rates at Internet cafes will vary so ask beforehand about the price.*

laminating ——
stamps ——
cards ——
translating ——
fax (sending & receiving) ——

- ΠΛΑΣΤΙΚΟΠΟΙΗΣΕΙΣ
- ΣΦΡΑΓΙΔΕΣ
- ΚΑΡΤΕΣ
- ΜΕΤΑΦΡΑΣΕΙΣ
- FAX (ΑΠΟΣΤΟΛΗ & ΛΗΨΗ)
- **ΜΕΤΑΞΑ ΧΑΡΑ** •

an internet café

The Greek for 'at' is **παπάκι** *papakee* (which literally means little duck).

I want to send an e-mail
thelo na steelo ena email
θέλω να στείλω ένα e-mail

do you have e-mail?
ekhete e-mail
έχετε e-mail;

how do you spell it?
pos grafete
πώς γράφεται;

did you get my e-mail?
peerate to e-mail moo
πήρατε το e-mail μου;

what is your e-mail address?
tee eene ee e-mail dhee-eftheensee sas
τι είναι η e-mail διεύθυνσή σας;

my e-mail address is...
ee e-mail dhee-eftheensee moo eene..
η e-mail διεύθυνσή μου είναι...

caroline dot zmith@harpercollins dot co dot uk
caroline teleea zmith papakee harpercollins teleea co teleea uk
caroline τελεία zmith παπάκι harpercollins τελεία co τελεία uk

do you have a website?
ekhete website
έχετε website;

can I book by e-mail?
boro na kano krateesee me e-mail
μπορώ να κάνω κράτηση με e-mail;

Website details on bill board.

photocopies

colour

photocopying/reprints

talking talking talking

I want to send a fax
thelo na steelo ena fax
θέλω να στείλω ένα φαξ

what's your fax number?
pyo eene to noomero too fax sas
ποιο είναι το νούμερο του φαξ σας;

please resend your fax
parakalo ksanasteelte to fax sas
παρακαλώ ξαναστείλτε το φαξ σας

your fax is constantly engaged
to fax sas eene seenekhos kateeleemeno
το φαξ σας είναι συνεχώς κατειλημμένο

where can I send a fax from?
poo boro na steelo ena fax
πού μπορώ να στείλω ένα φαξ;

do you have a fax?
ekhete fax
έχετε φαξ;

did you get my fax?
lavate to fax moo
λάβατε το φαξ μου;

I can't read it
dhen boro na to dheeavaso
δεν μπορώ να το διαβάσω

Out & About

Greece is well-known for the archaeological sites which highlight every period of its fascinating history. Tourist offices will have information on all the local sites. Check on opening times, as they do vary. Try to avoid walking round sites in the heat of the day in summer, though!

tourist information office

swimming pool

Street signs to places of interest are normally brown.

You can rent motor-bikes and scooters in many places. It's great fun and a good way to explore Greece. Be sure to check out the insurance situation carefully and make sure your bike is roadworthy.

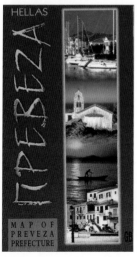

Local tourist information offices have free brochures, leaflets and maps.

Signs on the beach will often be in English.

keywords keywords keywords

βόλτα
volta
walk, trek

ορειβασία
oreevaseea
mountaineering

εκκλησία
ekleeseea
church

ναός
naos
temple

παλάτι
palatee
palace

θέατρο
thayatro
theatre

σινεμά
seenema
cinema

δημαρχείο
deemarkheeo
town hall

Throughout the summer you can see Greek plays and other shows performed in the ancient theatres.

Tickets for museums and visitor attractions often have English translations, as in this ticket for the Acropolis.

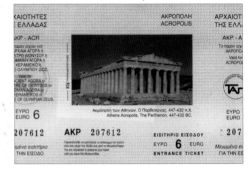

talking talking talking

excuse me! where is the tourist office?
seeghnomee! poo eene to tooreesteeko ghrafeeo
συγνώμη! πού είναι το τουριστικό γραφείο;

we want to visit...
theloome na epeeskeftoome...
θέλουμε να επισκεφτούμε...

have you any leaflets?
ekhete odheeghee-es
έχετε οδηγίες;

are there any excursions?
eeparkhoon orghanomenes ekdhromes
υπάρχουν οργανωμένες εκδρομές;

when does it leave?
pote fevyee
πότε φεύγει;

where does it leave from?
apo poo fevyee
από που φεύγει;

how much is it to get in?
poso kosteezee ee seemetokhee
πόσο κοστίζει η συμμετοχή;

is it open to the public?
eene aneekto sto keeno
είναι ανοικτό στο κοινό;

There is plenty of excellent walking and mountaineering to be done all over Greece, with clearly marked walking trails and refuge huts. The highest and most spectacular mountain is Mount Olympus, but there are many other scenic walks and climbs. Maps are available, showing you the National Parks and other areas where you can walk or drive.

Panathenaikos football ground.

Greek dancing is popular.

where can we...?	play tennis	play golf
poo boroome na...	peksoome tennis	peksoome golf
πού μπορούμε να...;	παίξουμε τέννις	παίξουμε γκολφ

how much is it...?	per hour	per day
poso kosteezee...	teen ora	teen mera
πόσο κοστίζει...;	την ώρα	την μέρα

is there a swimming pool?
ekhee peeseena
έχει πισίνα;

can you recommend a quiet beach?	is it sandy?
kserete kapya eeseekhee paraleea	ekhee amo
ξέρετε κάποια ήσυχη παραλία;	έχει άμμο;

is it dangerous?	is it a nudist beach?
eene epeekeendheeno	eene paraleea yeemneeston
είναι επικίνδυνο;	είναι παραλία γυμνιστών;

i There are many ferries to the islands and the high-speed 'flying dolphins' (ιπτάμενο δελφίνι *eeptameno dhelfeenee*) provide a fast service. You can visit their website **www.dolphins.gr.**

EPHIRA TRAVEL

ET   Tel. 0684031439
Fax. 0684032039

E-mail ephiratr @atenet.gr
ΓΡΑΜΜΗ ΠΑΞΩΝ
ΔΡΟΜΟΛΟΓΗΜΕΝΟ
ΠΛΟΙΟ ΓΑΪΟΣ
€. 4   ΜΟΝΗ ΔΙΑΔΡΟΜΗ
ΑΝΑΧΩΡΗΣΗ ΠΑΡΓΑ 9³⁰
ΑΝΑΧΩΡΗΣΗ ΠΑΞΟΙ 16⁰⁰

PAXOS LINE
WiTH GAIOS
€. 4   -ONE WAY
DEPARTURE PARGA 9 ³⁰
» » PAXOS 16 ⁰⁰

Prices are listed for various ticket types to different destinations. There are many day-trips available.

You can buy ferry tickets from travel agents or at the quayside.

High-speed boats provide a fast route to the islands.

is there a hydrofoil to...?
eeparkhee eeptameno dhelfeenee ya...
υπάρχει ιπτάμενο δελφίνι για...;

when is the next boat?
pote fevyee to epomeno pleeo
πότε φεύγει το επόμενο πλοίο;

can we hire a boat?
boroome na neekyasoome meea varka
μπορούμε να νοικιάσουμε μία βάρκα;

when does the ferry leave?
pote fevyee to fereebot
πότε φεύγει το φεριμπότ;

is there a boat to...?
eeparkhee pleeo ya...
υπάρχει πλοίο για...;

Accommodation

In major cities there are hotels classified by the star system. In general you are more likely to find hotels categorized in the Greek way: α A (alpha) = 1st class; β B (veeta) = 2nd class; γ Γ (gamma) = 3rd class. Most of these will also provide breakfast if you require it. The Tourist Offices will advise you about hotels and other accommodation. You can also stay in rooms, small guest-houses and self-catering apartments.

Accommodation of all kinds is plentiful in Greece. It's usually worth shopping around.

ΞΕΝΟΔΟΧΕΙΟ *hotel*
ΔΩΜΑΤΙΑ *rooms*
ΔΙΑΜΕΡΙΣΜΑΤΑ *apartments*
ΚΛΙΜΑΤΙΣΜΟΣ *air conditioning*
ΠΙΣΙΝΑ *swimming pool*
ΜΠΑΡ *bar*
ΠΑΡΚΙΝΚ *parking*
100m ΑΠΟ ΤΗΝ ΑΚΤΗ *100m from the beach*

do you have a room for tonight?
ekhete ena dhomateeo ya apopse
έχετε ένα δωμάτιο για απόψε;

for ... nights
ya ... neekhtes
για ... νύχτες

a single room
ena monokleeno dhomateeo
ένα μονόκλινο δωμάτιο

a double room
ena dheekleeno dhomateeo
ένα δίκλινο δωμάτιο

a room for three people
ena treekleeno dhomateeo
ένα τρίκλινο δωμάτιο

with bathroom
me banyo
με μπάνιο

with shower
me doos
με ντους

with a double bed
me dheeplo krevatee
με διπλό κρεβάτι

with twin beds
me dheeo krevateea
με δύο κρεβάτια

how much is it...?
poso kanee...
πόσο κάνει...;

per night
to vradhee
το βράδυ

per week
teen evdhomadha
την εβδομάδα

we'd like to stay...
tha thelame na meenoome...
θα θέλαμε να μείνουμε...

for one night
ya meea neekhtes
για μία νύχτες

for 3 nights
ya trees neekhtes
για τρεις νύχτες

talking talking talking

HOTEL ΑΘΩΣ

Hotel Athos

The word 'Reception' always
appears in English in Greek hotels.

Hotels have to post information about
their services on bedroom doors.

I booked a room
ekho kanee meea krateesee
έχω κάνει μία κράτηση

I'd like to see the room
tha eethela na dho to dhomateeo
θα ήθελα να δω το δωμάτιο

is breakfast included?
to proeeno eene steen teemee
το πρωινό είναι στην τιμή;

can you suggest somewhere else?
boreete na proteenete kapoo aloo
μπορείτε να προτείνετε κάπου αλλού;

my name is...
to onoma moo eene...
το όνομά μου είναι...

is there anything cheaper?
ekhete teepota ftheenotero
έχετε τίποτα φθηνότερο;

A 'garsonyera' or a 'stoodeeo' is a small apartment.
A 'deeamereesma' is a medium-sized apartment. A 'dhomateeo' is a room, usually without a kitchen. You will see signs for all types of accommodation, but if you are in a small place and there is no sign, just ask instead.

guest house

guest house Olga for rent : rooms and small apartments

apartments for rent

— *for rent*
— *studio apartments*
— *air-conditioned*

Not all areas have facilities for recycling.

city council of Athens recycling of paper

Paper-recycling bin.

keywords keywords keywords

υγρό πλυσίματος
eegro
pleeseematos
washing-up liquid

σκόνη πλυσίματος
skonee
pleeseematos
washing powder

σαπούνι
sapoonee
soap

ανοικτήρι
aneekteeree
tin-opener

κεριά
kereea
candles

σπίρτα
speerta
matches

φυάλη αεριού
feealee a-ereeoo
gas cylinder (large)

γκαζάκι
gazakee
camping gas

Logo of the Hostelling International organisation at the YHA hostel in Athens. The Greek Youth Hostel Asociation is the other hostelling organisation. There are also private hostels with economical rates, especially in cities.

Check out times vary according to where you are staying.

talking talking talking

can we have an extra set of keys?
boroome na ekhoome ena extra set kleedheea
μπορούμε να έχουμε ένα έξτρα σετ κλειδιά;

when does the cleaner come?
pote erkhete ee kathareestreea
πότε έρχεται η καθαρίστρια;

is there always hot water?
ekhee panta zesto nero
έχει πάντα ζεστό νερό;

who do we contact if there are problems?
se pee-on tha-pef-theen-thoome an eeparksoon provleemata
σε ποιόν θ' απευθυνθούμε αν υπάρξουν προβλήματα;

where is the nearest supermarket?
poo eene to kondeenotero supermarket
πού είναι το κοντινότερο supermarket;

where do we leave rubbish?
poo petame ta skoopeedheea
που πετάμε τα σκουπίδια;

when is the rubbish collected?
pote eene ee seeloghee skoopeedhee-on
πότε είναι η συλλογή σκουπίδιών;

what are the neighbours called?
pos leghonte ee gheetones
πώς λέγονται οι γείτονες;

Camping

There is no shortage of well-equipped campsites in Greece. Look for the tent/caravan sign, with CAMPING written in English. Prices are reasonable and facilities are good. Water is usually heated by solar power.

road sign for campsite

campsite sign

In smaller places you can have clothes washed or dry-cleaned at small laundries like this, where they charge per item. In towns there are bigger versions of the same thing. Self-service launderettes do not exist.

we're looking for a campsite
psakhnoome ya thesee kamping
ψάχνουμε για θέση κάμπινγκ

have you any vacancies?
ekhete thesees
έχετε θέσεις;

we'd like to stay for ... nights
theloome na meenoome ... vradya
θέλουμε να μείνουμε ... βράδια

how much is it per night...?
poso kosteezee tee neekhta...
πόσο κοστίζει τη νύχτα...;

for a tent
ee skenee
η σκηνή

per person
to atomo
το άτομο

is there a restaurant on the campsite?
eeparkhee esteeatoreeo sto camping
υπάρχει εστιατόριο στό κάμπινγκ;

how far is the beach?
poso makreea eene ee paraleea
πόσο μακριά είναι η παραλία;

can we camp here overnight?
boroome na perasoome edho tee neekhta
μπορούμε να περάσουμε εδώ τη νύχτα;

have you a list of campsites?
ekhete leesta me ta kamping
έχετε λίστα με τα κάμπινγκ;

talking talking talking talking

Typical pricelist for campsite. Tariffs can be listed in English as well as Greek.

Most sites have at least basic laundry facilities.

on-site laundrette

washing machines

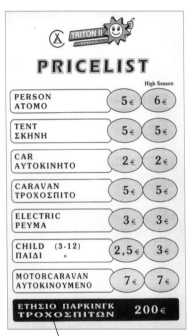

PRICELIST

			High Season
PERSON **ATOMO**	5€	6€
TENT **ΣΚΗΝΗ**	5€	5€
CAR **ΑΥΤΟΚΙΝΗΤΟ**	2€	2€
CARAVAN **ΤΡΟΧΟΣΠΙΤΟ**	5€	5€
ELECTRIC **ΡΕΥΜΑ**	3€	3€
CHILD (3-12) **ΠΑΙΔΙ** "	2,5€	3€
MOTORCARAVAN **ΑΥΤΟΚΙΝΟΥΜΕΝΟ**	7€	7€
ΕΤΗΣΙΟ ΠΑΡΚΙΝΓΚ **ΤΡΟΧΟΣΠΙΤΩΝ**		200€

annual parking fee for mobile homes

Dry cleaners are often open only in the morning.

talking

where can I do some washing?
poo boro na pleeno mereeka rookha
που μπορώ να πλύνω μερικά ρούχα;

do you have a laundry service?
ekhete eepeereseea pleendeereeoo
έχετε υπηρεσία πλυντηρίου;

when will my things be ready?
pote tha eene eteema ta praghmata moo
πότε θα είναι έτοιμα τα πράγματά μου;

is there a dry-cleaner's near here?
eeparkhee kathareesteereeo edho konda
υπάρχει καθαριστήριο εδώ κοντά;

can I borrow an iron?
boro na dhaneesto ena seedhero
μπορώ να δανειστώ ένα σίδερο;

where can I dry clothes?
poo boro na steghnoso rookha
πού μπορώ να στεγνώσω ρούχα;

Special Needs

Recent new facilities on the Metro and at the Venizelos Airport are superb. Elsewhere they are gradually improving, but it is still difficult to get around on public transport.

attention (no parking)

entrance to chemists

wheelchair access

Disabled lift access sign in the metro station.

Disabled lift access sign.

---

are there any toilets for the disabled?
eeparkhoon tooaletes ya atoma me eedheekes ananges
υπάρχουν τουαλέτες για άτομα με ειδικές ανάγκες;

do you have any bedrooms on the ground floor?
ekhete eepnodhomateea sto eesoyo
έχετε υπνοδωμάτια στο ισόγειο;

is there a ramp?
eeparkhee rampa
υπάρχει ράμπα;

where is the lift?
poo eene to asanser
πού είναι το ασανσέρ;

how many stairs are there?
poses skales eeparkhoon
πόσες σκάλες υπάρχουν;

do you have wheelchairs?
ekhete karotsakeea
έχετε καροτσάκια;

can you go to ... in a wheelchair?
borees na pas ... me karotsakee
μπορείς να πας ... με καροτσάκι;

where is the wheelchair-accessible entrance?
poo eene ee eesodhos me prosvasee ya ta karotsakeea
πού είναι η είσοδος με πρόσβαση για τα καροτσάκια;

is there a reduction for disabled people?
yeenete ekptosee sta atoma me eedheekes ananges
γίνεται έκπτωση στα άτομα με ειδικές ανάγκες;

talking talking talking talking

With Kids

Greek people make a fuss of children and always make them welcome. Greek children are generally polite and well-behaved. Greeks tend to eat altogether as a family, so you don't usually find special menus designed for children, except in the national/international fast-food eateries such as MacDonalds, Pizza Hut, Goody's etc. In the summer (schools close from mid-June to mid-September) children stay up late with their parents and most families have a 'siesta' in the afternoon.

keywords

παιδί
pedee
child

παιδικό κάθισμα
pedeeko katheesma
high-chair

κούνια
koonya
cot

παιδική χαρά
pedeekee hara
play park

πάνες
panes
nappies

Children should be securely strapped in the car.

Παιδικό κάθισμα. Η "ζωή" σας αξίζει.

your child deserves it

drive safely!

Οδηγείτε με ασφάλεια!

talking talking

a child's ticket
ena pedheeko eeseeteereeo
ένα παιδικό εισητήριο

he/she is ... years old
eene ... khronon
είναι ... χρονών

is there a reduction for children?
eeparkhee eedheekee teemee ya pedya
υπάρχει ειδική τιμή για παιδιά;

is there a children's menu?
eeparkhee pedheeko menoo
υπάρχει παιδικό μενού;

have you...?
ekhete...
έχετε...;

a high chair
meea pedheekee karekla
μία παιδική καρέκλα

a child's bed
ena pedheeko krevatee
ένα παιδικό κρεββάτι

is it safe for children?
eene asfales ya ta pedhya
είναι ασφαλές για τα παιδιά;

what is there for children to do?
tee boroon na kanoon ta pedhya
τι μπορούν να κάνουν τα παιδιά;

where is there a play park?
poo eene ee pedheekee khara
πού είναι η παιδική χαρά;

Health

The E111 (health insurance) form has been replaced by a new European Health Insurance card. Apply at the post office or online at www.dh.gov.uk to make sure you're covered. For minor ailments, ask the pharmacist for advice. You can consult a specialist for a reasonable price without a doctor's referral.

Doctor's sign. You can often see a doctor right away, or at least on the same day.

pharmacy

(name of pharmacist)

Parga Health Centre

ΕΘΝΙΚΟ ΣΥΣΤΗΜΑ ΥΓΕΙΑΣ
Πε.Σ.Υ. ΗΠΕΙΡΟΥ
ΚΕΝΤΡΟ ΥΓΕΙΑΣ ΠΑΡΓΑΣ
EMERGENCY & HEALTH CENTER
PRONTO SOCCORSO

Chemists work on a rota basis, so there is always one open.

ΕΦΗΜΕΡΙΑ ΦΑΡΜΑΚΕΙΩΝ ΑΥΓΟΥΣΤΟΣ 2002			
ΗΜΕΡΑ	ημ/νία	**ΕΠ/ΜΟ**	
ΠΕΜΠΤΗ	1	ΚΟΛΩΝΗΣ	KOLONIS
ΠΑΡΑΣΚΕΥΗ	2	ΛΕΝΑΣ	LENAS
ΣΑΒΒΑΤΟ	3	ΣΙΑΤΟΥΝΗΣ	SIATOYNIS
ΚΥΡΙΑΚΗ	4	ΣΙΑΤΟΥΝΗΣ	SIATOYNIS
ΔΕΥΤΕΡΑ	5	ΛΕΝΑΣ	LENAS

day — ΗΜΕΡΑ

days of the week

---

where is there a chemist?
poo eene ena farmakeeo
πού είναι ένα φαρμακείο;

I don't feel well
dhen esthanome kala
δεν αισθάνομαι καλά

have you something for...?
ekhete teepote ya...
έχετε τίποτε για...;

sunburn
ta engavmata
τα εγκαύματα

mosquito bites
tseebeemata koonoopeeon
τσιμπήματα κουνουπιών

diarrhoea
tee dheeareea
τη διάρροια

sunstroke
teen eeleeasee
την ηλίαση

toothache
ton ponodhonto
τον πονόδοντο

I have a rash
ekho ena eksantheema
έχω ένα εξάνθημα

is it safe to give children?
eene asfales ya ta pedhya
είναι ασφαλές για τα παιδιά;

talking talking talking

visiting times

ΩΡΕΣ ΕΠΙΣΚΕΠΤΗΡΙΟΥ
12.30 μμ - 2.30 μμ
17.30 μμ - 19.30 μμ

The dental system is reliable and efficient.

ΟΔΟΝΤΙΑΤΡΕΙΟ
DENTAL CLINIC

I feel ill
dhen esthanome kala
δεν αισθάνομαι καλά

I need a doctor
khreeazome yatro
χρειάζομαι γιατρό

my son is ill
o yos moo eene arostos
ο γιος μου είναι άρρωστος

my daughter is ill
ee koree moo eene arostee
η κόρη μου είναι άρρωστη

I'm on this medication
perno afta ta farmaka
παίρνω αυτά τα φάρμακα

I have high blood pressure
ekho eepertasee
έχω υπέρταση

I'm diabetic (m/f)
eeme dheeaveeteekos/ee
είμαι διαβητικός/ή

I'm pregnant
eeme engeeos
είμαι έγγυος

I'm on the pill
perno anteeseeleepteeka
παίρνω αντισυλληπτικά

I'm allergic to penicillin
ekho alergheea steen peneekeeleenee
έχω αλλεργία στην πενικιλλίνη

I'm breastfeeding
theelazo to moro moo
θηλάζω το μωρό μου

is it safe to take while breastfeeding?
eene asfales kata teen ghalookheea
είναι ασφαλές κατά την γαλουχία;

I need a dentist
khreeazome odhondeeatro
χρειάζομαι οδοντίατρο

I have toothache
ekho ponodhondo
έχω πονόδοντο

the filling has come out
moo efeeghe to sfragheesma
μου έφυγε το σφράγισμα

I have an abscess in the tooth
ekho ena aposteema sto dondee
έχω ένα απόστημα στο δόντι

it hurts
me ponaee
με πονάει

can you repair my dentures?
boreete na moo epeedheeorthosete teen odhondosteekheea
μπορείτε να μου επιδιορθώσετε την οδοντοστοιχία;

do I have to pay now?
prepee na pleeroso tora
πρέπει να πληρώσω τώρα;

talking talking talking talking talking talking

If you require hospital treatment, take your Health Insurance card and your passport with you. A proportion of the cost will be covered, depending on the type of hospital and the treatment.

general hospital (of preveza)

> ΑΠΑΓΟΡΕΥΕΤΑΙ
> ΤΟ ΚΑΠΝΙΣΜΑ

smoking prohibited

ΚΤΙΡΙΟ Α´ — Building A

- ⊕ Καρδιολογικό Τμήμα — Cardiology Dept
- ⊕ Καρδιολογική Μονάδα — Cardiology Unit
- 🛉 Ουρολογικό Τμήμα — Urology Dept
- 🔊 ΩΡΛ Τμήμα — ENT Dept

If you need to go to hospital

will he/she have to go to hospital?
prepee na bee sto nosokomeeo
πρέπει να μπει στο νοσοκομείο;

to the hospital, please
sto nosokomeeo parakalo
στο νοσοκομείο παρακαλώ

I need to go to casualty
prepee na pao sta epeeghonda pereestateeka
πρέπει να πάω στα επείγοντα περιστατικά

when are visiting hours?
pote ekhee epeeskepteereeo
πότε έχει επισκεπτήριο;

can you tell me what is the matter?
boreete na moo peete tee seemvenee
μπορείτε να μου πείτε τί συμβαίνει;

where is the hospital?
poo eene to nosokomeeo
πού είναι το νοσοκομείο;

which ward?
pya kleeneekee
ποια κλινική;

is it serious?
eene sovaro
είναι σοβαρό;

I need a receipt for the insurance
khreeazome apodheeksee ya teen asfaleesteekee moo etereea
χρειάζομαι απόδειξη για την ασφαλιστική μου εταιρεία

Emergency

i *If you experience a theft or other crime, you must go to the police (asteenomeea) and make a report. You will need the report for any related insurance claim. Emergency phone numbers: Police – 100, Medical emergency – 166, Fire Brigade – 199.*

ambulance

Vehicles connected with the council or government have orange number-plates.

There are often bush-fires in Greece in the summer,

so the fire-brigade has to be on the alert.

help!
voeetheea
βοήθεια!

can you help me?
boreete na me voeetheesete
μπορείτε να με βοηθήσετε;

there's been an accident
ekhee yeenee ateekheema
έχει γίνει ατύχημα

someone is injured
eeparkhoon travmatee-es
υπάρχουν τραυματίες

please call...
parakalo kaleste...
παρακαλώ καλέστε...

the police
teen asteenomeea
την αστυνομία

an ambulance
ena asthenoforo
ένα ασθενοφόρο

he was going too fast
etrekhe me meghalee takheeteeta
έτρεχε με μεγάλη ταχύτητα

where's the police station?
poo eene to asteenomeeko tmeema
πού είναι το αστυνομικό τμήμα;

I've been raped
me veeasan
με βίασαν

I want to report a theft
thelo na dheeloso meea klopee
θέλω να δηλώσω μία κλοπή

I've been robbed
ekho pesee theema klopees
έχω πέσει θύμα κλοπής

my car's been broken into
paraveeasan to aftokeeneeto moo
παραβίασαν το αυτοκίνητό μου

I've been attacked
ekho pesee theema efodhoo klepton
έχω πέσει θύμα εφόδου κλεπτών

I need a report for my insurance
khreeazome khartee pereeghrafees seemvandon ya teen asfaleea moo
χρειάζομαι χαρτί περιγραφής συμβάντων για την ασφάλεια μου

how much is the fine?
poso eene to prosteemo
πόσο είναι το πρόστιμο;

where do I pay it?
poo boro na to pleeroso
πού μπορώ να το πληρώσω;

talking talking talking talking

Food
&
Drink

Greek Food

Greek food is not only tasty but healthy, interesting, and reasonably priced. Greece's long and diverse history, along with its varied geography, is reflected in the wide range of dishes on offer. Unlike the UK, regional traditions are very much alive. The unifying theme is simplicity: unfussy, nutritious food with the emphasis on seasonality and fresh local produce.

Fish is of course well represented, as you would expect from a maritime nation. Other mainstays are lamb, goat and pork, cheese (including feta and halloumi), yoghurt, olive oil and salads, with lemon to pep up savoury dishes and honey to sweeten the desserts. Typical vegetables include aubergine/eggplant, courgettes/zucchini, cucumbers, tomatoes, peppers and vine leaves. This is the classic Mediterranean diet, credited with so many medical benefits, including lowering your risk of cancer and heart disease. Wine, whether red, white or rosé, is abundant, often with the famous resinous flavours traditionally associated with Greece. Greeks tend to drink a little and often; being visibly drunk is considered shameful.

It is often just as cheap to eat out as to cook for yourself, and there is no shortage of places to eat. Restaurants are informal, friendly places, where children are welcome. In the less grand places you can often see the food being prepared, and even go into the kitchen to see what's in the pot (tapsee), so you can choose by pointing at what you want. Ideal for those who are not confident of their Greek culinary vocabulary!

steefadho Beef in a rich sauce with onions, tomatoes, wine, peppercorns and spices.

Fried squid *(kalamareea)*, stuffed tomatoes *(domates yemeestes)*, green beans *(fasolakeea)* and yogurt and garlic dip *(tsatseekee)*.

Kebabs are great for a cheap, tasty meal. You will often spot the big doner kebabs from afar, and the little 'souvlakis' (pieces of meat on small skewers) lined up on the charcoal grill.

breeamee
A stew of potatoes, courgettes,
aubergines, onions, tomato, garlic
and herbs, simmered slowly in olive oil.

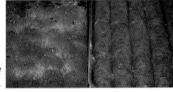

baklava and *kataeefee*
Cakes made with nuts and honey.

Moussaka, made with
mince, aubergines and
béchamel sauce.

Stuffed tomatoes (*tomates yemeestes*),
oven-baked. The filling is usually rice,
garlic, tomato and herbs, sometimes
with mince. There are also stuffed
peppers (*peepereees*) courgettes
(*kolookeethakeea*) and aubergines
(*meleetzanes*).

---

where can we have a snack?
poo boroome na fame katee prokheera
πού μπορούμε να φάμε κάτι πρόχειρα;

is there a good local restaurant?
eeparkhee ena kalo topeeko esteeatoreeo
υπάρχει ένα καλό τοπικό εστιατόριο;

not too expensive
okhee polee akreevo
όχι πολύ ακριβό

are there any vegetarian restaurants here?
eeparkhoon katholoo esteeatoreea ya khortofaghoos edho
υπάρχουν καθόλου εστιατόρια για χορτοφάγους εδώ;

can you recommend a local dish?
boreete na moo seesteesete ena topeeko fagheeto
μπορείτε να μου συστήσετε ένα τοπικό φαγητό;

what is this?
tee eene afto
τι είναι αυτό;

I'll have this
tha paro afto
θα πάρω αυτό

excuse me!
me seengkhoreete
με συγχωρείτε!

talking talking

i Snacking is easy and convenient, with food available on every street corner: cheese, spinach or sausage pies (teer**o**peetes, spanak**o**peetes, lookaneek**o**peetes), toasted sandwiches (sand-w**ee**ts), pitta bread (p**ee**ta), bread rolls (kooloor**a**keeya) and so on, or for the sweet-toothed, look**oo**mee (Turkish delight) and such honey-based treats as baklav**a** and kata**ee**fee.

keywords

κρέας	
kreas	
meat	
ψάρι	
psaree	
fish	
λαχανικά	
lakhaneeka	
vegetables	
φρούτα	
froota	
fruit	
κέικ	
cake	
cakes	
γλυκά	
gleeka	
cakes/desserts	

Pop-corn stands are popular.

all with the most pure ingredients

talking

I'd like a white coffee
*tha **ee**thela ena kafe me ghala*
θα ήθελα ένα καφέ με γάλα

a decaffeinated coffee
*ena dekafe**ee**ne*
ένα ντεκαφεϊνέ

a tea...	**with milk**	**with lemon**	**without sugar**
ena tsaee...	*me ghala*	*me lemonee*	*khorees zakharee*
ένα τσάι...	με γάλα	με λεμόνι	χωρις ζάχαρη

an orange juice please
*ena kheem**o** portokalee parakalo*
ένα χυμό πορτοκάλι παρακαλώ

an iced coffee
ena frape
ένα φραπέ

for me	**for her**	**for him**	**for us**
ya mena	*yaft**ee**n*	*yafton*	*ya mas*
για μένα	γι' αυτήν	γι' αυτόν	για μας

with ice please
me paghakeea parakalo
με παγάκια παρακαλώ

I'm very thirsty
*dheepsao pol**ee***
διψάω πολύ

a bottle of mineral water	**sparkling**	**still**
ena bookalee emfeealomeno nero	*aere**ee**ookho*	*aplo*
ένα μπουκάλι εμφιαλωμένο νερό	αεριούχο	απλό

snack and take-away van

take-away

Quick and easy sit-down or take-away place for a snack (doner kebab with slices of pork or chicken), wrapped up in a pitta bread with tomatoes, onions, chips and plain yogurt.

- KYΛIKEIO — buffet
- KAΦE — coffee
- ANAΨYKTIKA — soft drinks
- TOST — cheese & ham toasties
- ΣANTOYΪTΣ — sandwiches

keywords keywords keywords keywords

σοκολάτα
sokolata
chocolate

παγωτό
paghoto
ice cream

πάστες
pastes
slices of gateau

λεμόνι
lemonee
lemon

ροδάκινο
rodhakeeno
peach

φράουλα
fraoola
strawberry

τυρόπιτα
teeropeeta
cheese pie

πατάτες
patates
chips

φραπέ
frape
iced coffee

talking

I'd like a toasted sandwich
tha eethela ena tost
θα ήθελα ένα τοστ

what sandwiches do you have?
tee sandwich ekhete
τι σάντουϊτς έχετε;

a cheese pie
meea teeropeeta
μία τυρόπιτα

I'd like an ice cream
tha eethela ena paghoto
θα ήθελα ένα παγωτό

with chips
me patates
με πατάτες

with cheese
me teeree
με τυρί

with ham
me zambon
με ζαμπόν

what cakes do you have?
tee ghleeka ekhete
τι γλυκά έχετε;

what flavours do you have?
tee ghefsees ekhete
τι γεύσεις έχετε;

(i) Ask the restaurant whether they serve *mezedhes*. An alternative, if you want a mixture, is to order half-portions (*meesee mereedha*) of various dishes.

You are never far from a taverna.

— *traditional cuisine*
— *everything chargrilled*
— *views over the Ionian Sea*

seaside taverna

talking

I'd like to book a table	**for ... people**
tha eethela na krateeso ena trapezee	*ya ... atoma*
θα ήθελα να κρατήσω ένα τραπέζι	για ... άτομα
for tonight	**at 8 o'clock**
ya apopse	*stees okto to vradhee*
για απόψε	στις οκτώ το βράδυ
for tomorrow night	**for 5th August**
ya avreeo to vradhee	*ya tees 5 avghoostoo*
για αύριο το βράδυ	για τις 5 Αυγούστου
I booked a table	**in the name of...**
ekleesa ena trapezee	*sto onoma...*
έκλεισα ένα τραπέζι	στο όνομα...
in a non-smoking area	
stoos mee kapneezontes	
στους μη καπνίζοντες	

grill/bar

Specialities:
ΚΟΚΟΡΕΤΣΙ *spit-roasted liver and spleen, wrapped in intestines*

ΤΥΡΟΣΟΥΦΛΕ *cheese soufflé*

charcoal/grill house — restaurant — café-bar

Some restaurants have Greek dancing, as shown by the illustration.

a table for two
ena trapezee ya dheeo
ένα τραπέζι για δύο

the menu, please
ton katalogho parakalo
τον κατάλογο παρακαλώ

what is the dish of the day?
pyo eene to pyato tees eemeras
ποιο είναι το πιάτο της ημέρας;

can we see what you have?
boroome na dhoome tee ekhete
μπορούμε να δούμε τι έχετε;

what is this?
tee eene afto
τι είναι αυτό;

I'll have this
tha paro afto
θα πάρω αυτό

do you have any vegetarian dishes?
ekhete fa-yeeta ya khortofaghoos
έχετε φαγητά για χορτοφάγους;

please bring...
parakalo ferte...
παρακαλώ, φέρτε...

some more bread
ke alo psomee
και άλλο ψωμί

some more water
ke alo nero
και άλλο νερό

another bottle
alo ena bookalee
άλλο ένα μπουκάλι

the bill
to loghareeasmo
το λογαριασμό

talking talking talking talking

i Breakfast for many Greeks is simply coffee, perhaps with a bowl of yoghurt and honey. If you prefer something substantial to start the day, fresh bread (psom**ee**) with cheese (teer**ee**), olives (el**yes**) or jam (marmel**a**dha) is a common choice. You can buy it yourself from the bakery (**foo**rno), which will also sell teer**o**peetees (cheese pies).

menu of the day

Many restaurants have bilingual menus, like this one.

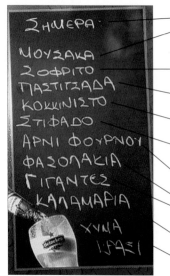

ΣΗΜΕΡΑ today

ΜΟΥΣΑΚΑΣ moosak**a**s moussaka with mince, aubergine/eggplant and béchamel sauce

ΣΟΦΡΙΤΟ sofr**ee**to tender beef in a creamy garlic sauce.

ΠΑΣΤΙΤΣΑΔΑ pasteets**a**da beef and pasta in tomato sauce

ΚΟΚΚΙΝΙΣΤΟ kokeen**ee**sto braised beef in red wine sauce

ΣΤΙΦΑΔΟ steef**a**do braised beef in onion and peppercorn sauce

ΑΡΝΙ ΦΟΥΡΝΟΥ arn**ee** f**oo**rnoo lamb cooked slowly in the oven

ΦΑΣΟΛΑΚΙΑ fasol**a**keea green beans

ΓΙΓΑΝΤΕΣ ghee**gh**antes large butter beans

ΚΑΛΑΜΑΡΙΑ kalam**a**reea rings of squid (calamari) in batter

ΧΥΜΑ ΚΡΑΣΙ kh**ee**ma kras**ee** wine from the barrel

Most people have lunch between 1 and 3pm, and it is usually a cooked meal, though fairly light: typically one main dish, with salad or chips, followed by a simple dessert such as fruit or yoghurt. The evening meal, which is the main one of the day, might be any time from about six until very late. It's accompanied by side-dishes and bread. Classic Greek dishes include moosak**a** (layers of aubergine, meat and béchamel sauce); soovl**a**keea (pieces of pork grilled on a skewer like a shish kebab); kl**e**fteeko (lamb casserole); and keft**e**dhes (herbed meat patties). These might be accompanied by Greek salad (khoree**a**teekee sal**a**ta), including chunks of tomato, cucumber, onions and feta cheese; tzatz**ee**kee (yoghurt, cucumber and garlic); or taramosal**a**ta (a purée of fish roes).

ΟΡΕΚΤΙΚΑ

appetisers

ΛΑΔΕΡΑ

cooked in oil

ΚΥΡΙΑ ΦΑΓΗΤΑ

main dishes

ΣΑΛΑΤΕΣ

salads

ΖΥΜΑΡΙΚΑ

pasta

ΤΗΣ ΩΡΑΣ

dishes of the day
usually fresh meat
or fish, barbecued
to order

cheese
ΤΥΡΙΑ

ΚΙΜΑΔΕΣ

mincemeat

fish

ΨΑΡΙΑ

Typical headings you will come across on restaurant menus.

Whole pigs roasting on spits. You buy the roast pork by the kilo.

i   Beer, though not native to Greece, is popular. The major international lager brands are widely available, usually brewed in Greece under licence.

Greek coffee (*eleeneekos kafes*), is small, strong and sweet, like that of Turkey and the Arab countries. Instead of being filtered, it's ground very fine and brewed in a pot with the sugar included, rather than added afterwards. If you prefer yours without sugar, you will need to ask for a 'plain' coffee (*sketo kafe*). Sweet is *gleeko*, and medium is *metreeo*. If you want it white, specify *me ghala* (with milk). The usual alternative to Greek coffee is instant, known by the name Nescafe regardless of brand, which can be served cold as a *frape*. Coffee is often served with a glass of water as a preliminary thirst-quencher, a welcome addition in a hot country. It is not common practice to finish a meal with coffee: in fact some restaurants do not serve it.

Tea (*tsaee*) is not quite so popular, but easily available. It will tend to be in the form of a teabag to dip in a glass of (fairly) hot water, which may be a disappointment to a British tea-drinker!

Bars, café-bars and bistros all serve beer and wine.

keywords keywords keywords

ΟΥΖΕΡΙ
oozeree
ouzo bar

μεζέδες
mezedes
snacks to go with ouzo

ΚΑΦΕ
café
café-bar

ΚΟΝΙΑΚ
konyak
brandy

ΜΠΥΡΑ ΜΥΘΟΣ
beera meethos
'Mythos' beer

ΜΠΥΡΑ ΚΟΡΩΝΑ
beera corona
'Corona' beer

International and
Greek beers are available.
Retsina is also popular,
and is sold chilled.

keywords keywords keywords keywords keywords

red
κόκκινο
kokeeno

white
άσπρο
aspro

rosé
ροζέ
roze

dry
ξηρό
kseero

sweet
γλυκό
gleeko

bottle
μπουκάλι
bookalee

glass
ποτήρι
poteeree

litre
λίτρο
leetro

half litre
μισό λίτρο
meeso leetro

house wine
σπιτικό κρασί
speeteeko krasee

carafe
καράφα
karafa

from the barrel
από το βαρέλι
apo to varelee

talking

a beer please
meea beera parakalo
μία μπύρα παρακαλώ

a glass of wine please
ena poteeree krasee parakalo
ένα ποτήρι κρασί παρακαλώ

a small beer
meea mekree beera
μία μικρή μπύρα

a large beer
meea meghalee beera
μία μεγάλη μπύρα

i Wine in Greece is very popular. The prices of bottled wines vary according to quality. It's fun to sample the various house-wines, served by the glass, carafe or jug, straight from the barrel.

Be adventurous and try the famous retsina (white wine flavoured with pine resin – originally, so they say, to deter the Turks from drinking it!) It makes a nice long drink diluted with soda, coke or iced water.

You will find an ever-increasing selection of quality wines throughout Greece in restaurants, supermarkets and specialist wine and spirit stores.

Perhaps the best-known Greek spirits are ouzo (**oo**zo, flavoured with aniseed, a little like French pastis) and Metaxa (Greek brandy). Ouzo is usually served with ice, and diluted to taste by the drinker, which makes the clear spirit turn cloudy. It can be found in ordinary bars or specialist ouzo-bars. Other famous Greek spirits include raki, from Crete, and ts**ee**pooro, an eau-de-vie distilled from the skins, stems, and pips of crushed grapes.

There are many types of the aniseed-flavoured spirit, ouzo. Metaxa brandy has three categories – 3-, 5- and 7-star.

enjoy your meal!	**cheers!**	**your health!**
kal**ee** o**r**eksee	ya mas	steen ee**ya** sas
καλή όρεξη!	γειά μας!	στην υγειά σας!
would you like a drink?	**it's my round**	
tha the**late ena** pot**o**	**ee**ne ee se**era** moo	
θα θέλατε ένα ποτό;	είναι η σειρά μου	

the wine list, please
ton katalogho krasyon parakalo
τον κατάλογο κρασιών, παρακαλώ

a carafe of wine
meea karafa krasee
μία καράφα κρασί

a glass of wine
ena poteeree krasee
ένα ποτήρι κρασί

a bottle of wine
ena bookalee krasee
ένα μπουκάλι κρασί

red
kokeeno
κόκκινο

white
lefko
λευκό

a bottle...
ena bookalee...
ένα μπουκάλι...

a carafe...
meea karafa...
μία καράφα...

of wine
krasee
κρασί

of dry wine
kseero krasee
ξηρό κρασί

of sweet wine
ghleeko krasee
γλυκό κρασί

of a local wine
topeeko krasee
τοπικό κρασί

talking talking talking

Flavours of Greece

Πηλιορίτικο μπουμπάρι (peeleeoreeteeko boobaree)
spicy sausage
Μακαρονόπιτα (makaronopeeta)
macaroni pie
Χαλβάς (halvas) fudge-like swee
made from sesame seeds and hor
Μεζέδες (mezedhes)
traditional snacks
Εξοχικό (exokheeko) beef or po
stuffed with vegetables and chee

Παστιτσάδα (pasteetsadha) braised beef
in spicy red sauce with pasta
Σοφρίτο (sofreeto) beef casseroled in a
creamy sauce with onions, garlic and herbs

Πίτα (peeta) various pies; you may buy
a large one to share, for a main course.
Γίδα βραστή (yeedha vrastee) goat-meat
soup, eaten with the juice of fresh lemon
Κυνήγι (keeneeghee) game
Φασολάδα (fasoladha)
a thick soup with haricot beans and
vegetables, served with lemon
Ψάρια φρέσκα (psareea freska) fresh fish
Γραβιέρα (gravee-era) gruyère-like cheese
Μπουγάτσα (boogatsa) vanilla custard pie
with cinnamon and icing-sugar
Μπακλαβάς (baklavas) filo pastries
with honey, nuts and syrup
Χαλβάς (khalvas) soft, gelatinous cake,
garnished with almonds
Wines
Ζίτσα (zeetsa); **Αβέρωφ** (averof)

Στην σούβλα (steen soovla) spit-roasts
Γουρουνόπουλο (ghooroonopoolo)
suckling pig roasted slowly with herbs
Χυλοπίτες με κοτόπουλο κρασάτο
(kheelopeetes me kotopoolo krasato)
Pie containing chicken marinated in wine
Τουρλού (toorloo)
ratatouille with aubergines, courgettes,
potatoes, onions and sometimes cheese
Σπανακόπιτα (spanakopeeta) spinach pie
Ελιές Καλαμάτας (elyes kalamatas)
Kalamata olives
Μηλόπιτα (meelopeeta)
apple pie with cinnamon
Δίπλες (dheeples)
pastries with honey and walnuts
Μελιτζανάκι γλυκό (meleetzanakee ghleeko)
sweet crystallized aubergine in syrup
Σύκα μαυροδάφνη (seeka mavrodhafnee)
figs in wine syrup
Σταφιδόπιτα (stafeedhopeeta) raisin pie
Wines
Νεμέας (nemeas); **Αχαΐα Κλάους** (akheya
klaoos); **Καμπάς** (kampas)

GREECE
MACE
Kastoria Véro
NORTHERN
GREECE
Ioánnina Trikal
EPIRUS CENTRAL
WESTERN
Arta GREECE
Larisa
STEREA ELLADA
Mesólongi
Pátra
PELOPONNE
Pýrgos Náf
Tripo
Kalámata S
CORFU
IONIAN
ISLANDS

Χοιρινό κρήτικο
(kheereeno kreeteeko)
pork chops baked with vegetab
in a spicy sauce
Σαλιγκάρια (saleengareea)
snails, prepared in various way
Ψάρια φρέσκα (psareea freska,
fresh fish and shellfish of all kind

Κοντοσούβλι *(kontos**oo**vlee)*
*lamb, pork or beef, spit-roasted with
herbs and spices*
μέλι θυμαρίσιο *(m**e**lee theemar**ee**seeo)*
thyme-flavoured honey
Τυρί Μετσόβου *(teer**ee** mets**o**voo)*
smoked cheese from Metsovo
Ούζο *(**oo**zo) aniseed-flavour spirit*
Τσίπουρο *(ts**ee**pooro) spirit*
Wines
Τσάνταλη *(tsantalee);* **Μπουτάρη**
(bootaree); **Κουρτάκη** *(koortakee);*
Καμπάς *(kamp**as**);* **Χατζημιχάλη**
(khadzeemeekhalee)

Σουτζουκάκια *(sootzookakya)*
meat balls in tomato sauce
Τας κεμπάμπ *(tash kebab) lamb, goat,
pork or beef in spicy sauce*
Ντολμάδες *(dolmadhes) spicy,
rice-stuffed vine-leaves*
Τυροκαυτερή *(teerokafter**ee**)*
feta cheese and red pepper dip
Τουρσί *(toor**see**)*
vegetables pickled in vinegar
Μπακλαβάς *(baklavas) and* **καταίφι**
*(kata**ee**fee) pastries of filo, with honey,
nuts and syrup*
Wines
Μακεδονικός *(makedhoneek**o**s);*
Τσάνταλη *(tsantalee);* **Μπουτάρη**
(bootaree); **Αγιορείτικο** *(ayor**ee**teeko
(made by monks on Mt Athos)*

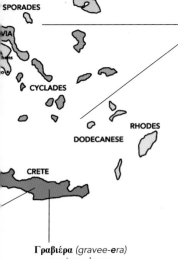

THRACE
•Dráma •Komotini
Kavála• Alexandroúpoli
THASSOS

NE AEGEAN
ISLANDS

SPORADES

CYCLADES

RHODES

DODECANESE

CRETE

Γραβιέρα *(gravee-**e**ra)
graviera cheese*
Μανούρι *(man**oo**ree)
soft cheese, similar to feta*
Σύκα *(s**ee**ka) figs*
Καρπούζι *(karp**oo**zee) watermelon*
Ρακί *(rak**ee**) raki, traditional spirit*
Wines
Κοκκινέλι *(kokeen**e**lee) (red only);*
Κρητικός *(kreeteek**o**s)*

Aegean Islands
Αρνάκι ψητό *(arnakee pseet**o**)
grilled lamb cutlets*
Παστίτσιο *(past**ee**tseeo)
pie made of spiced macaroni and mince
(similar to moussaka)*
Κακαβιά *(kakaveea) fish soup*
Χταπόδι κρασάτο *(khtap**o**dhee krasato)
octopus in wine sauce*
Μυδοπίλαφο *(meedhop**ee**lafo)
mussels and seafood cooked with rice*
Στρείδια *(str**ee**dheea) oysters*
Κάβουρας *(kavooras) crab*
Καλαμάρια *(kalamareea) squid*
Γλυκά κουταλιού *(ghleek**a** kootaly**oo**)
fruit preserved and crystallized in syrup*
Σύκα στο φούρνο με μαυροδάφνη
*(seek**a** sto f**oo**rno me mavrodh**a**fnee)
figs cooked in Mavrodafni red-wine
sauce with spices; from Chios and
Lesvos islands*
Wines
Σάμος *(samos);* **Σαντορίνη**
*(santor**ee**nee);* **Πάρος** *(paros)*

If you have specific dietary requirements, food allergies etc, it may be wise to tell the waiter.

talking talking talking talking talking talking

I'm vegetarian
eeme khortofaghos
είμαι χορτοφάγος

do you have any vegetarian dishes?
ekhete katee ya khortofaghoos
έχετε κάτι για χορτοφάγους;

I don't eat meat
dhen tro-o kreas
δεν τρώω κρέας

I don't eat pork
dhen tro-o kheereeno
δεν τρώω χοιρινό

I don't eat fish/shellfish
dhen tro-o psaree/ostraka
δεν τρώω ψάρι/όστρακα

which dishes have no meat/fish?
pya fa-yeeta dhen ekhoon kreas/psaree
ποια φαγητά δεν έχουν κρέας/ψάρι;

I have an allergy to peanuts
ekho alergheea sta feesteekeea
έχω αλλεργία στα φυστίκια

what do you recommend?
tee proteenete
τι προτείνετε;

I don't drink alcohol
dhen peeno alko-ol
δεν πίνω αλκοόλ

I'm on a diet   **is it raw?**
kano dheeeta   *eene omo*
κάνω δίαιτα   είναι ωμό;

what is this made with?
me tee eene fteeaghmeno afto
με τι είναι φτιαγμένο αυτό;

enjoy your meal!
kalee oreksee
καλή όρεξη

τηγανιτό
teeghaneeto
fried

βραστό
vrasto
boiled

ψητό
pseeto
roast

γεμιστό
yemeesto
stuffed

στο φούρνο
sto foorno
baked in the oven

στη σούβλα
stee soovla
on the spit

λαδερά
ladera
braised in olive oil

στη σχάρα
stee skhara
on the grill

στα κάρβουνα
sta karvoona
barbecued on charcoal

μαγειρευτά
mayeerefta
ready cooked (in casserole pots)

της ώρας
tees oras
while you wait

καπνιστό
kapneesto
smoked

μαγειρεμένο
mayeeremeno
cooked

ωμό
omo
raw

α A

αγγούρι *angooree* cucumber

αγγούρια

αγκινάρες *ankeenares* artichokes

αγκινάρες άλα πολίτα *ankeenares ala poleeta* artichokes with lemon juice and olive oil

αγριογούρουνο *aghreeoghooroono* wild boar

αεριούχο *aereeookho* fizzy, sparkling

αθερίνα *athereena* whitebait, usually fried

αλάτι *alatee* salt

αλεύρι *alevree* flour

αλευρόπιτα *alevropeeta* pie made with cheese, milk and eggs

αμύγδαλα *ameeghdhala* almonds

άνηθος *aneethos* dill

αρακάς *arakas* peas

αρνί *arnee* lamb

αρνί γιουβέτσι *arnee yoovetsee* roast lamb with small pasta

αρνί λεμονάτο *arnee lemonato* lamb braised in sauce with herbs and lemon juice

αρνί με βότανα *arnee me votana* lamb braised with vegetables and herbs

αρνίσιες μπριζόλες *arneesee-es breezoles* lamb chops

αρνί ψητό *arnee pseeto* roast lamb

αστακός *astakos* lobster (often served with lemon juice and olive oil)

άσπρο *aspro* white

άσπρο κρασί *aspro krasee* white wine

αυγά *avgha* eggs

αυγολέμονο *avgholemono* egg and lemon soup

αυγοτάραχο *avghotarakho* mullet roe (smoked)

αφέλια *afeleea* pork in red wine with seasonings (Cyprus)

αχινοί *akheenee* sea urchin roes

αχλάδι *akhladhee* pear

αχλάδι στο φούρνο *akhladhee sto foorno* baked pear in syrup sauce

αχνιστό *akhneesto* steamed

β B

βασιλικός *vaseeleekos* basil

βερίκοκο *vereekoko* apricot

βισινό κασέρι *veeseeno kaseree* sheep's cheese served with cherry preserve

βερίκοκα

γεμιστά *yemeesta* stuffed vegetables

γιαούρτι *yaoortee* yoghurt

γιαούρτι με μέλι *yaoortee me melee* yoghurt with honey

γιαχνί *yakhnee* cooked in tomato sauce and olive oil

γίγαντες *yeeghantes* large butter beans

γιουβαρλάκια *yoovarlakya* meatballs in lemon sauce

γκαζόζα *ghazoza* fizzy drink

γλυκά *ghleeka* desserts

γλυκά κουταλιού *ghleeka kootalyoo* crystallized fruits in syrup

γλώσσα *ghlosa* sole

γόπες *ghopes* bogue, a type of fish

γραβιέρα *ghravyera* cheese resembling gruyère

γύρος *yeeros* doner kebab

δεντρολίβανο

βλίτα *vleeta* wild greens (like spinach, eaten with olive oil and lemon)

βότκα *votka* vodka

βοδινό *vodheeno* beef

βουτήματα *vooteemata* biscuits to dip in coffee

βούτυρο *vooteero* butter

βραδινό *vradeeno* evening meal

βραστό *vrasto* boiled

γ Γ

γάλα *ghala* milk

γαλακτομπούρικο *ghalaktobooreeko* custard tart

γαλακτοπωλείο *ghalaktopoleeo* café/patisserie

γαρίδες *ghareedhes* shrimps; prawns

γαρίδες γιουβέτσι *ghareedhes yoovetsee* prawns in tomato sauce with feta

γαρύφαλλο *ghareefalo* clove (spice)

γαύρος *gavros* sardine-type fish (if salted: anchovy)

γίδα βραστή *yeeda vrastee* goat soup

δ Δ

δάφνη *dhafnee* bay leaf

δάκτυλα *dhakteela* almond cakes

δαμάσκηνα *dhamaskeena* plums, prunes

δείπνο *dheepno* dinner

δεντρολίβανο *dendroleevano* rosemary

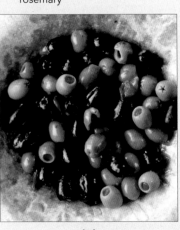

ελιές

δίπλες *dheeples* pastry with honey and walnuts

δολμάδες *dholmadhes* vine leaves, rolled up and stuffed with minced meat and rice

ε E

ελάχιστα ψημένο *elakheesta pseemeno* rare (meat)

ελαιόλαδο *eleoladho* olive oil

ελιές *elyes* olives

ελιές τσακιστές *elyes tsakeestes* cracked green olives with coriander seeds and garlic (Cyprus)

ελιοτή *elyotee* olive bread

εξοχικό *eksokheeko* stuffed pork or beef with vegetables and cheese

εστιατόριο *esteeatoreeo* restaurant

ζ Z

ζαμπόν *zambon* ham

ζαχαροπλαστείο *zakharoplasteeo* cake shop

ζάχαρη *zakharee* sugar

ζελατίνα *zelateena* brawn

ζεστή σοκολάτα *zestee sokolata* hot chocolate

ζεστό *zesto* hot, warm

θ Θ

Θαλασσινά *thalaseena* seafood

Θυμάρι *theemaree* thyme

ι I

Ιμάμ μπαϊλντί *eemam baeeldee* stuffed aubergines (eggplants)

κ K

κάβα *kava* wine shop

κάβουρας *kavooras* boiled crab

καγιανάς με παστό κρέας *kayanas me pasto kreyas* salted pork with cheese, tomatoes and eggs

κακαβιά *kakaveea* fish soup

κακάο *kakow* hot chocolate

καкαβιά

καλαμάκι *kalamakee* straw (for drinking); small skewer

καλαμάρια *kalamareea* squid

καλαμάρια τηγανιτά *kalamareea teeghaneeta* fried squid

καλαμπόκι *kalambokee* corn on the cob

καλαμπόκι

καλαμποκόπιτα *kalambokopeeta* corn bread

καλοψημένο *kalopseemeno* well done (meat)

κανέλα *kanella* cinnamon

κάπαρι *kaparee* pickled capers

καπνιστό *kapneesto* smoked

καπουτσίνο *kapootseeno* cappucino

καρυδόπιτα

καραβίδα karaveedha crayfish
καράφα karafa carafe
καρέκλα karekla chair
καρότο karoto carrot
καρπούζι karpoozee watermelon
καρύδι kareedhee walnut
καρυδόπιτα kareedhopeeta walnut cake
καρύδα kareedha coconut
κασέρι kaseree type of cheese
κάστανα kastana chestnuts
καταΐφι kataeefee small shredded pastry drenched in syrup
κατάλογος kataloghos menu
κατάλογος κρασιών kataloghos krasyon wine list
καταψυγμένο katapseeghmeno frozen
κατσίκι katseekee roast kid
καφενείο kafeneeo café
καφές kafes coffee (Greek-style)
  καφέδες kafedhes coffees (plural)
  καφές γλυκύς kafes ghleekees very sweet coffee
  καφές μέτριος kafes metreeos medium-sweet coffee
  καφές σκέτος kafes sketos coffee without sugar

κεράσια keraseea cherries
κεφαλοτύρι kefaloteeree type of cheese, often served fried in olive oil
κεφτέδες keftedhes meat balls
κιδώνι keedhonee quince
κιδώνι στο φούρνο keedhonee sto foorno baked quince
κιμάς keemas mince
κλέφτικο klefteeko casserole with lamb, potatoes and vegetables
κοκορέτσι kokoretsee traditional spit-roasted dish of spiced liver and other offal
κοκτέιλ kokteyl cocktail
κολατσιό kolatsyo brunch, elevenses
κολοκότες kolokotes pastries with pumpkin seeds and raisins
κολοκυθάκια kolokeethakeea courgettes, zucchini
κολοκυθόπιτα kolokeethopeeta courgette/zucchini pie
κολοκυθόπιτα γλυκιά kolokeethopeeta gleekya sweet courgette/zucchini pie
κονιάκ konyak brandy, cognac
κοντοσούβλι kontosoovlee spicy pieces of lamb, pork or beef, spit-roasted
κοτόπουλο kotopoolo chicken
κοτόπουλο ριγανάτο kotopoolo reeghanato grilled basted chicken with herbs

κεράσια

κουνουπίδι

κρύο *kreeo* cold
κυδώνια *keedhoneea* type of clams, cockles
κυνήγι *keeneeghee* game
κύριο πιάτο *keereeo pyato* main course

λ Λ

λαβράκι *lavrakee* sea-bass
λαγός *laghos* hare
λαδερά *ladhera* vegetable casserole
λάδι *ladhee* oil
λαδότυρο *ladhoteero* soft cheese with olive oil
λάχανα *lakhana* green vegetables

κοτόπουλο καπαμά *kotopoolo kapama* chicken casseroled with red peppers, onions, cinnamon and raisins
κουκιά *kookya* broad beans
κουλούρια *koolooreea* bread rings
κουνέλι *koonelee* rabbit
κουνουπίδι *koonoopeedhee* cauliflower
κουπέπια *koopepeea* stuffed vine leaves (Cyprus)
κουπές *koopes* meat pasties
κουραμπιέδες *kooramb-yedhes* small almond cakes eaten at Christmas
κρασί *krasee* wine
κρέας *kreas* meat
κρέμα *krema* cream
κρεμμύδια *kremeedheea* onions
κρητική σαλάτα *kreeteekee salata* watercress salad

λεμόνι

λαχανικά *lakhaneeka* vegetables (menu heading)
λάχανο *lakhano* cabbage, greens
λεμονάδα *lemonadha* lemon drink
λεμόνι *lemonee* lemon
λευκό *lefko* white (used for wine as well as **άσπρο**)
λίγο *leegho* a little, a bit
λουκάνικα *lookaneeka* type of highly seasoned sausage
λουκουμάδες *lookoomadhes* small fried dough balls in syrup
λουκούμι *lookoomee* Turkish delight
λουκούμια *lookoomeea* shortbread served at weddings
λούντζα *loondza* loin of pork, marinated and smoked

κουπέπια

μ M

μαγειρίτσα *mayeereetsa* soup made of lamb offal, special Easter dish

μαϊντανός *maeedanos* parsley

μακαρόνια *makaronya* spaghetti

μακαρόνια με κιμά *makaronya me keema* spaghetti bolognese

μαρίδες *mareedhes* small fish like sprats, served fried

μαρούλι *maroolee* lettuce

μαρτίνι *marteenee* martini

μαύρο κρασί *mavro krasee* red wine (although you'll hear *kokeeno krasee* more often)

μανιτάρια *maneetareea* mushrooms

μαυρομάτικα *mavromateeka* black-eyed peas

μεγάλο *meghalo* large, big

μεζές *mezes* (plural **μεζέδες** *mezedhes*) small snacks served free of charge with ouzo or retsina; assortment of mini-portions of various dishes, available on the menu (or on request) at some restaurants.

μεζεδοπωλείο *mezedhopoleeo* taverna/shop selling mezedhes

μέλι *melee* honey

μελιτζάνα *meleetzana* aubergine (eggplant)

μελιτζάνες ιμάμ *meleetzanes eemam* aubergines (eggplants) stuffed with tomato and onion

μελιτζάνα

μελιτζανοσαλάτα *meleetzanosalata* aubergine (eggplant) mousse (dip)

μελιτζανάκι γλυκό *meleetzanakee gleeko* crystallized sweet in syrup, made from aubergine/eggplant

μεσημεριανό *meseemereeano* lunch

μεταλλικό νερό *metaleeko nero* mineral water

μεταξά *metaksa* Metaxa (Greek brandy-type spirit)

μέτρια ψημένο *metreea pseemeno* medium-grilled (meat)

μη αεριούχο *mee aereeookho* still, not fizzy

μήλα *meela* apples

μηλόπιτα *meelopeeta* apple pie

μίλκο *meelko* chocolate milk

μιλκσέικ *meelkseik* milkshake

μικρό *meekro* small, little

μοσχάρι *moskharee* beef

μοσχάρι κοκινιστό *moskharee kokeeneesto* beef in wine sauce with tomatoes and onions

μανιτάρια

μήλα

μουσακάς *moosakas* moussaka, layers of aubergine (eggplant), minced meat and potato, with white sauce

μπακαλιάρος *bakaleearos* cod

μπακαλιάρος παστός *bakaleearos pastos* salt cod

μπακλαβάς *baklavas* filo-pastry with nuts soaked in syrup

μπάμιες *bameeyes* okra, ladies' fingers (vegetable)

μπαράκι *barakee* bar

μπαρμπούνι *barboonee* red mullet

μπέικον *baykon* bacon

μπιφτέκι *beeftekee* beef rissole/ burger

μπουγάτσα *booghatsa* cheese or custard pastry sprinkled with sugar and cinnamon

μπουκάλι *bookalee* bottle

μπουρέκι *boorekee* cheese potato and courgette pie

μπουρέκια *boorekeea* puff pastry filled with meat and cheese (Cyprus)

μπουρδέτο *boordheto* fish or meat in a thick sauce of onions, tomatoes and red peppers

μπριάμ(ι) *breeam(ee)* ratatouille

μπριζόλα *breezola* steak/chop

μπριζόλα αρνίσια *breezola arneeseea* lamb chop

μπακλαβάς

μπριζόλα μοσχαρίσια *breezola moskhareeseea* beef steak/chop

μπριζόλα χοιρινή *breezola kheereenee* pork chop

μπύρα *beera* beer

μύδια *meedheea* mussels

ν N

νες, νεσκαφέ *nes, nescafe* instant coffee (of any brand)

νες με γάλα *nes me ghala* coffee (instant) with milk

νες φραπέ *nes frappe* iced coffee

νερό *nero* water

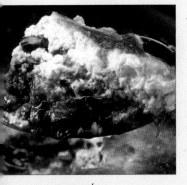

μουσακάς

οβελιστήριο

ντολμάδες *dolmadhes* vine leaves, rolled up and stuffed with rice and sometimes mince

ντομάτες *domates* tomatoes

ντομάτες γεμιστές *domates yemeestes* tomatoes stuffed with rice and herbs, and sometimes with mince

ξ Ξ

ξιφίας *kseefeeas* swordfish

ξύδι *kseedhee* vinegar

ο Ο

οβελιστήριο *oveleesteereeo* shop selling souvlakia and doner kebabs

οινοπωλείο *eenopoleeo* wine shop

ομελέτα *omeletta* omelette

ορεκτικά *orekteeka* first courses/ starters (menu heading)

ούζερι *oozeree* small bar selling ouzo and other drinks, maybe with mezedhes (μεζέδες)

ούζο *oozo* ouzo (traditional aniseed-flavoured spirit)

ουίσκι *weeskee* whisky

οχταπόδι *okhtapodhee* octopus (see also χταπόδι)

οχταπόδι κρασάτο *okhtapodhee krasato* octopus in red wine sauce

π Π

παγάκια *paghakya* ice-cubes

παγωτό *paghoto* ice-cream

παϊδάκια *pa-eedhakeea* grilled lamb chops

παντζάρια *pandzareea* beetroot with seasonings

παξιμάδια *pakseemadheea* crispy bread (baked twice)

παξιμαδοκούλουρα *pakseemadhokooloora* tomato and cheese bread

παπουτσάκια *papootsakeea* stuffed aubergines (eggplants)

πασατέμπο *pasatempo* pumpkin seeds

πάστα *pasta* cake, pastry

παστό *pasto* salted

παστιτσάδα *pasteetsada* beef with tomatoes, onions, red wine, herbs, spices and pasta

παστίτσιο *pasteetseeo* baked pasta dish with a middle layer of meat and white sauce

πατσάς *patsas* tripe soup

πατάτες *patates* potatoes

πατάτες τηγανιτές *patates teeghaneetes* chips, fries

πεπόνι *peponee* melon

πέστροφα *pestrofa* trout

πηλιορίτικο μπουμπάρι *peeleeoreeteeko boobaree* spicy sausage

ραδίκια

σαρδέλλες

πιάτο της ημέρας *pyato tees eemeras* dish of the day

πικάντικο *peekanteeko* spicy

πιλάφι *peelafee* rice

πιπέρι *peeperee* pepper

πιπεριές *peeperyes* peppers

πιπεριές γεμιστές *peeperyes yemeestes* stuffed peppers with rice, herbs and sometimes mince

πίτα or **πίττα** *peeta* pitta (flat-unleavened bread); pie with different fillings, such as meat, cheese, vegetables

πλακί *plakee* fish in tomato sauce

πορτοκαλάδα *portokaladha* orangeade

πορτοκάλια *portokalya* oranges

πουργούρι *poorghooree* cracked wheat (Cyprus)

πουργούρι πιλάφι *poorghooree peelafee* salad made of cracked wheat (Cyprus)

πράσα με σησάμι *prasa me seesamee* leeks baked and sprinkled with sesame seeds

πρωινό *proeeno* breakfast

ρ P

ραβιόλι *raveeolee* pastry stuffed with cheese (Cyprus)

ραδίκια *radheekeea* chicory

ρακή, ρακί *rakee* raki, strong spirit a bit like schnapps

ρεβίθια *reveetheea* chickpeas

ρέγγα *renga* herring

ρέγγα καπνιστή *renga kapneestee* smoked herring, kipper

ρετσίνα *retseena* retsina, traditional resinated white wine

ρίγανη *reeghanee* oregano

ροδάκινο *rodhakeeno* peach

ροζέ κρασί *roze krasee* rosé wine

ρολό με κιμά *rolo me keema* meatloaf

ρύζι *reezee* rice

ρυζόγαλο *reezoghalo* rice pudding

ρώσσικη σαλάτα *roseekee salata* Russian salad (pieces of egg, potatoes, gherkins, peas and carrots in mayonnaise)

σκόρδο

σς Σ

σαγανάκι *saghanakee* cheese coated in flour and fried in olive oil

σαλάτα *salata* salad

σαλατικά *salateeka* salads (menu heading)

σαλάχι *salakhee* ray

σαλιγκάρια *saleengareea* snails

σαλιγκάρια γιαχνί *saleengareea yakhnee* snails in tomato sauce

σπανακόπιτα

σάντουιτς *sandweets* sandwich (sometimes a filled roll, sometimes a toasted sandwich with your own chosen combination of fillings)

σαραγλί *saranghlee* pastry with walnuts, sesame seeds and syrup; sometimes chocolate too

σαρδέλλες *sardheles* sardines

σέλινο *seleeno* celery, celeriac

σεφταλιά *seftalya* minced pork pasty

σικαλέσιο ψωμί *seekaleseeo psomee* rye bread

σικώτι *seekotee* liver

σκορδαλιά *skordhalya* garlic and potato mash

σκορδαλιά με ψάρι τηγανιτό *skordhalya me psaree teeghaneeto* fried fish served with garlic and potato mash

σκόρδο *skordho* garlic

σόδα *sodha* soda

σουβλάκι *soovlakee* meat kebab

παράγγι

σουβλατζίδικο *soovlatseedeeko* shop selling souvlakia, doner kebabs, etc

σούπα *soopa* soup

σουπιά *soopya* cuttlefish

σουτζουκάκια *sootzookakeea* highly seasoned meat balls

σοφρίτο *sofreeto* beef stew with creamy garlic sauce (Corfu)

σπανάκι *spanakee* spinach

σπανακόπιτα *spanakopeeta* spinach pie

σπαράγγι *sparang-ee* asparagus

σπαράγγια και αγγινάρες *sparang-eea ke angeenares* asparagus and artichokes with lemon

σπαράγγια σαλάτα *sparang-eea salata* asparagus salad

σταφύλια *stafeeleea* grapes

στη σούβλα *stee soovla* spit-roasted

στιφάδο *steefadho* braised beef in spicy onion and tomato sauce

στο φούρνο *sto foorno* baked in the oven

στρείδια *streedheea* oysters

σύκα *seeka* figs

σύκα στο φούρνο με μαυροδάφνη *seeka sto foorno me mavrodafnee* figs cooked in red wine sauce with spices

σχάρας *skharas* grilled

φασολάδα

τζατζίκι

τ T

ταραμοσαλάτα *taramosalata* mousse of cod roe

ταχίνι *takheenee* sesame seed paste

τζατζίκι *tzatzeekee* yoghurt, garlic and cucumber dip

τηγανιτό *teeghaneeto* fried

τόννος ψητός *tonos pseetos* grilled tuna with vegetables

τραπανός *trapanos* soup made of cracked wheat and yoghurt (Cyprus)

τραπέζι *trapezee* table

τσάι *tsaee* tea

τσιπούρα *tseepoora* type of sea bream

τσουρέκι *tsoorekee* festive bread

τυρί *teeree* cheese

τυροκαυτερή *teerokafteree* spicy dip made of cheese and peppers

τυρόπιτα *teeropeeta* cheese pie

τυροσαλάτα *teerosalata* starter made of cream cheese and herbs

φ Φ

φάβα *fava* yellow split peas or lentils, served in a purée with olive oil and capers

φαγγρί *fangree* sea bream

φακές *fakes* lentils

φασολάδα *fasoladha* soup made with white beans and vegetables, eaten with lemon

φασολάκια *fasolakeea* green beans

φασόλια *fasoleea* haricot beans

φέτα *feta* feta cheese, tangy white cheese used in salads and other dishes; a slice

φλαούνες *flaoones* Easter cheese cake (Cyprus)

φράουλες *fraooles* strawberries

φραπέ *frappe* iced coffee

φρέσκο *fresko* fresh

φυστίκια *feesteekya* peanuts

φυστίκια Αιγίνης *feesteekya egheenees* pistacchios

χ X

χαλβάς *khalvas* sesame seed sweet

χαλούμι *khaloomee* ewe's- or goat's-milk cheese, often grilled

χέλι καπνιστό *khelee kapneesto* smoked eel

χοιρινό *kheereeno* pork

χοιρινό κρητικό *kheereeno kreeteeko* baked pork chops (Crete)

χοιρομέρι *kheeromeree* marinated, smoked ham

φασολάκια

φέτα

χόρτα *khorta* wild greens (similar to spinich) eaten cold with oil and lemon

χορτοφάγος *khortofaghos* vegetarian

χούμους *khoomoos* dip made with puréed chickpeas, hummus (Cyprus)

χταπόδι *khtapodhee* octopus, grilled or as a side-salad

χωριάτικη σαλάτα *khoreeateekee salata* salad, Greek-style, with tomatoes, feta cheese, cucumber, onions, olives and oregano

ψ Ψ

ψάρι *psaree* fish

ψάρια καπνιστά *psareea kapneesta* smoked fish

ψάρια πλακί *psareea plakee* baked whole fish with vegetables and tomatoes

ψαρόσουπα *psarosoopa* seafood soup

ψαροταβέρνα *psarotaverna* fish taverna

ψησταριά *pseestareea* grill house

ψητό *pseeto* roast/grilled

ψωμάκι *psomakee* bread roll, bread bun

ψωμί *psomee* bread

ψωμι ολικής αλέσεως *psomee oleekees aleseos* wholemeal bread

ψωμί

ψάρι

Phonetic Menu Reader

A

aereeookho fizzy, sparkling

afeleea pork in red wine with seasonings (Cyprus)

aghreeoghooroono wild boar

akheenee sea urchin roes

akhladhee pear

akhladhee sto foorno baked pear in syrup sauce

akhneesto steamed

alatee salt

alevree flour

alevropeeta pie made with cheese, milk and eggs

ameeghdhala almonds

aneethos dill

angooree cucumber

ankeenares ala poleeta artichokes with lemon juice and olive oil

ankeenares artichokes

arakas peas

arnee lamb

  arnee lemonato lamb braised in sauce with herbs and lemon juice

  arnee me votana lamb braised with vegetables and herbs

  arnee pseeto roast lamb

  arnee yoovetsee roast lamb with small pasta

  arneesee-es breezoles lamb chops

aspro krasee white wine

aspro white

astakos lobster (often served with lemon juice and olive oil)

athereena whitebait, usually fried

avgha eggs

avgholemono egg and lemon soup

avghotarakho mullet roe (smoked)

B

bakaleearos cod

bakaleearos pastos salt cod

baklavas filo-pastry with nuts soaked in syrup

bameeyes okra, ladies' fingers (vegetable)

barakee bar

barboonee red mullet

baykon bacon

beeftekee beef rissole/burger

beera beer

booghatsa cheese or custard pastry sprinkled with sugar and cinnamon

bookalee bottle

boordheto fish or meat in a thick sauce of onions, tomatoes and red peppers

boorekee cheese potato and courgette pie

boorekeea puff pastry filled with meat and cheese (Cyprus)

breeam(ee) ratatouille

breezola steak/chop

breezola arneeseea lamb chop

breezola kheereenee pork chop

breezola moskhareeseea beef steak/chop

D

dendroleevano rosemary

dhafnee bay leaf

dhakteela almond cakes

dhamaskeena plums, prunes

dheeples pastry with honey and walnuts

dheepno dinner

dholmadhes vine leaves, rolled up and stuffed with minced meat and rice

dolmadhes vine leaves, rolled up and stuffed with rice and sometimes mince

domates tomatoes

domates yemeestes tomatoes stuffed with rice and herbs, and sometimes with mince

E

eemam baeeldee stuffed aubergines (eggplants)

eenopoleeo wine shop

eksokheeko stuffed pork or beef with vegetables and cheese

elakheesta pseemeno rare (meat)

eleoladho olive oil

elyes olives

elyes tsakeestes cracked green olives with coriander seeds and garlic (Cyprus)

elyotee olive bread

esteeatoreeo restaurant

F

fakes lentils

fangree sea bream

fasoladha soup made with white beans and vegetables, eaten with lemon

fasolakeea green beans

fasoleea haricot beans

fava yellow split peas or lentils, served in a purée with olive oil and capers

feesteekya peanuts

feesteekya egheenees pistacchios

feta feta cheese, tangy white cheese used in salads and other dishes; a slice

flaoones Easter cheese cake (Cyprus)

fraooles strawberries

frappe iced coffee

fresko fresh

G

gavros sardine-type fish (if salted: anchovy)

ghala milk

ghalaktobooreeko custard tart

ghalaktopoleeo café/patisserie

ghareedhes shrimps; prawns

ghareedhes yoovetsee prawns in tomato sauce with feta

ghareefalo clove (spice)

ghazoza fizzy drink

ghleeka desserts

ghleeka kootalyoo crystallized fruits in syrup

ghlosa sole

ghopes bogue, a type of fish

ghravyera cheese resembling gruyère

K

kafedhes coffees (plural)

kafeneeo café

kafes coffee (Greek-style)

kafes ghleekees very sweet coffee

kafes metreeos medium-sweet coffee

kafes sketos coffee without sugar

kakaveea fish soup

kakow hot chocolate

kalamakee straw (for drinking); small skewer

kalamareea squid

kalamareea teeghaneeta fried squid

kalambokee corn on the cob

kalambokopeeta corn bread

kalopseemeno well done (meat)

kanella cinnamon

kaparee pickled capers

kapneesto smoked

kapootseeno cappucino

karafa carafe

karaveedha crayfish

kareedha coconut

kareedhee walnut

kareedhopeeta walnut cake

karekla chair

karoto carrot

karpoozee watermelon

kaseree type of cheese

kastana chestnuts

kataeefee small shredded pastry drenched in syrup

kataloghos menu

kataloghos krasyon wine list

katapseeghmeno frozen

katseekee roast kid

kava wine shop

kavooras boiled crab

kayanas me pasto kreyas salted pork with cheese, tomatoes and eggs

keedhonee quince

keedhonee sto foorno baked quince

keedhoneea type of clams, cockles

keemas mince

keeneeghee game

keereeo pyato main course

kefaloteeree type of cheese, often served fried in olive oil

keftedhes meat balls

keraseea cherries

khaloomee ewe's- or goat's-milk cheese, often grilled

khalvas sesame seed sweet

kheereeno pork

kheereeno kreeteeko baked pork chops (Crete)

kheeromeree marinated, smoked ham

khelee kapneesto smoked eel

khoomoos dip made with puréed chickpeas, hummus (Cyprus)

khoreeateekee salata salad, Greek-style, with tomatoes, feta cheese, cucumber, onions, olives and oregano

khorta wild greens (similar to spinich) eaten cold with oil and lemon

khortofaghos vegetarian

khtapodhee octopus, grilled or as a side-salad

klefteeko casserole with lamb, potatoes and vegetables

kokoretsee traditional spit-roasted dish of spiced liver and other offal

kokteyl cocktail

kolatsyo brunch, elevenses

kolokeethakeea courgettes, zucchini

kolokeethopeeta courgette/zucchini pie

kolokeethopeeta gleekya sweet courgette/zucchini pie

kolokotes pastries with pumpkin seeds and raisins

kontosoovlee spicy pieces of lamb, pork or beef, spit-roasted

konyak brandy, cognac

kookya broad beans

koolooreea bread rings

koonelee rabbit

koonoopeedhee cauliflower

koopepeea stuffed vine leaves (Cyprus)

koopes meat pasties

kooramb-yedhes small almond cakes eaten at Christmas

kotopoolo chicken

kotopoolo kapama chicken casseroled with red peppers, onions, cinnamon and raisins

kotopoolo reeghanato grilled basted chicken with herbs

krasee wine

kreas meat

kreeo cold

kreeteekee salata watercress salad

krema cream

kremeedheea onions

kseedhee vinegar

kseefeeas swordfish

L

ladhee oil

ladhera vegetable casserole

ladhoteero soft cheese with olive oil

laghos hare

lakhana green vegetables

lakhaneeka vegetables (menu heading)

lakhano cabbage, greens

lavrakee sea-bass

leegho a little, a bit

lefko white (used for wine as well as άσπρο)

lemonadha lemon drink

lemonee lemon

lookaneeka type of highly seasoned sausage

lookoomadhes small fried dough balls in syrup

lookoomee Turkish delight

lookoomeea shortbread served at weddings

loondza loin of pork, marinated and smoked

M

maeedanos parsley

makaronya spaghetti

makaronya me keema spaghetti bolognese

maneetareea mushrooms

mareedhes small fish like sprats, served fried

maroolee lettuce

marteenee martini

mavro krasee red wine (although you'll hear *kokeeno krasee* more often)

mavromateeka black-eyed peas

mayeereetsa soup made of lamb offal, special Easter dish

mee aereeookho still, not fizzy

meedheea mussels

meekro small, little

meela apples

meelko chocolate milk

meelkseik milkshake

meelopeeta apple pie

meghalo large, big

melee honey

meleetzana aubergine (eggplant)

meleetzanakee gleeko crystallized sweet in syrup, made from aubergine/eggplant

meleetzanes eemam aubergines (eggplants) stuffed with tomato and onion

meleetzanosalata aubergine (eggplant) mousse (dip)

meseemereeano lunch

metaksa Metaxa (Greek brandy-type spirit)

metaleeko nero mineral water

metreea pseemeno medium-grilled (meat)

mezedhopoleeo taverna/shop selling mezedhes

mezes (plural μεζέδες *mezedhes*) small snacks served free of charge with ouzo or retsina; assortment of mini-portions of various dishes, available on the menu (or on request) at some restaurants.

moosakas moussaka, layers of aubergine (eggplant), minced meat and potato, with white sauce

moskharee beef

moskharee kokeeneesto beef in wine sauce with tomatoes and onions

N

nero water

nes frappe iced coffee

nes me ghala coffee (instant) with milk

nes, nescafe instant coffee (of any brand)

O

okhtapodhee octopus (see also χταπόδι)

okhtapodhee krasato octopus in red wine sauce

omeletta omelette

oozeree small bar selling ouzo and other drinks, maybe with mezedhes (μεζέδες)

oozo ouzo (traditional aniseed-flavoured spirit)

orekteeka first courses/starters (menu heading)

oveleesteereeo shop selling souvlakia and doner kebabs

P

pa-eedhakeea grilled lamb chops

paghakya ice-cubes

paghoto ice-cream

pakseemadheea crispy bread (baked twice)

pakseemadhokooloora tomato and cheese bread

pandzareea beetroot with seasonings

papootsakeea stuffed aubergines (eggplants)

pasatempo pumpkin seeds

pasta cake, pastry

pasteetsada beef with tomatoes, onions, red wine, herbs, spices and pasta *pasteetseeo* baked pasta dish with a middle layer of meat and white sauce

pasto salted

patates potatoes

patates teeghaneetes chips, fries

patsas tripe soup

peekanteeko spicy

peelafee rice

peeleeoreeteeko boobaree spicy sausage

peeperee pepper

peeperyes peppers

peeperyes yemeestes stuffed peppers with rice, herbs and sometimes mince

peeta pitta (flat unleavened bread); pie with different fillings, such as meat, cheese, vegetables

peponee melon

pestrofa trout

plakee fish in tomato sauce

poorghooree cracked wheat (Cyprus)

poorghooree peelafee salad made of cracked wheat (Cyprus)

portokaladha orangeade

portokalya oranges

prasa me seesamee leeks baked and sprinkled with sesame seeds

proeeno breakfast

psaree fish

psareea kapneesta smoked fish

psareea plakee baked whole fish with vegetables and tomatoes

psarosoopa seafood soup

psarotaverna fish taverna

pseestareea grill house

pseeto roast/grilled

psomakee bread roll, bread bun

psomee bread

psomee oleekees aleseos wholemeal bread

pyato tees eemeras dish of the day

R

radheekeea chicory

rakee raki, strong spirit a bit like schnapps

raveeolee pastry stuffed with cheese (Cyprus)

reeghanee oregano

reezee rice

reezoghalo rice pudding

renga herring

renga kapneestee smoked herring, kipper

retseena retsina, traditional resinated white wine

reveetheea chickpeas

rodhakeeno peach

rolo me keema meatloaf

roseekee salata Russian salad (pieces of egg, potatoes, gherkins, peas and carrots in mayonnaise)

roze krasee rosé wine

S

saghanakee cheese coated in flour and fried in olive oil

salakhee ray

salata salad

salateeka salads (menu heading)

saleengareea snails

saleengareea yakhnee snails in tomato sauce

sandweets sandwich (sometimes a filled roll, sometimes a toasted sandwich with your own chosen combination of fillings)

saranghlee pastry with walnuts, sesame seeds and syrup; sometimes chocolate too

sardheles sardines

seeka figs

seeka sto foorno me mavrodafnee figs cooked in red wine sauce with spices

seekaleseeo psomee rye bread

seekotee liver

seftalya minced pork pasty

seleeno celery, celeriac

skharas grilled

skordhalya garlic and potato mash

skordhalya me psaree teeghaneeto fried fish served with garlic and potato mash *skordho* garlic

sodha soda

sofreeto beef stew with creamy garlic sauce (Corfu)

soopa soup

soopya cuttlefish

sootzookakeea highly seasoned meat balls

soovlakee meat kebab

soovlatseedeeko shop selling souvlakia, doner kebabs, etc

spanakee spinach

spanakopeeta spinach pie

sparang-ee asparagus

sparang-eea ke angeenares asparagus and artichokes with lemon

sparang-eea salata asparagus salad

stafeeleea grapes

stee soovla spit-roasted

steefadho braised beef in spicy onion and tomato sauce

sto foorno baked in the oven

streedheea oysters

T

takheenee sesame seed paste

taramosalata mousse of cod roe

teeghaneeto fried

teeree cheese

teerokafteree spicy dip made of cheese and peppers

teeropeeta cheese pie

teerosalata starter made of cream cheese and herbs

thalaseena seafood

theemaree thyme

tonos pseetos grilled tuna with vegetables

trapanos soup made of cracked wheat and yoghurt (Cyprus)

trapezee table

tsaee tea

tseepoora type of sea bream

tsoorekee festive bread

tzatzeekee yoghurt, garlic and cucumber dip

V

vaseeleekos basil

veeseeno kaseree sheep's cheese served with cherry preserve

vereekoko apricot

vleeta wild greens (like spinach, eaten with olive oil and lemon)

vodheeno beef

vooteemata biscuits to dip in coffee

vooteero butter

votka vodka

vradeeno evening meal

vrasto boiled

W

weeskee whisky

Y

yakhnee cooked in tomato sauce and olive oil

yaoortee yoghurt

yaoortee me melee yoghurt with honey

yeeda vrastee goat soup

yeeghantes large butter beans

yeeros doner kebab

yemeesta stuffed vegetables

yoovarlakya meatballs in lemon sauce

Z

zakharee sugar

zakharoplasteeo cake shop

zambon ham

zelateena brawn

zestee sokolata hot chocolate

zesto hot, warm

DICTIONARY

english > greek

greek > english

A

24-hour adj εικοσιτετράωρος/η/ο
eekoseetetraoros-ee-o
24-hour access η εικοσιτετράωρη
πρόσβαση ee eekoseetetraoree
prosvasee

24/7 adj μόνιμος/η/ο moneemos-ee-o
adv μόνιμα moneema

a ένας enas (masculine ο words)
μία meea (feminine η words)
ένα ena (neuter το words)

abbey το μοναστήρι to monasteeree

abortion η άμβλωση ee amvlosee

about: a book about Athens ένα
βιβλίο για την Αθήνα ena veevleeo
ya teen Atheena
at about ten o'clock περίπου στις
δέκα pereepoo stees dheka

above πάνω από pano apo

abscess το απόστημα to aposteema

accident το ατύχημα to ateekheema

accommodation το κατάλυμα
to kataleema

ache ο πόνος o ponos

Acropolis η Ακρόπολη ee Akropolee

activities οι δραστηριότητες
ee dhrasteereeoteetes

adaptor το πολύμπριζο
to poleebreezo

address η διεύθυνση
ee dheeeftheensee
what is your address? ποια είναι
η διεύθυνσή σας; pya eene ee
dhee-eftheensee sas

address book η ατζέντα ee atzenda

adhesive tape η συγκολλητική
ταινία ee seengoleeteekee teneea

admission charge η είσοδος ee
eesodhos

adult ο ενήλικος o eneeleekos

advance: in advance
προκαταβολικώς prokatavoleekos

Aegean Sea το Αιγαίο (πέλαγος)
to egheo (pelaghos)

after μετά meta

afternoon το απόγευμα to apoyevma

aftershave το αφτερσέιβ to aftershave

afterwards αργότερα arghotera

again πάλι palee//ξανά ksana

ago: a week ago πριν μια βδομάδα
preen meea vdhomadha

AIDS ΕΙΤΖ e-eetz

air ambulance το ελικόπτερο-
ασθενοφόρο to eleekoptero-
asthenoforo

airbag ο αερόσακος o aerosakos

air conditioning ο κλιματισμός
o kleemateesmos

air-conditioning unit το
κλιματιστικό to kleemateesteeko

air freshener το αποσμητικό χώρου
to aposmeeteeko khoroo

airline η αεροπορική εταιρία
ee aeroporeekee etereea

air mail αεροπορικώς aeroporeekos

air mattress το στρώμα για τη
θάλασσα to stroma ya tee thalasa

airplane το αεροπλάνο to aeroplano

airport το αεροδρόμιο
to aerodhromeeo

airport bus το λεωφορείο για
το αεροδρόμειο to leoforeeo
ya to aerodhromeeo

air ticket το αεροπορικό εισιτήριο
to aeroporeeko eeseeteereeo

aisle (in aircraft) ο διάδρομος
o dheeadhromos

alarm (emergency) ο συναγερμός
o seenayermos

alarm clock το ξυπνητήρι
to kseepneeteeree

alcohol το αλκοόλ *to alko-ol*

alcohol-free χωρίς αλκοόλ *khorees alko-ol*

alcoholic οινοπνευματώδης
eenopnevmatodhees

all όλος *olos*
all the milk όλο το γάλα *olo to ghala*
all the time όλον τον καιρό *olon ton kero*

allergic to αλλεργικός σε
aleryeekos se

alley το δρομάκι *to dhromakee*

allowance: *duty-free allowance*
η επιτρεπόμενη ποσότητα
ee epeetrepomenee posoteeta

all right (agreed) εντάξει *endaksee*

almond το αμύγδαλο *to ameeghdhalo*

also επίσης *epeesees*

always πάντα *panda*

ambulance το ασθενοφόρο
to asthenoforo

America η Αμερική *ee amereekee*

American ο Αμερικανός/η
Αμερικανίδα *o amereekanos/ee amereekaneedha*

amphitheatre το αμφιθέατρο
to amfeetheatro

anaesthetic το αναισθητικό
to anestheeteeko

anchor η άγκυρα *ee ankeera*

anchovy η αντζούγια *ee andzooya*

and και *ke*

angina η στηθάγχη *ee steethangkhee*

angry θυμωμένος *theemomenos*

another άλλος *alos*
another beer άλλη μία μπίρα *alee meea beera*

answer η απάντηση *ee apandeesee*

to answer απαντώ *apando*

answerphone ο αυτόματος
τηλεφωνητής *o aftomatos teelefoneetees*

antacid το αντιόξινο *to andeeokseeno*

antibiotics τα αντιβιοτικά
ta andeeveeoteeka

antihistamine το αντιισταμινικό
to andeestameeneeko

antiques οι αντίκες *ee andeekes*

antiseptic το αντισηπτικό
to andeeseepteeko

anywhere οπουδήποτε
opoodheepote

apartment το διαμέρισμα
to dheeamereesma

apartment block η πολυκατοικία
ee poleekateekeea

aperitif το απεριτίφ *to apereeteef*

apple το μήλο *to meelo*

appendicitis η σκωληκοειδίτιδα
ee skoleeko-eedheeteedha

application form η αίτηση
ee eteesee

appointment το ραντεβού
to randevoo

apricot το βερίκοκο *to vereekoko*

archaeology η αρχαιολογία
ee arkheoloyeea

architecture η αρχιτεκτονική
ee arkheetektoneekee

arm το μπράτσο *to bratso*

armbands (for swimming)
τα μπρατσάκια *ta bratsakya*

around γύρω *yeero*

to arrest συλλαμβάνω *seelamvano*

arrivals οι αφίξεις *ee afeeksees*

to arrive φτάνω *ftano*

art gallery η πινακοθήκη
ee peenakotheekee

arthritis η αρθρίτιδα
ee arthreeteedha

artichoke η αγκινάρα
ee angheenara

ashtray το τασάκι *to tasakee*

asparagus το σπαράγγι *to sparang-ee*

aspirin η ασπιρίνη *ee aspeereenee*
soluble aspirin διαλυόμενη
ασπιρίνη *dhealeeomenee
aspeereenee*

asthma το άσθμα *to asthma*

at σε *se*
at the (masculine, neuter) στο *sto*
at the (feminine) στη *stee*

atlas ο άτλαντας *o atlandas*

attractive (person) ελκυστικός
elkeesteekos

aubergine η μελιτζάνα
ee meleetzana

aunt η θεία *ee theea*

Australia η Αυστραλία
ee afstraleea

Australian ο Αυστραλός/η
Αυστραλίδα *o afstralos/ee
afstraleedha*

authentic αυθεντικός/ή/ό
afthenteekos/ee/o

automatic αυτόματος *aftomatos*

autoteller το ΑΤΜ *to ey tee em*

autumn το φθινόπωρο
to ftheenoporo

avalanche η χιονοστιβάδα
ee khyonosteevadha

avocado το αβοκάντο *to avokado*

awful φοβερός *foveros*

awning (for caravan etc) η τέντα
ee tenda

B

baby το μωρό *to moro*

baby food οι βρεφικές τροφές
ee vrefeekes trofes

baby milk το βρεφικό γάλα
to vrefeeko ghala

baby's bottle το μπιμπερό
to beebero

baby seat (in car) το παιδικό
κάθισμα *to pedheeko katheesma*

baby-sitter η μπεϊμπισίτερ
ee babysitter

baby wipes τα υγρά μαντηλάκια
για μωρά *ta eeghra mandeelakya ya
mora*

back (of a person) η πλάτη *ee platee*

backpack το σακκίδιο *to sakeedheeo*

bad (of food) χαλασμένος
khalasmenos
(of weather) κακός *kakos*

bag (small) η τσάντα *ee tsanda*
(suitcase) η βαλίτσα *ee valeetsa*

baggage οι αποσκευές *ee
aposkeves*

baggage reclaim η παραλαβή
αποσκευών *ee paralavee aposkevon*

bait (for fishing) το δόλωμα
to dholoma

baker's ο φούρνος *o foornos*

balcony το μπαλκόνι *to balkonee*

bald (person) φαλακρός *falakros*

ball η μπάλα *ee bala*

banana η μπανάνα *ee banana*

band (musical) η ορχήστρα
ee orkheestra

bandage ο επίδεσμος o epeedhesmos

bank η τράπεζα ee trapeza

banknote το χαρτονόμισμα
to khartonomeesma

bar το μπαρ to bar

barbecue η ψησταριά
ee pseestarya

barber ο κουρέας o kooreas

barrel το βαρέλι to varelee

basil ο βασιλικός o vaseeleekos

basket το καλάθι to kalathee

basketball το μπάσκετ to basket

bath (tub) το μπάνιο to banyo
to take a bath κάνω μπάνιο
kano banyo

bathing cap ο σκούφος του
μπάνιου o skoofos too banyoo

bathroom το μπάνιο to banyo

battery η μπαταρία ee batareea

beach η πλαζ ee plaz//η παραλία
ee paraleea

bean (haricot) το φασόλι to fasolee
(broad) το κουκί to kookee
(green) το φασολάκι to fasolakee
(soya) η σόγια ee soya

beautiful όμορφος omorfos

because επειδή epeedhee

bed το κρεβάτι to krevatee
double bed διπλό κρεβάτι
dheeplo krevatee
single bed μονό κρεβάτι
mono krevatee
twin beds δύο μονά κρεβάτια
dheeo mona krevatya
sofa bed καναπές kanapes

bedroom η κρεβατοκάμαρα
ee krevatokamara

beef το μοσχάρι to moskharee

beer η μπύρα ee beera

beetroot το παντζάρι to pandzaree

before (time) πριν (από) preen (apo)
(place) μπροστά από brosta apo

to begin αρχίζω arkheezo

behind πίσω από peeso apo

to believe πιστεύω peestevo

bell (electric) το κουδούνι to
koodhoonee

below κάτω από kato apo

belt η ζώνη ee zonee

beside δίπλα dheepla

best ο καλύτερος o kaleeteros

better (than) καλύτερος (από)
kaleeteros (apo)

between μεταξύ metaksee

bib η σαλιάρα ee salyara

bicycle το ποδήλατο to podheelato

bicycle pump η τρόμπα ποδηλάτου
ee trompa podheelatoo

big μεγάλος meghalos

bigger μεγαλύτερος meghaleeteros

bikini το μπικίνι to beekeenee

bill ο λογαριασμός o logharyasmos

bin το καλάθι των αχρήστων
to kalathee ton akhreeston

bin liner η σακούλα σκουπιδιών
ee sakoola skoopeedhyon

binoculars τα κυάλια ta keealya

bird το πουλί to poolee

birth η γέννηση ee yeneesee

birth certificate το πιστοποιητικό
γεννήσεως to peestopyeeteeko
yeneeseos

birthday τα γενέθλια ta yenethleea
happy birthday! χρόνια πολλά
khronya pola

νΝ ξΞ οΟ πΠ ρΡ σςΣ τΤ υΥ φΦ χΧ ψΨ ωΩ

biscuit το μπισκότο *to beeskoto*

bit: *a bit (of)* λίγο *leegho*

bite *(insect)* το τσίμπημα *to tseebeema*

bitten: *I have been bitten* με δάγκωσε *me dhangkose*

bitter πικρός *peekros*

black μαύρος *mavros*

blackcurrant το μαύρο φραγκοστάφυλο *to mavro frangostafeelo*

blank *adj (disk, tape)* κενός η/ο *kenos-ee-o*

blanket η κουβέρτα *ee kooverta*

bleach το λευκαντικό *to lefkandeeko*

to bleed αιμορραγώ *emoragho*

blister η φουσκάλα *ee fooskala*

blocked *(pipe)* βουλωμένος *voolomenos*
(nose) κλειστή *kleestee*

blood group η ομάδα αίματος *ee omadha ematos*

blood pressure η πίεση αίματος *ee peeyesee ematos*

blouse η πουκαμίσα *ee pookameesa*

blow-dry στέγνωμα *steghnoma*

blowout *n (of tyre)* το κλατάρισμα *to klatareesma*

blue γαλάζιος *ghalazeeos*//μπλε *ble*

boarding card το δελτίο επιβιβάσεως *to dhelteeo epeeveevaseos*

boarding house η πανσιόν *ee pansyon*

boat *(small)* η βάρκα *ee varka*
(ship) το πλοίο *to pleeo*

boat trip η βαρκάδα *ee varkadha*

to boil βράζω *vrazo*

boiled βραστός *vrastos*
boiled water βραστό νερό *vrasto nero*

bone το κόκκαλο *to kokalo*
(fishbone) το αγκάθι *to angkathee*

book *n* το βιβλίο *to veevleeo*

to book *(room, tickets)* κλείνω *kleeno*

booking: *to make a booking* κλείνω θέση *kleeno thesee*

booking office *(railways, airlines, etc.)* το εκδοτήριο *to ekdhoteereeo*
(theatre) το ταμείο *to tameeo*

bookshop το βιβλιοπωλείο *to veevleeopoleeo*

boots οι μπότες *ee botes*

border *(frontier)* τα σύνορα *ta seenora*

boring βαρετός *varetos*

boss ο/η προϊστάμενος *o/ee proeestamenos*

both και οι δυο *ke ee dheeo*

bottle το μπουκάλι *to bookalee*

bottle-opener το ανοιχτήρι *to aneekhteeree*

bowl το μπωλ *to bol*

box *(container)* το κιβώτιο *to keevotyo*
(cardboard) το κουτί *to kootee*

box office το ταμείο *to tameeo*

boy το αγόρι *to aghoree*

boyfriend ο φίλος *o feelos*

bra το σουτιέν *to sootyen*

bracelet το βραχιόλι *to vrakheeolee*

to brake φρενάρω *frenaro*

brake cable το καλόδιο φρένου *to kalodheeo frenoo*

brake fluid το υγρό των φρένων *to eeghro ton frenon*

brake lights τα φώτα φρενών
ta fota frenon

brakes τα φρένα ta frena

brandy το κονιάκ to konyak

bread το ψωμί to psomee
(wholemeal) ψωμί ολικής αλέσεως
psomee oleekees aleseos

to break σπάζω spazo

breakdown η βλάβη ee vlavee

breakdown van το συνεργείο
διασώσεως to seenergheeo
dheeasoseos

breakfast το πρωινό to proeeno

breast το στήθος to steethos

to breathe αναπνέω anapneo

bride η νύφη ee neefee

bridegroom ο γαμπρός o ghambros

briefcase ο χαρτοφύλακας
o khartofeelakas

to bring φέρνω ferno

Britain η Βρετανία ee vretaneea

British ο Βρετανός/η Βρετανίδα
o vretanos/ee vretaneedha

broadband n η ευρηζωνική
σύνδεση (DSL) ee evreezoneekee
seendhesee (DSL)

brochure η μπροσούρα ee brosoora

broken σπασμένος spasmenos
broken down χαλασμένος
khalasmenos

bronze μπρούντζινος broondzeenos

brooch η καρφίτσα ee karfeetsa

brother ο αδελφός o adhelfos

brown καφέ kafe

bruise η μελανιά ee melaneea

brush η βούρτσα ee voortsa

bucket ο κουβάς o koovas

buffet ο μπουφές o boofes

buffet car το βαγόνι εστιατόριο
to vaghonee esteeatoreeo

bulb (light) ο γλόμπος o ghlobos

bumbag η τσαντάκι μέσης ee
tsantakee mesees

buoy η σημαδούρα ee seemadhoora

bureau de change (bank) ξένο
συνάλλαγμα kseno seenalaghma

to burn καίω keo

burnt καμένος kamenos

to burst σκάζω skazo

bus το λεωφορείο to leoforeeo

business η δουλειά ee dhoolya

business centre το εμπορικό
κέντρο to emboreeko kendro

bus station ο σταθμός του
λεωφορείου o stathmos too
leoforeeoo

bus stop η στάση του λεωφορείου
ee stasee too leoforeeoo

bus terminal το τέρμα του
λεωφορείου to terma too leoforeeoo

bus tour η εκδρομή με λεωφορείο
ee ekdhromee me leoforeeo

busy απασχολημένος
apaskholeemenos

but αλλά ala

butcher's το κρεοπωλείο
to kreopoleeo

butter το βούτυρο to vooteero

button το κουμπί to koombee

to buy αγοράζω aghorazo

C

cab το ταξί to taksee

cabbage το καμπρολάχανο
to kambrolakhano

cabin η καμπίνα ee kabeena

cable car το τελεφερίκ to telefereek

cable TV η δορυφορική τηλεώραση
ee dhoreeforeekee teeleorasee

café το καφενείο *to kafeneeo*

cake το γλύκισμα *o ghleekeesma*

cake shop το ζαχαροπλαστείο
to zakharoplasteeo

calculator το κομπιουτεράκι
to kompyooterakee

calendar το ημερολόγιο
to eemeroloyo

to call φωνάζω *fonazo*

call n (telephone) η κλήση *ee kleesee*
long-distance call η υπεραστική
κλήση *ee eeperasteekee kleesee*

calm ήσυχος *eeseekhos*

camcorder η βιντεοκάμερα
ee veedeokamera

camera η φωτογραφική μηχανή
ee fotoghrafeekee meekhanee

camera phone το τηλέφωνο με
κάμερα *to teelefono me kamera*

to camp κατασκηνώνω
kataskeenono

camping gas το γκαζάκι *to gazakee*

camping stove το πετρογκάζ
to petrogas

campsite το κάμπινγκ *to camping*

to can vb : I can μπορώ *boro*
you can μπορείς *borees*
he can μπορεί *boree*
we can μπορούμε *boroome*

can (of food) η κονσέρβα *ee konserva*
(for oil) ο τενεκές *o tenekes*

Canada ο Καναδάς *o kanadhas*

Canadian ο Καναδός/η Καναδή
o Kanadhos/ee Kanadhee

candle το κερί *to keree*

to cancel ακυρώνω *akeerono*

canoe το κανό *to kano*

can-opener το ανοιχτήρι
to aneekhteeree

cappuccino το καπουτσίνο
to kapootseeno

car το αυτοκίνητο *to aftokeeneeto*

car alarm ο συναγερμός *o seena-yermos*

car ferry το φεριμπότ *to fereebot*

car keys τα κλειδιά αυτοκινήτου
ta kleedhya aftokeeneetoo

car park το πάρκινγκ *to parking*

car port η σκεπαστή θέση
στάθμευσης *ee skepastee thesee stathmefsees*

car radio το ραδιόφωνο
αυτοκινήτου *to radhyofono aftokeeneetoo*

car seat (for children) το παιδικό
κάθισμα αυτοκινήτου *to pedheeko katheesma aftokeeneetoo*

car wash το πλυντήριο
αυτοκινήτων *to pleenteereeo aftokeeneeton*

carafe η καράφα *ee karafa*

caravan το τροχόσπιτο
to trokhospeeto

card η κάρτα *ee karta*

cardigan η ζακέτα *ee zaketa*

careful προσεκτικός *prosekteekos*

carpet το χαλί *to khalee*

carriage (railway) το βαγόνι
to vaghonee

carrot το καρότο *to karoto*

to carry κουβαλώ *koovalo*

case (matter) η υπόθεση
ee eepothesee
(suitcase) η βαλίτσα *ee valeetsa*

to cash (cheque) εξαργυρώνω
eksar-yeerono

cash τα μετρητά ta metreeta

cash desk το ταμείο to tameeo

cash dispenser το ΑΤΜ to ey tee em

cashier ο ταμίας o tameeas

casino το καζίνο to kazeeno

cassette η κασέτα ee kaseta

cassette-player το κασετόφωνο to kasetofono

castle το κάστρο to kastro

casualty department τα επείγοντα περιστατικά ta epeeghonda pereestateeka

cat η γάτα ee ghata

catalogue ο κατάλογος o kataloghos

to catch πιάνω pyano (bus, train, etc.) παίρνω perno

Catholic καθολικός katholikos

cauliflower το κουνουπίδι to koonoopeedhee

cave η σπηλιά ee speelya

CD το CD to see dee

CD ROM το CD ROM to see dee rom

celery το σέλινο to seleeno

cemetery το νεκροταφείο to nekrotafeeo

cents (euro) λεπτά lepta

centimetre το εκατοστό to ekastosto

central κεντρικός kendreekos

central locking (car) η αυτόματη κλειδαριά ee aftomatee kleedharya

centre το κέντρο to kendro

century ο αιώνας o eonas

certificate το πιστοποιητικό to peestopyeeteeko

chain η αλυσίδα ee aleeseedha

chair η καρέκλα ee karekla

champagne η σαμπάνια ee sambanya

change η αλλαγή ee alaghee (money) τα ρέστα ta resta

to change αλλάζω alazo

changing room (beach, sports) το αποδυτήριο to apodheeteereeo

charcoal το κάρβουνο to karvoono

charge η τιμή ee teemee

charge n η φόρτηση ee forteesee I've run out of charge έμεινα από μπαταρία emeena apo batareea

to charge φορτίζω forteezo I need to charge my phone πρέπει να φορτίσω το κινητό μου prepee na forteeso to keeneeto moo

charter flight το τσάρτερ to tsarter

chatroom (internet) chatroom

cheap φτηνός fteenos

cheap rate (for phone, etc) η φτηνή ταρίφα ee fteenee tareefa

cheaper φτηνότερος fteenoteros

to check ελέγχω elenkho

to check in περνώ από τον έλεγχο εισιτηρίων perno apo ton elenkho eeseeteereeon

check-in desk ο έλεγχος εισιτηρίων o elenkhos eeseeteereeon

cheek το μάγουλο to maghoolo

cheerio! γεια ya

cheers! γεια μας! ya mas

cheese το τυρί to teeree

chemist's το φαρμακείο to farmakeeo

cheque η επιταγή ee epeetaghee

cheque card η κάρτα επιταγών ee karta epeetaghon

cherry το κεράσι to kerasee

chestnut το κάστανο to kastano

chewing gum η τσίχλα *ee tseekhla*

chicken το κοτόπουλο *to kotopoolo*

chickenpox η ανεμοβλογιά
ee anemovloya

chickpeas τα ρεβίθια *ta reveetheea*

child το παιδί *to pedhee*

children τα παιδιά *ta pedhya*

chilli (meal) το τσίλι *to tseelee*
(vegetable) η καυτερή πιπεριά
ee kafteree peepereea

chilled: is the wine chilled?
είναι κρύο το κρασί; *eene kreeo
to krasee*

chips πατάτες τηγανητές *patates
teeghaneetes*

chocolate η σοκολάτα *ee sokolata*

Christmas τα Χριστούγεννα
ta khreestooyena
merry Christmas! καλά
Χριστούγεννα *kala khreestooyena*

church η εκκλησία *ee ekleeseea*

cigar το πούρο *to pooro*

cigarette το τσιγάρο *to tseegharo*

cigarette paper το τσιγαρόχαρτο
to tseegharokharto

cinema ο κινηματογράφος
o keeneematoghrafos

cistern το καζανάκι *to kazanakee*

city η πόλη *ee polee*

clean καθαρός *katharos*

to clean καθαρίζω *kathareezo*

cleansing cream η κρέμα
καθαρισμού *ee krema kathareesmoo*

client ο πελάτης/η πελάτισσα
o pelatees/ee pelateesa

cliffs οι γκρεμοί *ee gremee*

climbing η ορειβασία *ee oreevaseea*

climbing boots οι μπότες
ορειβασίας *ee botes oreevaseeas*

clingfilm το σελοφάν *to selofan*

cloakroom η γκαρνταρόμπα
ee gardaroba

clock το ρολόι *to roloee*

to close κλείνω *kleeno*

close adj (near) κοντινός *kondeenos*
(weather) αποπνιχτικός
apopneekhteekos

closed κλειστός *kleestos*

cloth το πανί *to panee*
(for floor) το σφουγγαρόπανο
to sfoongaropano

clothes τα ρούχα *ta rookha*

clothes line το σκοινί για τα ρούχα
to skeenee ya ta rookha

clothes peg το μανταλάκι
to mandalakee

cloudy συννεφιασμένος
seenefyasmenos

clove (spice) το γαρίφαλο
to ghareefalo

club (society) η λέσχη *ee leskhee*
(nightclub) το nightclub *to naeetklab*

coach (railway) το βαγόνι
to vaghonee
(bus) το πούλμαν *to poolman*
(instructor) ο προπονητής
o proponeetees

coach station ο σταθμός
λεωφορείων *o stathmos leoforeeon*

coach trip το ταξίδι με πούλμαν
to takseedhee me poolman

coast η ακτή *ee aktee*

coastguard η ακτοφυλακή
ee aktofeelakee

coat το παλτό *to palto*

coat hanger η κρεμάστρα
ee kremastra

cockroach η κατσαρίδα
ee katsareedha

cocktail bar το κοκτέιλ μπαρ
to kokteyl bar

cocoa το κακάο *to kakao*

coffee ο καφές *o kafes*
black coffee σκέτος καφές
sketos kafes
white coffee καφές με γάλα
kafes me ghala

coin το νόμισμα *to nomeesma*

colander το σουρωτήρι
to sooroteeree

cold κρύος *kreeos*
I have a cold είμαι κρυωμένος
eeme kreeomenos
I'm cold κρυώνω *kreeono*

cold sore ο έρπητας *o erpeetas*

colour το χρώμα *to khroma*

colour blind δαλτωνικός
dhaltoneekos

colour film το έγχρωμο φιλμ
to enkhromo feelm

comb η χτένα *ee khtena*

to come έρχομαι *erkhome*

to come back γυρίζω *yeereezo*

to come in μπαίνω *beno*

comfortable αναπαυτικός
anapafteekos

communion *(holy)* η θεία κοινωνία
ee theea keenoneea

company *(firm)* η εταιρία *ee etereea*

compartment *(train)* το βαγόνι
to vaghonee

compass η πυξίδα *ee peekseedha*

to complain παραπονούμαι
paraponoome

compulsory υποχρεωτικός
eepokhreoteekos

computer το κομπιούτερ
to kompyooter

computer software το software
to software

concert η συναυλία *ee seenavleea*

concert hall το μέγαρο μουσικής
to megharo mooseekees

condition η κατάσταση *ee
katastasee*

condom το προφυλακτικό
to profeelakteeko

conductor *(bus)* ο εισπράκτορας
o eespraktoras
(train) ο ελεγκτής *o elenktees*

conference η διάσκεψη *ee
dheeaskepsee*

to confirm επιβεβαιώνω
epeeveveono

congratulations! συγχαρητήρια
seenkhareeteereea

connection *(trains, etc)* η σύνδεση
ee seendhesee

to be constipated έχω
δυσκοιλιότητα *ekho
dheeskeeleeoteeta*

consulate το προξενείο
to prokseneeo

to contact έρχομαι σε επαφή
erkhome se epafee

contact lenses οι φακοί επαφής
ee fakee epafees

contact lens cleaner το
καθαριστικό διάλυμα *to
kathareesteeko dheealeema*

contraceptives τα αντισυλληπτικά
ta andeeseeleepteeka

contract το συμβόλαιο *to seemvoleo*

to cook μαγειρεύω *magheerevo*

cooker η κουζίνα *ee koozeena*

cool δροσερός *dhroseros*

cool box *(for picnics)* το ψυγειάκι
to psee-yeeakee

copper ο χάλκος *o khalkos*

to copy *(photocopy)* φωτοτυπώ *fototeepo*

copy *n* το αντίγραφο *to andeeghrafo*

coral το κοράλλι *to koralee*

cordless phone το ασύρματο τηλέφωνο *to aseermato teelefono*

corkscrew το τιρμπουσόν *to teerbooson*

corn *(sweet corn)* το καλαμπόκι *to kalambokee*

corner η γωνία *ee ghoneea*

cornflakes τα κορνφλέικς *ta kornfleiks*

cortisone η κορτιζόνη *ee korteezonee*

cosmetics τα καλλυντικά *ta kaleendeeka*

to cost κοστίζω *kosteezo*
how much does it cost? πόσο κάνει; *poso kanee*

cotton το βαμβάκι *to vamvakee*

cotton buds οι μπατονέτες *ee batonetes*

cotton wool το βαμβάκι *to vamvakee*

couchette η κουκέτα *ee kooketa*

cough ο βήχας *o veekhas*

country η χώρα *ee khora*
(not town) η εξοχή *ee eksokhee*

couple *(two people)* το ζευγάρι *to zevgharee*

courgette το κολοκυθάκι *to kolokeethakee*

courier *(for tourists)* ο/η συνοδός *o/ee seenodhos*

course *(meal)* το πιάτο *to pyato*

cousin ο εξάδελφος/η εξαδέλφη *o eksadhelfos/ee eksadhelfee*

cover charge το κουβέρ *to koover*

crab το καβούρι *to kavooree*

craft fair ο εκθεσιακός χώρος χειροποίητων *o ektheseeakos khoros kheeropee-eeton*

cramp η κράμπα *ee krampa*

cranberry juice ο χυμός φρούτου <γκράνμπερι> *o kheemos frootoo 'cranberry'*

to crash συγκρούομαι *seengkrooome*

crash η σύγκρουση *ee seengroosee*

crash helmet το κράνος *to kranos*

cream η κρέμα *ee krema*

credit *n (on mobile phone)* οι μονάδες *ee monadhes*

credit card η πιστωτική κάρτα *ee peestoteekee karta*

crime το έγκλημα *to engkleema*

crisps τα πατατάκια *ta patatakya*

croquette η κροκέτα *ee kroketa*

cross ο σταυρός *o stavros*

to cross διασχίζω *dheeaskheezo*

crossroads το σταυροδρόμι *to stavrodhromee*

crowded γεμάτος *yematos*

cruise η κρουαζιέρα *ee krooazyera*

crutches οι πατερίτσες *ee patereetses*

cucumber το αγγούρι *to angooree*

cup το φλυτζάνι *to fleedzanee*

cupboard το ντουλάπι *to doolapee*

currant η σταφίδα *ee stafeedha*

current *(electric)* το ρεύμα *to revma*

cushion το μαξιλάρι *to makseelaree*

customer ο πελάτης *o pelatees*

customs το τελωνείο *to teloneeo*

to cut το κόβω *kovo*

cut *(wound)* το κόψιμο *to kopseemo*

cutlery τα μαχαιροπήρουνα
ta makheropeeroona

to cycle ποδηλατώ podheelato

cyst η κύστη ee keestee

cystitis η κυστίτιδα ee keesteeteedha

D

daily ημερήσιος eemereeseeos

dairy products τα γαλακτοκομικά
προϊόντα ta ghalaktokomeeka
proeeonda

damage η ζημιά ee zeemya

damp υγρός eeghros

dance n ο χορός o khoros

to dance χορεύω khorevo

danger ο κίνδυνος o keendheenos

dangerous επικίνδυνος
epeekeendheenos

dark (colour) σκούρο skooro
it's dark είναι σκοτεινά
eene skoteena

date η ημερομηνία ee eemeromeeneea
what's the date? τι ημερομηνία
είναι; tee eemeromeeneea eene

date of birth η ημερομηνία
γεννήσεως ee eemeromeeneea
yeneeseos

daughter η κόρη ee koree

day η μέρα ee mera

dead νεκρός nekros

dear αγαπητός aghapeetos
(expensive) ακριβός akreevos

debit card η κάρτα ανάληψης
ee karta analeepsees

decaffeinated χωρίς καφεΐνη
khorees kafe-eenee

deck chair η ξαπλώστρα
ee ksaplostra

to declare δηλώνω dheelono

deep βαθύς vathees

deep freeze η κατάψυξη
ee katapseeksee

to defrost ξεπαγώνω ksepaghono

delay η καθυστέρηση
ee katheestereesee

delayed καθυστερισμένος
katheestereesmenos

delicious νόστιμος nosteemos

dentist ο/η οδοντίατρος
o/ee odhondeeatros

dentures η οδοντοστοιχία
ee odhondosteekheea

deodorant το αποσμητικό
to aposmeeteeko

department store
το πολυκατάστημα
to poleekatasteema

departure η αναχώρηση
ee anakhoreesee

departure lounge η αίθουσα
αναχωρήσεων ee ethoosa
anakhoreeseon

deposit (part payment)
η προκαταβολή ee prokatavolee

dessert το επιδόρπιο
to epeedhorpeeo

details οι λεπτομέρειες
ee leptomereeyes

detergent το απορρυπαντικό
to aporeepandeeko

detour: to make a detour
βγαίνω από το δρόμο vyeno apo
to dhromo

to develop αναπτύσσω anapteeso

diabetic διαβητικός dheeaveeteekos

to dial παίρνω αριθμό perno
areethmo

dialling code ο τηλεφωνικός
κώδικας o teelefoneekos kodheekas

diamond το διαμάντι *to dheeamandee*

diapers οι πάνες *ee panes*

diarrhoea η διάρροια *ee dheeareea*

diary το ημερολόγιο *to eemeroloyo*

dictionary το λεξικό *to lekseeko*

diesel το ντίζελ *to deezel*

diet η δίαιτα *ee dhee-eta*
 I'm on a diet κάνω δίαιτα *kano dhee-eta*

different διαφορετικός *dheeaforeteekos*

difficult δύσκολος *dheeskolos*

digital camera η ψηφιακή φωτογραφική μηχανή *ee pseefeeakee fotografeekee meekhanee*

dinghy η μικρή βάρκα *ee meekree varka*

dining room η τραπεζαρία *ee trapezareea*

dinner το δείπνο *to dheepno*

direct άμεσος *amesos*

directory *(telephone)* ο τηλεφωνικός κατάλογος *o teelefoneekos kataloghos*

directory enquiries οι πληροφορίες καταλόγου *ee pleeroforeeyes kataloghoo*

dirty βρώμικος *vromeekos*

disabled ανάπηρος *anapeeros*

disco η ντισκοτέκ *ee deeskotek*

discount η έκπτωση *ee ekptosee*

dish το πιάτο *to pyato*

dish towel η πετσέτα πιάτων *ee petseta pyaton*

dishwasher το πλυντήριο πιάτων *to pleenteereeo pyaton*

disinfectant το απολυμαντικό *to apoleemandeeko*

disk *(floppy)* η δισκέτα *ee dheesketa*

distilled water το απεσταγμένο νερό *to apestaghmeno nero*

diversion η παράκαμψη *ee parakampsee*

divorced χωρισμένος/χωρισμένη *khoreesmenos/khoreesmenee*

dizzy ζαλισμένος *zaleesmenos*

to do: *I do* κάνω *kano*
 you do κάνεις *kanees*

doctor ο/η γιατρός *o/ee yatros*

documents τα έγγραφα *ta engrafa*

dog το σκυλί *to skeelee*

doll η κούκλα *ee kookla*

dollar το δολάριο *to dholareeo*

door η πόρτα *ee porta*

donkey το γαϊδούρι *to ghaeedhooree*

donor card η κάρτα δότη *ee karta dhotee*

double διπλός *dheeplos*

double bed το διπλό κρεββάτι *to dheeplo krevatee*

double room το δίκλινο δωμάτιο *to dheekleeno dhomateeo*

down: *to go down* κατεβαίνω *kateveno*

Down's syndrome το σύνδρομο Down *to seendhromo Down*
 he/she has Down's syndrome αυτός/αυτή έχει το σύνδρομο Down *aftos/aftee ekhee to seendhromo Down*

downstairs κάτω *kato*

drachmas δραχμές *dhrakhmes*

drain η αποχέτευση *ee apokhetefsee*

draught *(of air)* το ρεύμα *to revma*

draught lager η μπίρα από βαρέλι *ee beera apo varelee*

drawer το συρτάρι *to seertaree*

drawing το σχέδιο *to skhedheeo*

dress το φόρεμα *to forema*

to dress ντύνομαι *deenome*

dressing (for salad) το λαδολέμονο
to ladholemono

dressing gown η ρόμπα *ee roba*

drill τρυπώ *treepo*

drink *n* το ποτό *to poto*
to have a drink παίρνω ένα ποτό
perno ena poto

to drink πίνω *peeno*

drinking water το πόσιμο νερό
to poseemo nero

to drive οδηγώ *odheegho*

driver ο οδηγός *o odheeghos*

driving licence η άδεια οδήγησης
ee adheea odheegheesees

to drown πνίγομαι *pneeghome*

drug (illegal) το ναρκωτικό
to narkoteeko
(medicine) το φάρμακο *to farmako*

drunk μεθυσμένος *metheesmenos*

dry *adj* στεγνός *steghnos*

to dry στεγνώνω *steghnono*

dry-cleaners το καθαριστήριο
to kathareesteereeo

duck η πάπια *ee papya*

due: when is the train due? πότε
θα φτάσει το τραίνο; *pote tha
ftasee to treno*

dummy η πιπίλα *ee peepeela*

during κατά τη διάρκεια *kata tee
dheearkeea*

dust η σκόνη *ee skonee*

duvet το πάπλωμα *to paploma*

duvet cover η παπλωματοθήκη
ee paplomatotheekee

DVD το DVD *to dee vee dee*

DVD player το DVD player *to dee
vee dee player*

E

each κάθε *kathe*
100 cents each εκατό ευρώ ο
καθένας *ekato evro o kathenas*

ear το αυτί *to aftee*

earache: I have earache με πονάει
το αυτί μου *me ponaee
to aftee moo*

earlier νωρίτερα *noreetera*

early νωρίς *norees*

earrings τα σκουλαρίκια
ta skoolareekya

earthquake ο σεισμός *o seesmos*

east η ανατολή *ee anatolee*

Easter το Πάσχα *to paskha*

easy εύκολος *efkolos*

to eat τρώω *tro-o*

ecological οικολογικός/η/ο
eekologheekos

eco-tourism ο οικοτουρισμός
o eekotooreesmos

eel το χέλι *to khelee*

egg το αβγό *to avgho*
fried eggs αβγά τηγανητά
avgha teeghaneeta
boiled eggs αβγά βραστά
avgha vrasta
poached eggs αβγά ποσέ
avgha pose

either ... or ή ... ή *ee ... ee//
είτε ... είτε *eete ... eete*

elastic το λάστιχο *to lasteekho*

elastic band το λαστιχάκι
to lasteekhakee

electrician ο ηλεκτρολόγος
o eelektrologhos

electricity meter ο μετρητής ηλεκτρισμού *o metreetees eelektreesmoo*

electric razor η ξυριστική μηχανή *ee kseereesteekee meekhanee*

electric toothbrush η ηλεκτρική οδοντόβουρτσα *ee eelektreekee odhontovoortsa*

electronic ηλεκτρονικός/ή/ ό *eelektroneekos-ee-o*

electronic organizer το ηλεκτρονικό organizer *to eelektroneeko organizer*

e-mail το e-mail *to e-mail*

e-mail address η e-mail διεύθυνση *ee e-mail dheeeftheensee*

embassy η πρεσβεία *ee presveea*

emergency: it's an emergency είναι επείγον περιστατικό *eene epeeghon pereestateeko*

empty άδειος *adheeos*

end το τέλος *to telos*

engaged (to marry) αρραβωνιασμένος/η *aravonyasmenos/ee* (toilet) κατειλημμένη *kateeleemenee* (phone) μιλάει *meelaee*

engine η μηχανή *ee meekhanee*

England η Αγγλία *ee angleea*

English (thing) αγγλικός *angleekos*

Englishman/woman ο Άγγλος/η Αγγλίδα *o anglos/ee angleedha*

to enjoy oneself διασκεδάζω *dheeaskedhazo*

enough αρκετά *arketa* *enough bread* αρκετό ψωμί *arketo psomee*

enquiry desk/office το γραφείο πληροφοριών *to ghrafeeo pleeroforeeon*

to enter μπαίνω *beno*

entertainment η ψυχαγωγία *ee pseekhaghoyeea*

entrance η είσοδος *ee eesodhos*

entrance fee η τιμή εισόδου *ee teemee eesodhoo*

envelope ο φάκελος *o fakelos*

equipment ο εξοπλισμός *o eksopleesmos*

escalator η κυλιόμενη σκάλα *ee keelyomenee skala*

especially ειδικά *eedheeka*

essential απαραίτητος *apareteetos*

euro ευρώ *evro*

Europe η Ευρώπη *ee evropee*

even number ο ζυγός αριθμός *o zeeghos areethmos*

evening το βράδυ *to vradhee* *this evening* απόψε *apopse* *in the evening* το βράδυ *to vradhee*

every κάθε *kathe*

everyone όλοι *olee*

everything όλα *ola*

exact ακριβής *akreevees*

examination η εξέταση *ee eksetasee*

excellent εξαιρετικός *eksereteekos*

except εκτός από *ektos apo*

excess luggage επί πλέον αποσκευές *epee pleon aposkeves*

exchange rate η τιμή του συναλλάγματος *ee teemee too seenalaghmatos*

excursion η εκδρομή *ee ekdhromee*

excuse me με συγχωρείτε *me seeghkhoreete*

exhaust pipe η εξάτμιση *ee eksatmeesee*

exhibition η έκθεση *ee ekthesee*

exit η έξοδος *ee eksodhos*

expensive ακριβός *akreevos*

expert ο/η ειδικός *o/ee eedheekos*

to expire λήγω *leegho*

expired έχει λήξει *ekhee leeksee*

to explain εξηγώ *ekseegho*

express (train) η ταχεία *ee takheea*

express letter το κατεπείγον γράμμα *to katepeeghon ghrama*

extra: it costs extra κοστίζει επιπλέον *kosteezee epeepleon* extra money περισσότερα χρήματα *pereesotera khreemata*

eyes τα μάτια *ta matya*

F

fabric το ύφασμα *to eefasma*

face το πρόσωπο *to prosopo*

facilities οι ευκολίες *ee efkoleeyes*

factor (sunblock) ο δείκτης *o dheektees* factor 25 δείκτης 25 *dheektees 25*

factory το εργοστάσιο *to erghostaseeo*

to faint λιποθυμώ *leepotheemo*

fainted λιποθύμησε *leepotheemeese*

fair adj (hair) ξανθός *ksanthos* fair hair ξανθά μαλλιά *ksantha mallya*

fair n (commercial) η έκθεση *ee ekthese* (fun fair) το λουνα-πάρκ *to loonapark*

to fall πέφτω *pefto* he/she has fallen έπεσε *epese*

family η οικογένεια *ee eekoyenya*

famous διάσημος *dheeaseemos*

fan (electric) ο ανεμιστήρας *o anemeesteeras*

fan belt το λουρί του ψυγείου *to looree too pseegheeo*

far μακριά *makreea*

fare (bus, train) το εισιτήριο *to eeseeteereeo*

farm το αγρόκτημα *to aghrokteema*

farmers' market η λαϊκή αγορά *ee la-eekee aghora*

fast γρήγορα *ghreeghora*

fat adj χοντρός *khondros*

fat n το λίπος *to leepos*

father ο πατέρας *o pateras*

father-in-law ο πεθερός *o petheros*

fault (mistake) το λάθος *to lathos* it is not my fault δε φταίω εγώ *dhe fteo egho*

favourite ο πιο αγαπημένος *o pyo aghapeemenos*

fax το φαξ *fax*

feather (of bird) το φτερό *to ftero*

to feed ταΐζω *taeezo*

to feel αισθάνομαι *esthanome* I feel sick θέλω να κάνω εμετό *thelo na kano emeto*

female θηλυκός *theeleekos*

ferry το φεριμπότ *to fereebot*

festival το φεστιβάλ *to festeeval* // το πανηγύρι *to paneegheeree*

to fetch φέρνω *ferno*

fever ο πυρετός *o peeretos*

few: a few μερικοί/μερικές/ μερικά *mereekee (masculine)/ mereekes (feminine)/mereeka (neuter)*

fiancé(e) ο αρραβωνιαστικός/η αρραβωνιαστικιά *o aravonyasteekos/ee aravonyasteekya*

field το χωράφι *to khorafee*

file (nail) η λίμα ee leema
(computer) το αρχείο to arkheeo

to fill γεμίζω yemeezo
fill it up! (car) γεμίστε το yemeeste to

fillet το φιλέτο to feeleto

filling (in cake, etc.) η γέμιση
ee yemeesee
(in tooth) το σφράγισμα
to sfragheesma

film (for camera) το φιλμ to feelm
(in cinema) η ταινία ee teneea

Filofax® η ατζέντα ee adzenda

filter το φίλτρο to feeltro

to finish τελειώνω teleeono

fire (heater) η θερμάστρα
ee thermastra
fire! φωτιά! fotya!
fire brigade η πυροσβεστική
ee peerosvesteekee
fire extinguisher ο πυροσβεστήρας
o peerosvesteeras

fireworks τα πυροτεχνήματα
ta peerotekhneemata

first πρώτος protos

first aid οι πρώτες βοήθειες
ee protes voeetheeyes

first class (seat, etc.) η πρώτη θέση
ee protee thesee

first floor ο πρώτος όροφος
o protos orofos

first name το όνομα to onoma

fish το ψάρι to psaree

to fish ψαρεύω psarevo

fishing rod το καλάμι ψαρέματος
to kalamee psarematos

fit (healthy) υγιής eeyees

to fix φτιάχνω fteeakhno
(arrange) κανονίζω kanoneezo

fizzy (drink) αεριούχο aeryookho

flash (on camera) το φλας to flas

flask το θερμός to thermos

flat (apartment) το διαμέρισμα
to dheeamereesma

flat tyre: I have a flat tyre έχω
σκασμένο λάστιχο ekho skasmeno
lasteekho

flea ο ψύλλος o pseelos

flight η πτήση ee pteesee

flippers (swimming)
τα βατραχοπέδιλα
ta vatrakhopedheela

flood η πλημμύρα ee pleemeera

floor το πάτωμα to patoma
(storey) ο όροφος o orofos

floppy disk η δισκέτα ee dheesketa

flour το αλεύρι to alevree

flower το λουλούδι to looloodhee

flu η γρίππη ee ghreepee

to fly πετώ peto

fly η μύγα ee meegha

to follow ακολουθώ akolootho

food το φαγητό to fa-yeeto

food poisoning η τροφική
δηλητηρίαση ee trofeekee
dheeleeteereeasee

foot το πόδι to podhee

football το ποδόσφαιρο
to podhosfero

for για ya

foreign ξένος ksenos

forest το δάσος to dhasos

to forget ξεχνώ ksekhno

fork το πηρούνι to peeroonee
(in road) η διακλάδωση
ee dheeakladhosee

fortnight το δεκαπενθήμερο
to dhekapentheemero

fountain το σιντριβάνι
to seendreevanee

fracture *(of bone)* το κάταγμα
to kataghma

France η Γαλλία ee ghaleea

free ελεύθερος eleftheros
(costing nothing) δωρεάν dhorean

to freeze *(food)* ψύχω pseekho

freezer ο καταψύκτης
o katapseektees

French *(thing)* γαλλικός ghaleekos

French beans τα φασολάκια
ta fasolakya

frequent συχνός seekhnos

fresh φρέσκος freskos

fridge το ψυγείο to psee-gheeo

fried τηγανητός teeghaneetos

friend ο φίλος/η φίλη o feelos/
ee feelee

from από apo

front *(part)* το μπροστινό (μέρος)
to brosteeno (meros)
in front μπροστά brosta

frozen *(water)* παγωμένος
paghomenos
(food) κατεψυγμένος
katepseeghmenos

fruit τα φρούτα ta froota

fruit juice ο χυμός φρούτων
o kheemos frooton

fruit salad η φρουτοσαλάτα
ee frootosalata

frying pan το τηγάνι to teeghanee

fuel τα καύσιμα ta kafseema

fuel pump η αντλία καυσίμων
ee andleea kafseemon

full γεμάτος yematos

full board (η) πλήρης διατροφή
(ee) pleerees dheeatrofee

fumes *(of car)* τα καυσαέρια
ta kafsaereea

funeral η κηδεία ee keedheea

funny αστείος asteeos

fur η γούνα ee ghoona

furniture τα έπιπλα ta epeepla

fuse η ασφάλεια ee asfaleea

fuse box ο ηλεκτρικός πίνακας
o eelektreekos peenakas

G

gallery *(art)* η πινακοθήκη
ee peenakotheekee

game το παιγνίδι to peghneedhee
(to eat) το κυνήγι to keeneeghee

garage *(for parking car)* το γκαράζ
to garaz

garden ο κήπος o keepos

garlic το σκόρδο to skordho

gas το γκάζι to gazee

gas cooker η γκαζιέρα ee gazyera

gas cylinder η φιάλη γκαζιού
ee feealee gazyoo

gate *(at airport)* η έξοδος ee eksodhos

gears οι ταχύτητες ee takheeteetes
first gear πρώτη protee
second gear δεύτερη dhefteree
third gear τρίτη treetee
fourth gear τετάρτη tetartee
neutral νεκρά nekra
reverse όπισθεν opeesthen

gearbox το κιβώτιο ταχυτήτων
to keevotyo takheeteeton

gear cable το καλώδιο με μεγάλη
ταχύτητα διάδοσης πληροφοριών
(για P/C) to kalodheeo me
meghalee takheeteeta dheeadhosees
pleeroforeeon (ya PC)

gents *(toilet)* ανδρών andhron

genuine γνήσιος ghneeseeos

germs τα μικρόβια ta meekroveea

German measles η ερυθρά
ee ereethra

to get παίρνω *perno*
(fetch) φέρνω *ferno*

to get in (car, etc.) μπαίνω *beno*

to get off (from bus) κατεβαίνω από
kateveno apo

to get on (bus) ανεβαίνω στο
λεωφορείο *aneveno sto leoforeeo*

to get through (on the phone)
συνδέομαι *seendheome*

gift το δώρο *to dhoro*

gift shop το κατάστημα δώρων
to katasteema dhoron

gin το τζιν *to gin*

ginger το τζίντζερ *to dzeendzer*

girl το κορίτσι *to koreetsee*

girlfriend η φίλη *ee feelee* //
η φιλενάδα *ee feelenadha*

to give δίνω *dheeno*

to give back επιστρέφω *epeestrefo*

glass (to drink from) το ποτήρι
to poteeree
a glass of water ένα ποτήρι νερό
ena poteeree nero

glasses (spectacles) τα γυαλιά
ta yalya

gloves τα γάντια *ta ghandeea*

glucose η γλυκόζη *ee ghleekozee*

glue n η κόλλα *ee kola*

to glue κολλώ *kolo*

gluten η γλουτένη *ee ghlootenee*

GM-free μη γενετικά μεταλαγμένα
mee yeneteeka metalaghmena

to go πηγαίνω *peegheno*
I go/I am going πηγαίνω
peegheno
you go/you are going πηγαίνεις
peeghenees

we go/we are going πηγαίνουμε
peeghenoome

to go back γυρίζω πίσω *yeereezo
peeso*

to go down κατεβαίνω *kateveno*

to go in μπαίνω *beno*

to go out βγαίνω *vyeno*

to go up ανεβαίνω *aneveno*

goat η κατσίκα *ee katseeka*

goggles τα γυαλιά *ta yalya*

gold ο χρυσός *o khreesos*
(made of gold) χρυσός *khreesos*

golf το γκολφ *to golf*

golf course το γήπεδο του γκολφ
to yeepedho too golf

good καλός *kalos*

good afternoon χαίρετε *kherete*

goodbye αντίο *adeeo*

good day καλημέρα *kaleemera*

good evening καλησπέρα
kaleespera

good morning καλημέρα
kaleemera

good night καληνύχτα *kaleeneekhta*

goose η χήνα *ee kheena*

GPS (global positioning system)
το GPS *to jee pee ess*

gram το γραμμάριο *to ghramareeo*

grandfather ο παππούς *o papoos*

grandmother η γιαγιά *ee yaya*

grandparents ο παππούς και η
γιαγιά *o papoos ke ee yaya*

grapefruit το γκρέιπ-φρουτ
to grapefruit

grapes τα σταφύλια *ta stafeelya*

grated cheese το τυρί τριμένο
to teeree treemeno

grater ο τρίφτης *o treeftees*

greasy λιπαρός *leeparos*

great μεγάλος *meghalos*

Greece η Ελλάδα *ee eladha*

Greek (person) ο Έλληνας/η Ελληνίδα *o eleenas/ee eleeneedha*

Greek adj ελληνικός *eleeneekos*

green πράσινος *praseenos*

grey γκρίζος *greezos*

grilled της σχάρας *tees skharas*

grocer's το μπακάλικο *to bakaleeko*//το παντοπωλείο *to pandopoleeo*

ground n το έδαφος *to edhafos*

ground adj (coffee, etc.) αλεσμένος *alesmenos*

ground floor το ισόγειο *to eesoyeeo*

groundsheet ο μουσαμάς εδάφους *o moosamas edhafoos*

group η ομάδα *ee omadha*

to grow μεγαλώνω *meghalono*

guarantee η εγγύηση *ee enghee-yeesee*

guard (on train) ο υπεύθυνος τρένου *o eepeftheenos trenoo*

guava το γκουάβα *to gooava*

guest ο φιλοξενούμενος *o feeloksenoomenos*

guesthouse ο ξενώνας *o ksenonas*

guide ο/η ξεναγός *o/ee ksenaghos*

to guide ξεναγώ *ksenagho*

guidebook ο οδηγός *o odheeghos*

guided tour η περιήγηση με ξεναγό *ee peree-eeyeesee me ksenagho*

gym shoes τα αθλητικά παπούτσια *ta athleeteeka papootsya*

gynaecologist ο/η γυναικολόγος *o/ee yeenekologhos*

H

haemorrhoids οι αιμορροΐδες *ee emoroeedhes*

hair τα μαλλιά *ta malya*

hairbrush η βούρτσα *ee voortsa*

haircut το κούρεμα *to koorema*

hairdresser ο κομμωτής/η κομμώτρια *o komotees/ee komotreea*

hairdryer το πιστολάκι *to peestolakee*

half το μισό *to meeso*
half an hour μισή ώρα *meesee ora*

half board (η) ημιδιατροφή *(ee) eemeedheeatrofee*

half-bottle το μικρό μπουκάλι *to meekro bookalee*

half price μισή τιμή *meesee teemee*

ham το ζαμπόν *to zambon*

hamburger το χάμπουργκερ *to khamboorgher*

hammer το σφυρί *to sfeeree*

hand το χέρι *to kheree*

handbag η τσάντα *ee tsanda*

handicapped ανάπηρος *anapeeros*

handkerchief το μαντήλι *to mandeelee*
(tissue) το χαρτομάντηλο *to khartomandeelo*

hand luggage οι χειραποσκευή *ee kheeraposkevee*

hand-made χειροποίητος *kheeropee-eetos*

hands-free kit (for phone) τα ακουστικά *ta akoosteeka*

to hang up (phone) κλείνω *kleeno*

to happen συμβαίνω *seemveno*
what happened? τι συνέβη; *tee seenevee*

happy χαρούμενος *kharoomenos*

harbour το λιμάνι *to leemanee*

hard (difficult) δύσκολος *dheeskolos*

hard-boiled (egg) σφιχτό *sfeekhto*

hardware shop το σιδηροπωλείο
to seedheeropoleeo

harvest ο θερισμός *o thereesmos*

hat το καπέλο *to kapelo*

hay fever η αλλεργική ρινίτιδα
ee aleryeekee reeneeteedha

hazelnut το φουντούκι *to foondookee*

he αυτός *aftos*

head το κεφάλι *to kefalee*

headache: *I have a headache* έχω
πονοκέφαλο *ekho ponokefalo*

headlights τα φώτα *ta fota*

headphones τα ακουστικά
ta akoosteeka

health η υγεία *ee eegheea*

to hear ακούω *akoo-o*

hearing aid το ακουστικό
βαρηκοΐας *to akoosteeko
vareekoeeas*

heart η καρδιά *ee kardhya*

heart attack η καρδιακή προσβολή
ee kardheeakee prosvolee

heartburn η καούρα *ee kaoora*

heater η θερμάστρα *ee thermastra*

heating η θέρμανση *ee thermansee*

heavy βαρύς *varees*

hello γεια σας *ya sas*

helmet ο κράνος *o kranos*

to help βοηθώ *voeetho*
help! βοήθεια *voeetheea*

hepatitis η ηπατίτιδα
ee eepateeteedha

herb το βότανο *to votano*

herbal tea το τσάι του βουνού
to tsaee too voonoo

here εδώ *edho*

hernia η κήλη *ee keelee*

high ψηλός *pseelos*

high blood pressure η ψηλή
πίεση *ee pseelee peeyesee*

high chair η ψηλή παιδική
καρέκλα *ee pseelee pedheekee
karekla*

hill ο λόφος *o lofos*
(slope) η πλαγιά *ee pla-ya*

hill walking η ορειβασία
ee oreevaseea

to hire νοικιάζω *neekyazo*

to hit χτυπώ *khteepo*

hitchhiking το οτοστόπ *to otostop*

HIV positive θετικός για ΕΙΤΖ
theteekos ya aids

to hold κρατώ *krato*

hold-up η καθυστέρηση
ee katheestereesee

hole η τρύπα *ee treepa*

holidays οι διακοπές *ee dheeakopes*

home το σπίτι *to speetee*
at home στο σπίτι *sto speetee*

homeopathic (remedy etc)
ομοιοπαθητικός/ή/ό
omeeopatheeteekos-ee-o

homeopathy η ομοιοπαθητική
ee omeeopatheeteekee

honey το μέλι *to melee*

honeymoon ο μήνας του μέλιτος
o meenas too meleetos

hook (fishing) το αγκίστρι
to angkeestree

to hope ελπίζω *elpeezo*

hors d'œuvre τα ορεκτικά
ta orekteeka

horse το άλογο *to alogho*

hospital το νοσοκομείο
to nosokomeeo

hot ζεστός *zestos*
I'm hot ζεσταίνομαι *zestenome*
it's hot έχει ζέστη *ekhee zestee*
hot water το ζεστό νερό *to zesto nero*

hotel το ξενοδοχείο *to ksenodhokheeo*

hour η ώρα *ee ora*

house το σπίτι *to speetee*

housewife η νοικοκυρά *ee neekokeera*

house wine το κρασί χύμα
to krasee kheema

how πώς *pos*
how long? πόση ώρα; *posee ora*
how much? πόσο; *poso*
how many? πόσα; *posa*
how are you? πώς είστε;
pos eeste

hungry: *I'm hungry* πεινώ *peeno*

to hurry: *I'm in a hurry* βιάζομαι
vyazome

to hurt: *that hurts* με πονάει *me pona-ee*

husband ο σύζυγος *o seezeeghos*

hydrofoil το ιπτάμενο δελφίνι
to eeptameno dhelfeenee

hypodermic needle η υποδερμική
βελόνα *ee eepodhermeekee velona*

I

I εγώ *egho*

ice ο πάγος *o paghos*

ice cream/ice lolly το παγωτό
to paghoto

iced *(drink)* παγωμένος *paghomenos*

icon η εικόνα *ee eekona*

if αν *an*

ignition η ανάφλεξη *ee anafleksee*

ignition key το κλειδί μίζας
to kleedhee meezas

ill άρρωστος *arostos*

immediately αμέσως *amesos*

immobilizer *(on car)* το immobilizer

immunisation ο εμβολιασμός
o emvoleeasmos

important σπουδαίος *spoodheos*

impossible αδύνατο *adheenato*

in *(inside)* μέσα *mesa*
(into) σε *se*
(with countries, towns) στο/στη/στο
sto/stee/sto

included συμπεριλαμβάνεται
seembereelamvanete

indigestion η δυσπεψία
ee dheespepseea

indoors εσωτερικά *esotereeka*

infectious μεταδοτικός
metadhoteekos

information οι πληροφορίες
ee pleeroforeeyes

information office το γραφείο
πληροφοριών *to ghrafeeo
pleeroforeeon*

inhaler η συσκευή εισπνοής
ee seeskevee eespnoees

injection η ένεση *ee enesee*

injured τραυματισμένος
travmateesmenos

ink το μελάνι *to melanee*

inner tube η σαμπρέλα *ee sambrela*

insect το έντομο *to endomo*

insect bite το τσίμπημα
to tseembeema

insect repellent
το εντομοαπωθητικό
to endomoapotheeteeko

inside n (interior) το εσωτερικό
to esotereeko
inside the car μέσα στο
αυτοκίνητο mesa sto aftokeeneeto
it's inside είναι μέσα eene mesa

instant coffee στιγμιαίος καφές
steeghmee-eos kafes

instructor ο εκπαιδευτής
o ekpedheftees

insulin η ινσουλίνη ee eensooleenee

insurance η ασφάλεια ee asfalea

insurance certificate η βεβαίωση
ασφαλίσεως ee veveosee
asfaleeseos

insured ασφαλισμένος
asfaleesmenos

interesting ενδιαφέρων
endheeaferon

international διεθνής dhee-ethnees

internet το ίντερνετ to eenternet

internet access η πρόσβαση στο
ίντερνετ ee prosvasee sto eenternet
do you have internet access?
έχεις/έχετε πρόσβαση στο
ίντερνετ ekhees/ekhete prosvasee
sto eenternet?

interpreter ο/η διερμηνέας
o/ee dhee-ermeeneas

interval (theatre) το διάλειμμα
to dheealeema

into σε se

into the στο/στη/στο sto/stee/sto

invitation η πρόσκληση
ee proskleesee

to invite προσκαλώ proskalo

invoice το τιμολόγιο to teemoloyo

iPod® το ipod to 'ipod'

Ireland η Ιρλανδία ee eerlandheea

Irish (person) ο Ιρλανδός/η Ιρλανδή
o eerlandhos/ee eerlandhee

iron (for clothes) το σίδερο to seedhero
(metal) ο σίδηρος o seedheeros

to iron σιδερώνω seedherono

ironmonger's το σιδηροπωλείο
to seedheeropoleeo

island το νησί to neesee

it το to

Italy η Ιταλία ee eetaleea

itch η φαγούρα ee faghoora

itemised bill ο αναλυτικός
λογαριασμός o analeeteekos
logharyasmos

IUD το σπιράλ to speeral

J

jack ο γρύλος o ghreelos

jacket το μπουφάν to boofan

jam η μαρμελάδα ee marmeladha

jar το βάζο to vazo

jaundice ο ίκτερος o eekteros

jeans το τζιν to jean

jelly το ζελέ to zele

jellyfish η τσούχτρα ee tsookhtra

jersey το πουλόβερ to poolover

to jetski το jetski to jetski

jetty ο μώλος o molos

jeweller's το κοσμηματοπωλείο
to kosmeematopoleeo

jewellery τα κοσμήματα
ta kosmeemata

job η δουλειά ee dhoolya

to jog κάνω τζόκινγκ kano jogging

joint το άρθρωση to arthrosee

joke το αστείο to asteeo

journey το ταξίδι to takseedhee

jug η κανάτα ee kanata

juice ο χυμός *o kheemos*

jump leads τα καλώδια μπαταρίας *ta kalodheea batareeas*

junction *(crossroads)* η διασταύρωση *ee dheeastavrosee*

just: just two μόνο δύο *mono dheeo*
I've just arrived μόλις έφτασα *molees eftasa*

K

to keep κρατώ *krato*

kettle ο βραστήρας *o vrasteeras*

key το κλειδί *to kleedhee*

keycard *(electronic key eg in hotel)* η κάρτα-κλειδί *ee karta-kleedhee*

key-ring το μπρελόκ *to brelok*

kid *(young goat)* το κατσικάκι *to katseekakee*

kidneys τα νεφρά *ta nefra*

kilo το κιλό *to keelo*

kilometre το χιλιόμετρο *to kheelyometro*

kind *n (sort)* το είδος *to eedhos*

kind *adj* ευγενικός *ef-gheneekos*

king ο βασιλιάς *o vaseelyas*

kiosk το περίπτερο *to pereeptero*

to kiss φιλώ *feelo*

kitchen η κουζίνα *ee koozeena*

kitchen paper το χαρτί κουζίνας *to khartee koozeenas*

kitten το γατάκι *to ghatakee*

kiwi fruit το ακτινίδιο *to akteeneedheeo*

knee το γόνατο *to ghonato*

knee highs οι κάλτσες *ee kaltses*

knickers *(women's)* η κυλότα *ee keelota*

knife το μαχαίρι *to makheree*

to knock down *(by car)* χτυπώ με αυτοκίνητο *khteepo me aftokeeneeto*

to knock over *(vase, glass)* ρίχνω κάτω *reekhno kato*

L

label η ετικέτα *ee eteeketa*

lace η δαντέλα *ee dhandela*

laces *(of shoe)* τα κορδόνια *ta kordhoneea*

ladder η σκάλα *ee skala*

ladies *(toilet)* γυναικών *yeenekon*

lady η κυρία *ee keereea*

lager η μπίρα *ee beera*

lake η λίμνη *ee leemnee*

lamb το αρνάκι *to arnakee*

lamp η λάμπα *ee lamba*

to land *(plane)* προσγειώνω *prosgheeono*

landslide η καθίζηση *ee katheezeesee*

language η γλώσσα *ee ghlosa*

laptop το λάπτοπ *to laptop*

laptop bag η θήκη φορητού υπολογιστή *ee theekee foreetoo eepologheestee*

large μεγάλος *meghalos*

last τελευταίος *telefteos*

late *(in the day)* αργά *argha*
I am late *(for an appointment)* έχω αργήσει *ekho argheesee*

later αργότερα *arghotera*

laundrette το πλυντήριο *to pleendeereeo*

laundry service η υπηρεσία πλυντηρίου *ee eepeereseea pleendeereeoo*

lavatory η τουαλέτα *ee tooaleta*

lawyer o/η δικηγόρος
o/ee dheekeeghoros

laxative το καθαρτικό
to katharteeko

lay-by η βοηθητική λωρίδα
ee voeetheeteekee loreedha

lazy τεμπέλης *tembelees*

lead (electric) το καλώδιο
to kalodheeo

leader (guide) o/η ξεναγός
o/ee ksenaghos

leadfree αμόλυβδος *amoleevdhos*

leaf το φύλλο *to feelo*

leak η διαρροή *ee dheearoee*

learning disability το μαθησιακό
πρόβλημα *to matheeseeako
provleema*
he/she has a learning disability
αυτός/αυτή έχει μαθησιακό
πρόβλημα *aftos/aftee ekhee
matheeseeako provleema*

to learn μαθαίνω *matheno*

least: at least τουλάχιστο
toolakheesto

leather το δέρμα *to dherma*

leather goods τα δερμάτινα είδη
ta dhermateena eedhee

to leave (go away) φεύγω *fevgho*

leek το πράσσο *to praso*

left: (on/to the) left αριστερά
areestera

left-luggage (office) η φύλαξη
αποσκευών *ee feelaksee aposkevon*

leg το πόδι *to podhee*

lemon το λεμόνι *to lemonee*

lemonade η λεμονάδα *ee lemonadha*

lemongrass είδος βοτάνων
<λέμονγκρας> *eedhos votanon
'lemongrass'*

lemon tea το τσάι με λεμόνι
to tsaee me lemonee

to lend δανείζω *dhaneezo*

length το μήκος *to meekos*

lens ο φακός *o fakos*

lentils οι φακές *ee fakes*

less: less milk λιγότερο γάλα
leeghotero ghala

lesson το μάθημα *to matheema*

to let (allow) επιτρέπω *epeetrepo*
(hire out) νοικιάζω *neekyazo*

letter το γράμμα *to ghrama*

letterbox το γραμματοκιβώτιο
to ghramatokeevotyo

lettuce το μαρούλι *to maroolee*

level crossing η σιδηροδρομική
διασταύρωση *ee
seedheerodhromeekee
dheeastavrosee*

library η βιβλιοθήκη *ee
veevleeotheekee*

licence η άδεια *ee adheea*

to lie down ξαπλώνω *ksaplono*

lifeboat η ναυαγοσωστική λέμβος
ee navaghososteekee lemvos

lifeguard ο ναυαγοσώστης
o navaghosostees

life insurance η ασφάλεια ζωής
ee asfaleea zoees

life jacket το σωσίβιο *to soseeveeo*

lift το ασανσέρ *to asanser*

lift pass (skiing) το εισιτήριο
to eeseeteereeo

light το φως *to fos*

light bulb η λάμπα *ee lampa*

lighter (to light a cigarette)
ο αναπτήρας *o anapteeras*

lightning ο κεραυνός *o keravnos*

to like : *I like* μου αρέσει *moo aresee*

lilo το φουσκωτό στρώμα
to fooskoto stroma

lime *(fruit)* το γλυκολέμονο
to ghleekolemono

line η γραμμή *ee ghramee*

lip reading η χειλοανάγνωση
ee kheeloanaghnosee

lip salve το προστατευτικό στικ
to prostatefteeko steek

lipstick το κραγιόν *to kra-yon*

liqueur το λικέρ *to leeker*

to listen ακούω *akoo-o*

litre το λίτρο *to leetro*

litter τα σκουπίδια *ta skoopeedhya*

little μικρός *meekros*
a little λίγο *leegho*

to live μένω *meno*
he lives in London μένει στο
Λονδίνο *menee sto londheeno*

liver το συκώτι *to seekotee*

living room το καθιστικό
to katheesteeko

lizard η σαύρα *ee savra*

lobster ο αστακός *o astakos*

local τοπικός *topeekos*

lock η κλειδαριά *ee kleedharya*

to lock κλειδώνω *kleedhono*
I'm locked out κλειδώθηκα έξω
kleedhotheeka ekso

locker *(luggage)* η θήκη *ee theekee*

log book *(for car)* η άδεια
κυκλοφορίας
ee adheea keekloforeeas

lollipop το γλειφιτζούρι
to ghleefeedzooree

London το Λονδίνο *to londheeno*

long μακρύς *makrees*

to look at κοιτάζω *keetazo*

to look after φροντίζω *frondeezo*

to look for ψάχνω *psakhno*

lorry το φορτηγό *to forteegho*

to lose χάνω *khano*

lost χαμένος *khamenos*
I've lost my wallet έχασα το
πορτοφόλι μου *ekhasa to portofolee
moo*
I am lost χάθηκα *khatheeka*

lost-property office το γραφείο
απωλεσθέντων αντικειμένων
*to ghrafeeo apolesthendon
andeekeemenon*

lot: *a lot (of)* πολύς *polees*

lotion η λοσιόν *ee losyon*

loud δυνατός *dheenatos*

loudspeaker το ηχείο *to eekheeo*

lounge *(at airport)* η αίθουσα
ee ethoosa
(in hotel, house) το σαλόνι *to salonee*

to love αγαπώ *aghapo*

low χαμηλός *khameelos*

low-alcohol beer η μπίρα χαμηλή
σε αλκοόλ *ee beera khameelee se
alko-ol*

low-fat λάϊτ *laeet*

luggage οι αποσκευές *ee aposkeves*

luggage allowance το
επιτρεπόμενο βάρος αποσκευών
to epeetrepomeno varos aposkevon

luggage rack ο χώρος αποσκευών
o khoros aposkevon

luggage tag η ετικέτα *ee eteeketa*

luggage trolley το καροτσάκι
αποσκευών *to karotsakee aposkevon*

lump η εξόγκωση *ee eksongosee*

lunch το μεσημεριανό
to meseemereeano

lung ο πνεύμονας *o pnevmonas*
luxury η πολυτέλεια *ee poleeteleea*

M

machine η μηχανή *ee meekhanee*
mad τρελός *trelos*
magazine το περιοδικό *to pereeodheeko*
magnifying glass ο μεγενθυτικός φακός *o meghentheeteekos fakos*
maiden name το πατρώνυμο *to patroneemo*
main course *(of meal)* το κύριο πιάτο *to keereeo pyato*
mains *(electric)* ο κεντρικός αγωγός *o kendreekos aghoghos*
to make κάνω *kano*
make-up το μακιγιάζ *to makeeyaz*
male αρσενικός *arseneekos*
man ο άντρας *o andras*
manager ο διαχειριστής *o dheeakheereestees*
mango το μάνγκο *to mango*
manicure το μανικιούρ *to maneekyor*
many πολλοί *polee*
  many people πολλοί άνθρωποι *polee anthropee*
map ο χάρτης *o khartees*
marble το μάρμαρο *to marmaro*
margarine η μαργαρίνη *ee marghareenee*
marina η μαρίνα *ee mareena*
market η αγορά *ee aghora*
market day η μέρα της αγοράς *ee mera tees aghoras*
marmalade η μαρμελάδα πορτοκαλιού *ee marmeladha portokalyoo*

marriage certificate το πιστοποιητικό γάμου *to peestopyeeteeko ghamoo*
married παντρεμένος *pandremenos*
mass *(in church)* η Θεία Λειτουργία *ee theea leetoorgheea*
massage το μασάζ *to masaj*
match *(game)* ο αγώνας *o aghonas*
matches τα σπίρτα *ta speerta*
material το υλικό *to eeleeko*
matter: it doesn't matter δεν πειράζει *dhen peerazee*
  what's the matter with you? τι έχεις; *tee ekhees*
mayonnaise η μαγιονέζα *ee ma-yoneza*
Mb *(megabyte)* Mb
meal το γεύμα *to yevma*
to mean εννοώ *eno-o*
measles η ιλαρά *ee eelara*
meat το κρέας *to kreas*
mechanic ο μηχανικός *o meekhaneekos*
medicine *(drug)* το φάρμακο *to farmako*
Mediterranean η Μεσόγειος *ee mesoyeeos*
medium sweet *(wine)* μέτριο γλυκύ *metreeo ghleekee*
  (steak, size) μέτριο *metreeo*
to meet συναντώ *seenando*
meeting η συνάντηση *ee seenandeesee*
megabyte το μεγαμπάιτ *to megabaeet*
  128 megabytes 128 μεγαμπάιτ *128 megabaeet*
melon το πεπόνι *to peponee*
  (watermelon) το καρπούζι *to karpoozee*

member *(of club)* το μέλος *to melos*

memory stick *(for camera etc)*
το τσιπάκι μνήμης *to tseepakee mneemees*

men οι άντρες *ee andres*

menu ο κατάλογος *o kataloghos*//
το μενού *to menoo*

message το μήνυμα *to meeneema*

metal το μέταλο *to metalo*

meter ο μετρητής *o metreetees*

metre το μέτρο *to metro*

microphone το μικόφωνο
to meekrofono

microwave *(oven)* ο φούρνος
μικροκυμάτων *o foornos
meekrokeematon*

midday το μεσημέρι *to meseemeree*

midnight τα μεσάνυχτα
ta mesaneekhta

migraine η ημικρανία
ee eemeekraneea

mile το μίλι *to meelee*

milk το γάλα *to ghala*

milkshake το μιλκσέικ *to meelkseyk*

millimetre το χιλιοστόμετρο
to kheelyostometro

million το εκατομμύριο
to ekatomeereeo

mince ο κιμάς *o keemas*

to mind: do you mind if...?
σας ενοχλεί αν...; *sas enokhlee an...*

mineral water το επιτραπέζιο νερό
to epeetrapezeeo nero
(sparkling) το αεριούχο μεταλλικό
νερό *to aeryookho metaleeko nero*

minidisk το μινιντίσκ *to minidisk*

minimum ελάχιστος *elakheestos*

minor road ο παράδρομος
o paradhromos

mint *(herb)* ο δυόσμος *o dheeosmos*

minute το λεπτό *to lepto*

mirror ο καθρέφτης *o kathreftees*

to miss *(train, etc.)* χάνω *khano*

Miss η Δεσποινίς *ee dhespeenees*

missing χαμένος *khamenos*
he's missing λείπει *leepee*

mistake το λάθος *to lathos*

misunderstanding η παρεξήγηση
ee parekseeyeesee

mobile *(phone)* το κινητό (τηλέφωνο)
to keeneeto (teelefono)

mobile number ο αριθμός κινητού
o areethmos keeneetoo

moisturizer η υδατική κρέμα
ee eedhateekee krema

monastery το μοναστήρι
to monasteeree

money τα χρήματα *ta khreemata*//
τα λεφτά *ta lefta*

money order η ταχυδρομική
επιταγή *ee takheedhromeekee
epeetaghee*

month ο μήνας *o meenas*

monument το μνημείο
to mneemeeo

moon το φεγγάρι *to fengaree*

more περισσότερο *pereesotero*
more bread κι άλλο ψωμί *kee alo
psomee*

morning το πρωί *to proee*

mosaic το μωσαϊκό *to mosaeeko*

mosque το τζαμί *to dzamee*

mosquito το κουνούπι
to koonoopee

most το περισσότερο *to pereesotero*

moth η πεταλουδίτσα
ee petaloodheetsa

mother η μητέρα *ee meetera*

mother-in-law η πεθερά *ee pethera*

motor η μηχανή *ee meekhanee*

motorbike η μοτοσικλέτα
ee motoseekleta

motorboat το ταχύπλοο
to takheeplo-o

motorway ο αυτοκινητόδρομος
o aftokeeneetodhromos

mountain το βουνό *to voono*

mouse το ποντίκι *to pondeekee*

mousse το μους *to moos*

moustache το μουστάκι
to moostakee

mouth το στόμα *to stoma*

to move κινούμαι *keenoome*

MP3 player το MP3 *to empee three*

Mr Κύριος *keereeos*

Mrs Κυρία *keereea*

much πολύς *polees*
  too much πάρα πολύ *para polee*
  very much πάρα πολύ *para polee*

mumps οι μαγουλάδες
ee maghooladhes

muscle ο μυς *o mees*

museum το μουσείο *to mooseeo*

mushroom το μανιτάρι
to maneetaree

music η μουσική *ee mooseekee*

mussel το μύδι *to meedhee*

must: *I must go* πρέπει να πάω
prepee na pao
  you must go πρέπει να πας *prepee
na pas*
  he/she must go πρέπει να πάει
prepee na paee
  we must go πρέπει να πάμε
prepee na pame

mustard η μουστάρδα
ee moostardha

N

nail *(metal)* το καρφί *to karfee*
  (on finger, toe) το νύχι *to neekhee*

nail polish το βερνίκι νυχιών
to verneekee neekhyon

nail polish remover το ασετόν
to aseton

nailbrush η βούρτσα των νυχιών
ee voortsa ton neekhyon

naked γυμνός *yeemnos*

name το όνομα *to onoma*

napkin η πετσέτα *ee petseta*

nappy η πάνα *ee pana*

narrow στενός *stenos*

nationality η υπηκοότητα
ee eepeeko-oteeta

navy blue μπλε μαρέν *ble maren*

near κοντά *konda*

necessary απαραίτητος *apareteetos*

neck ο λαιμός *o lemos*

necklace το κολιέ *to kolye*

to need: *I need...* χρειάζομαι...
khreeazome...

needle η βελόνα *ee velona*
  a needle and thread βελόνα και
κλωστή *velona ke klostee*

negative *(photography)*
το αρνητικό *to arneeteeko*

neighbour ο γείτονας/η γειτόνισσα
o yeetonas/ee yeetoneesa

nephew ο ανιψιός *o aneepsyos*

never ποτέ *pote*
  I never go there δεν πηγαίνω
ποτέ εκεί *dhen peegheno pote ekee*

new καινούριος *kenooryos*

news *(TV, radio)* οι ειδήσεις
ee eedheesees

newspaper η εφημερίδα
ee efeemereedha

New Year: *happy New Year!* καλή χρονιά! *kalee khronya*

New Zealand η Νέα Ζηλανδία *ee nea zeelandheea*

next επόμενος *epomenos*

nice *(thing)* ωραίος *oreos*
(person) καλός *kalos*

niece η ανιψιά *ee aneepsya*

night η νύχτα *ee neekhta*

nightclub το nightclub *to naeetklab*

nightdress το νυχτικό
to neekhteeko

no όχι *okhee*

nobody κανένας *kanenas*

noise ο θόρυβος *o thoreevos*

non-alcoholic μη οινοπνευματώδης *mee eenopnevmatodhees*

none κανένα *kanena*

non-smoking μη καπνίζοντες *mee kapneezondes*

north ο βορράς *o voras*

Northern Ireland η Βόρεια Ιρλανδία *ee voreea eerlandheea*

nose η μύτη *ee meetee*

not μη *mee*/δεν *dhen*
I am not δεν είμαι *dhen eeme*
don't stop μη σταματάς *mee stamatas*

note *(banknote)* το χαρτονόμισμα *to khartonomeesma*
(letter) το σημείωμα *to seemeeoma*

note pad το σημειωματάριο
to seemeeomatareeo

nothing τίποτα *teepota*

now τώρα *tora*

nudist beach η παραλία γυμνιστών *ee paraleea yeemneeston*

number ο αριθμός *o areethmos*

number plate η πινακίδα κυκλοφορίας *ee peenakeedha keekloforeeas*

nurse η νοσοκόμα *ee nosokoma*

nut *(peanut)* το φιστίκι *to feesteekee*
(walnut) το καρύδι *to kareedhee*
(hazelnut) το φουντούκι
to foondookee
(for bolt) το παξιμάδι
to pakseemadhee

O

oar το κουπί *to koopee*

occasionally κάπου-κάπου *kapoo-kapoo*

octopus το χταπόδι *to khtapodhee*

odd number ο μονός αριθμός
o monos areethmos

of: *of course* βέβαια *vevea*

off *(light, machine, etc)* σβυστός *sveestos*
it's off (rotten) είναι χαλασμένο *eene khalasmeno*

to offer προσφέρω *prosfero*

office το γραφείο *to ghrafeeo*

often συχνά *seekhna*

oil το λάδι *to ladhee*

oil filter το φίλτρο του λαδιού
to feeltro too ladhyoo

ointment η αλοιφή *ee aleefee*

OK εντάξει *endaksee*

old *(person)* ηλικιωμένος *eeleekyomenos*
(thing) παλιός *palyos*
how old are you? πόσων χρονών είστε; *poson khronon eeste*

olive oil το ελαιόλαδο
to eleoladho

olives οι ελιές *ee elyes*

omelette η ομελέτα *ee omeleta*

on πάνω pano (light, TV) ανοιχτός
aneekhtos
on the table (πάνω) στο τραπέζι
(pano) sto trapezee

once μία φορά meea fora

one ένας/μία/ένα enas (masculine)/
meea (feminine)/ena (neuter)

one-way (street) ο μονόδρομος
o monodhromos
(ticket) το απλό εισιτήριο to aplo
eeseeteereeo

onion το κρεμμύδι to kremeedhee

only μόνο mono

to open ανοίγω aneegho

open adj ανοικτός aneektos

operator (telephone)
η τηλεφωνήτρια ee teelefoneetreea

opposite απέναντι apenandee

or ή ee

orange (fruit) το πορτοκάλι
to portokalee
(colour) πορτοκαλί portokalee

orange juice ο χυμός πορτοκάλι
o kheemos portokalee

orchard το περιβόλι to pereevolee

to order παραγγέλλω parang-elo

organic βιολογικής καλλιέργιας
veeologheekees kalee-ergheeas

organize οργανώνω orghanono

original αρχικός arkheekos

Orthodox (religion) ορθόδοξος
orthodhoksos

other άλλος alos

out (light, etc.) σβησμένος
sveesmenos
he's out λείπει leepee

outdoors στην ύπαιθρο steen
eepethro

outside έξω ekso

outskirts τα προάστια ta proasteea

oven ο φούρνος o foornos

over πάνω από pano apo
over there εκεί πέρα ekee pera

to owe: you owe me μου χρωστάς
moo khrostas

owner ο ιδιοκτήτης
o eedheeokteetees

oxygen το οξυγόνο to okseeghono

oyster το στρείδι to streedhee

P

to pack πακετάρω paketaro

package το δέμα to dhema

package tour η οργανωμένη
εκδρομή ee orghanomenee
ekdhromee

packet το πακέτο to paketo

paddling pool η λιμνούλα για
παιδιά ee leemnoola ya pedhya

padlock το λουκέτο to looketo

paid πληρωμένος pleeromenos

pain ο πόνος o ponos

painful οδυνηρός odheeneeros
it's painful πονάει ponaee

painkiller το παυσίπονο to
pafseepono

painting ο πίνακας o peenakas

pair το ζευγάρι to zevgharee

palace το παλάτι to palatee

pale χλομός khlomos

palmtop computer ο υπολογιστής
παλάμης o eepologheestees
palamees

pan η κατσαρόλα ee katsarola

pancake η κρέπα ee krepa

panties η κυλότα ee keelota

pants (men's underpants) το σλιπ
to sleep

panties (women's) η κυλότα ee keelota

paper το χαρτί to khartee

paramedic (in general, in hospitals etc.)
ο παραιατρικός o para-yatreekos
(in ambulance only) ο διασώστης
o dheeasostees

parcel το δέμα to dhema

pardon παρακαλώ parakalo
I beg your pardon με συγχωρείτε
me seenkhoreete

parents οι γονείς o ghonees

park n το πάρκο to parko

to park (in car) παρκάρω parkaro

parsley ο μαϊντανός o ma-eendanos

part το μέρος to meros

party (group) η ομάδα ee omadha
(celebration) το πάρτυ to party

passenger ο επιβάτης o epeevatees

passenger ο επιβάτης o epeevatees

passionfruit το φρούτο
<πάσιονφρουτ> to frooto
'passionfruit'

passport control ο έλεγχος
διαβατηρίων o elengkhos
dheeavateereeon

pasta τα ζυμαρικά ta zeemareeka

pastry η ζύμη ee zeemee
(cake) το γλύκισμα to ghleekeesma

path το μονοπάτι to monopatee

pavement το πεζοδρόμιο
to pezodhromeeo

to pay πληρώνω pleerono

payment η πληρωμή ee pleeromee

PDA το PDA to pee day ay

peach το ροδάκινο to rodhakeeno

peak hour η ώρα αιχμής ee ora
ekhmees

peanut το φιστίκι to feesteekee

pear το αχλάδι to akhladhee

peas ο αρακάς o arakas

pebble το πετραδάκι
to petradhakee

pedestrian (person) ο πεζός o pezos

pedestrian crossing
η διασταύρωση πεζών
ee dheeastavrosee pezon

pedicure το πεντικιούρ to pedeekyor

to peel ξεφλουδίζω ksefloodheezo

peg (for tent) ο πάσσαλος o pasalos
(for clothes) το μανταλάκι
to mandalakee

pen το στυλό to steelo

pencil το μολύβι to moleevee

penicillin η πενικιλλίνη
ee peneekeeleenee

penknife ο σουγιάς o sooyas

pensioner ο/η συνταξιούχος
o/ee seendaksyookhos

pepper (spice) το πιπέρι
to peeperee
(vegetable) η πιπεριά ee peeperya

per: per hour την ώρα teen ora

perfect τέλειος teleeos

performance η παράσταση
ee parastasee

perfume το άρωμα to aroma

perhaps ίσως eesos

period (menstruation) η περίοδος
ee pereeodhos

perm η περμανάντ ee permanand

permit άδεια adheea

person το άτομο to atomo

pet το κατικοίδιο ζώο
to kateekeedhyo zo-o

petrol η βενζίνη ee venzeenee

petrol station το βενζινάδικο
to venzeenadheeko//το πρατήριο
βενζίνης *to pratereeo venzeenees*

pharmacist ο φαρμακοποιός
o farmakopeeos

phone *see* **telephone**

phonecard η τηλεκάρτα
ee teelekarta

photocopier το φωτοτυπικό
to fototeepeeko

photocopy η φωτοτυπία
ee fototeepeea

photograph η φωτογραφία
ee fotoghrafeea

phrase book το βιβλιαράκι
φράσεων *to veevleearakee fraseon*

picture η εικόνα *ee eekona*

pie η πίτα *ee peeta*

piece το κομμάτι *to komatee*

pier η αποβάθρα *ee apovathra*

pill το χάπι *to khapee*

pillow το μαξιλάρι *to makseelaree*

pillowcase η μαξιλαροθήκη
ee makseelarotheekee

pin η καρφίτσα *ee karfeetsa*

pine το πεύκο *to pefko*

pineapple ο ανανάς *o ananas*

pink ροζ *roz*

pipe η πίπα *ee peepa*

pistachio nut το φυστίκι Αιγίνης
to feesteekee eyeenees

pitch *(place for tent/caravan)*
ο χώρος *o khoros*

plaster *(for broken limb)* ο γύψος
o yeepsos

plastic πλαστικός *plasteekos*

plate το πιάτο *to pyato*

platform η αποβάθρα *ee apovathra*

to play παίζω *pezo*

playroom το δωμάτιο των παιδιών
to dhomateeo ton pedhyon

please παρακαλώ *parakalo*

pleased ευχαριστημένος
efkhareesteemenos

pliers η πένσα *ee pensa*

plug *(electric)* το φις *to fees*

plum το δαμάσκηνο *to damaskeeno*

plumber ο υδραυλικός
o eedhravleekos

poisonous δηλητηριώδης
dheeleeteereeodhees

police η αστυνομία *ee asteenomeea*

policeman ο αστυνόμος
o asteenomos

police station το αστυνομικό
τμήμα *to asteenomeeko tmeema*

polish *(for shoes)* το βερνίκι
to verneekee

polluted μολυσμένος *moleesmenos*

pollution η ρύπανση *ee reepansee*

pony trekking η ιππασία
ee eepaseea

pool *(for swimming)* η πισίνα
ee peeseena

popular δημοφιλής *dheemofeelees*
(fashionable) κοσμικός *kosmeekos*

pork το χοιρινό *to kheereeno*

port *(harbour)* το λιμάνι
to leemanee

porter ο αχθοφόρος *o akhthoforos*

possible δυνατός *dheenatos*

to post *(letter)* ταχυδρομώ
takheedhromo

postbox το ταχυδρομικό κουτί
to takheedhromeeko kootee

postcard η καρτποστάλ
ee kartpostal

postcode ο κωδικός *o kodheekos*

post office το ταχυδρομείο
to takheedhromeeo

pot η κατσαρόλα *ee katsarola*

potato η πατάτα *ee patata*

pottery τα κεραμικά *ta kerameeka*

pound (money) η λίρα *ee leera*

powdered milk το γάλα σε σκόνη
to ghala se skonee

pram το καροτσάκι *to karotsakee*

prawn η γαρίδα *ee ghareedha*

to prefer προτιμώ *proteemo*

pregnant έγγυος *engeeos*

to prepare ετοιμάζω *eteemazo*

prescription η συνταγή
ee seendaghee

present (gift) το δώρο *to dhoro*

pretty ωραίος *oreos*

price η τιμή *ee teemee*

price list ο τιμοκατάλογος
o teemokataloghos

priest ο παπάς *o papas*

printout η εκτύπωση *ee ekteeposee*

private ιδιωτικός *eedheeoteekos*

prize το βραβείο *to vraveeo*

probably πιθανώς *peethanos*

problem το πρόβλημα *to provleema*

programme το πρόγραμμα
to proghrama

prohibited απαγορευμένος
apaghorevmenos

to pronounce προφέρω *profero*
how do you pronounce this? πώς
το προφέρετε; *pos to proferete*

Protestant διαμαρτυρόμενος
dheeamarteeromenos

prune το δαμάσκηνο ξερό
to dhamaskeeno ksero

public δημόσιος *dheemoseeos*

public holiday η γιορτή *ee yortee*

to pull τραβώ *travo*

pullover το πουλόβερ *to poolover*

puncture το τρύπημα
to treepeema

purple πορφυρός *porfeeros*

purse το πορτοφόλι *to portofolee*

to push σπρώχνω *sprokhno*

push chair το καροτσάκι (μωρού)
to karotsakee (moroo)

to put βάζω *vazo*
to put down βάζω κάτω *vazo kato*

pyjamas η πιζάμα *ee peezama*

Q

quality η ποιότητα *ee peeoteeta*

quay η προκυμαία *ee prokeemea*

queen η βασίλισσα *ee vaseeleesa*

question η ερώτηση *ee eroteesee*

queue η ουρά *ee oora*

quick γρήγορος *ghreeghoros*

quickly γρήγορα *ghreeghora*

quiet ήσυχος *eeseekhos*

quilt (duvet) το πάπλωμα *to paploma*

R

rabbit το κουνέλι *to koonelee*

rabies η λύσσα *ee leesa*

racket η ρακέτα *ee raketa*

radiator (car) το ψυγείο *to pseeyeeo*

radio το ραδιόφωνο *to radheeofono*

radish το ραπανάκι *to rapanakee*

railway station ο σιδηροδρομικός
σταθμός *o seedheerodhromeekos
stathmos*

rain η βροχή *ee vrokhee*

'N ξΞ οΟ πΠ ρΡ σςΣ τΤ υΥ φΦ χΧ ψΨ ωΩ

raincoat το αδιάβροχο
  to adheeavrokho

raining: *it's raining* βρέχει *vrekhee*

raisin η σταφίδα *ee stafeedha*

rare σπάνιος *spanyos*
  (steak) μισοψημένος
  meesopseemenos

rash *(skin)* το εξάνθημα
  to eksantheema

raspberries τα βατόμουρα
  ta vatomoora

rat ο αρουραίος *o arooreos*

rate ο ρυθμός *o reethmos*
  rate of exchange η ισοτιμία
  ee eesoteemeea

raw ωμός *omos*

razor το ξυράφι *to kseerafee*

razor blade το ξυραφάκι
  to kseerafakee

to read διαβάζω *dheeavazo*

ready έτοιμος *eteemos*

real πραγματικός *praghmateekos*

reason ο λόγος *o loghos*

receipt η απόδειξη *ee apodheeksee*

recently τελευταία *teleftea*

reception *(desk)* η ρεσεψιόν
  ee resepsyon

recipe η συνταγή *ee seendaghee*

to recommend συνιστώ *seeneesto*

record *(music, etc.)* ο δίσκος
  o dheeskos

red κόκκινος *kokeenos*

reduction η έκπτωση *ee ekptosee*

refund η επιστροφή χρημάτων
  ee epeestrofee khreematon

registered *(letter)* συστημένο
  seesteemeno

regulations οι κανονισμοί
  ee kanoneesmee

to reimburse αποζημιώνω
  apozeemeeono

relations *(family)* οι συγγενείς
  ee seenghenees

to relax ξεκουράζομαι
  ksekoorazome

reliable *(person)* αξιόπιστος
  akseeopeestos
  (car, method) δοκιμασμένος
  dhokeemasmenos

to remain απομένω *apomeno*

to remember θυμάμαι *theemame*

to rent νοικιάζω *neekyazo*

rental το νοίκι *to neekee*

to repair επιδιορθώνω
  epeedheeorthono

to repeat επαναλαμβάνω
  epanalamvano

reservation η κράτηση *ee krateesee*

to reserve κρατώ *krato*

reserved κρατημένος *krateemenos*

rest ξεκούραση *ksekoorasee*
  the rest *(the others)* οι υπόλοιποι
  ee eepoleepee

to rest ξεκουράζομαι *ksekoorazome*

restaurant το εστιατόριο
  to esteeatoreeo

restaurant car το βαγόνι ρεστωράν
  to vaghonee restoran

to retire βγαίνω στη σύνταξη
  vyeno stee seendaksee

retired συνταξιούχος
  seendaksyookhos

to return *(go back, give back)*
  επιστρέφω *epeestrefo*

return ticket το εισιτήριο με
  επιστροφή *to eeseeteereeo me
  epeestrofee*

reverse-charge call κλήση
πληρωτέα από τον παραλήπτη
*kleesee pleerotea apo ton
paraleeptee*

rheumatism οι ρευματισμοί
ee revmateesmee

rice το ρύζι *to reezee*

rich (person, food) πλούσιος
plooseeos

riding (equestrian) η ιππασία
ee eepaseea

right (correct, accurate) σωστός
sostos
(on/to the) right δεξιά *dheksea*

ring το δαχτυλίδι
to dhakhteeleedhee

ripe ώριμος *oreemos*

river το ποτάμι *to potamee*

road ο δρόμος *o dhromos*

road map ο οδικός χάρτης
o odheekos khartees

roast το ψητό *to pseeto*

to rob ληστεύω *leestevo*

roll (of bread) το ψωμάκι
to psomakee

roof η στέγη *ee steghee*

roof rack η σχάρα *ee skhara*

room (in house, etc.) το δωμάτιο
to dhomateeo
(space) ο χώρος *o khoros*

room service η υπηρεσία
δωματίου *ee eepeereseea
dhomateeoo*

rope το σχοινί *to skheenee*

rosé ροζέ *roze*

rotten (fruit) χαλασμένος
khalasmenos

rough (sea) τρικυμισμένη
treekeemeesmenee

round (shape) στρογγυλός
strongeelos
round Greece γύρω στην Ελλάδα
yeero steen eladha

route ο δρόμος *o dhromos*

to row (boat) κάνω κουπί *kano
koopee*

rowing boat η βάρκα με κουπιά
ee varka me koopya

royal βασιλικός *vaseeleekos*

rubber (substance) το καουτσούκ
to ka-ootsook
(eraser) η γόμα *ee goma*

rubber band το λαστιχάκι
to lasteekhakee

rubbish τα σκουπίδια
ta skoopeedhya

rucksack ο σάκκος *o sakos*

ruins τα ερείπια *ta ereepya*

rum το ρούμι *to roomee*

to run τρέχω *trekho*

rush hour η ώρα αιχμής *ee ora
ekhmees*

rusty σκουριασμένος *skooryasmenos*

S

sad λυπημένος *leepeemenos*

safe adj (harmless) αβλαβής *avlavees*
(not dangerous) ακίνδυνος
akeendheenos
(secure, sure) ασφαλής *asfalees*

safe n το χρηματοκιβώτιο
to khreematokeevotyo

safety pin η παραμάνα
ee paramana

sailing η ιστιοπλοΐα
ee eesteeoploeea

salad η σαλάτα *ee salata*

salad dressing το λαδολέμονο
to ladholemono

sale (in shop) το ξεπούλημα
to ksep**oo**leema

salmon ο σολομός o sol**o**m**o**s

salt το αλάτι to al**a**tee

same ίδιος eedheeos

sand η άμμος ee **a**mos

sandals τα πέδιλα ta p**e**dheela

sandwich το σάντουϊτς to sandwich

sanitary towel η σερβιέτα
ee servy**e**ta

sardine η σαρδέλα ee sardh**e**la

satnav (satellite navigation system,
for car) το GPS to GPS

sauce η σάλτσα ee s**a**ltsa

saucepan η κατσαρόλα ee katsar**o**la

saucer το πιατάκι to pyat**a**kee

sausage το λουκάνικο to
look**a**neeko

savoury πικάντικος peek**a**ndeekos

to say λέω l**e**o

scarf (long) το κασκόλ to kask**o**l
(square) το μαντήλι to mand**ee**lee

school (primary) το σχολείο
to skhol**ee**o
(for 12- to 15-year-olds) το γυμνάσιο
to yeemn**a**seeo
(for 15- to 18-year-olds) το λύκειο
to l**ee**keeo

scissors το ψαλίδι to psal**ee**dhee

Scotland η Σκωτία ee skot**ee**a

Scottish (person) ο Σκωτσέζος/η
Σκωτσέζα o skots**e**zos/ee skots**e**za

screw η βίδα ee v**ee**dha

screwdriver το κατσαβίδι
to katsav**ee**dhee

sculpture το γλυπτό to ghleept**o**

sea η θάλασσα ee th**a**lasa

seafood τα θαλασσινά ta thalaseen**a**

seasickness η ναυτία ee naft**ee**a

seaside (beach, seafront) η παραλία
ee paral**ee**a

seat (in theatre) η θέση ee th**e**see
(in car, etc.) το κάθισμα
to k**a**theesma

second δεύτερος dh**e**fteros

second class (ticket, etc.) δεύτερη
θέση dh**e**fteree th**e**see

second-hand μεταχειρισμένος
metakheereesm**e**nos

security check ο έλεγχος
ασφάλειας o **e**lengkhos asf**a**lyas

to see βλέπω vl**e**po

self-service το σελφ σέρβις to self
service

to sell πουλώ pool**o**

Sellotape® το σελοτέιπ to selot**e**yp

send στέλνω st**e**lno

separate χωριστός khoreest**o**s

serious σοβαρός sovar**o**s

to serve σερβίρω serv**ee**ro

service (in restaurant, etc.)
η εξυπηρέτηση
ee ekseepeer**e**teesee

service charge το ποσοστό
υπηρεσίας to posost**o** eepeeres**ee**as

set menu το καθορισμένο μενού
to kathoreesm**e**no men**oo**

several διάφοροι dhe**e**aforee

to sew ράβω r**a**vo

shade η σκιά ee skee**a**

shallow ρηχός reekh**o**s

shampoo το σαμπουάν
to samboo**a**n

shampoo and set λούσιμο και
στέγνωμα l**oo**seemo ke st**e**ghnoma

to share μοιράζω meer**a**zo

to shave ξυρίζομαι kseer**ee**zome

shaver η ξυριστική μηχανή
ee kseereesteekee meekhanee

shaving cream η κρέμα ξυρίσματος
ee krema kseereesmatos

she αυτή *aftee*

sheep το πρόβατο *to provato*

sheet το σεντόνι *to sendonee*

shellfish τα όστρακα *ta ostraka*

ship το πλοίο *to pleeo*

shirt το πουκάμισο *to pookameeso*

shock absorber το αμορτισέρ
to amorteeser

shoe το παπούτσι *to papootsee*

to shop ψωνίζω *psoneezo*

shop το μαγαζί *to maghazee*

shop assistant *(woman)*
η πωλήτρια *ee poleetreea*
(man) ο πωλητής *o poleetees*

short κοντός *kondos*

short cut ο συντομότερος δρόμος
o seendomoteros dhromos

shorts το σορτς *to shorts*

show *n (in theatre, etc.)*
η παράσταση *ee parastasee*

to show δείχνω *dheekhno*

shower *(in bath)* το ντους *to doos*
(rain) η μπόρα *ee bora*

shrimp η γαρίδα *ee ghareedha*

shut *(closed)* κλειστός *kleestos*

to shut κλείνω *kleeno*

shutters τα παντζούρια
ta pantzooreea

sick *(ill)* άρρωστος *arostos*
to be sick *(vomit)* κάνω εμετό *kano
emeto*

sightseeing: to go sightseeing
επισκέπτομαι τα αξιοθέατα
epeeskeptome ta akseeotheata

sign *(roadsign, notice, etc.)*
η πινακίδα *ee peenakeedha*

signature η υπογραφή *ee
eepoghrafee*

silk το μετάξι *to metaksee*

silver ασημένιος *aseemeneeos*

SIM card η κάρτα SIM *ee karta
seem*

similar παρόμοιος *paromeeos*

simple απλός *aplos*

to sing τραγουδώ *traghoodho*

single *(not married)* ελεύθερος
eleftheros
(not double) μονός *monos*

single bed το μονό κρεβάτι
to mono krevatee

single room το μονόκλινο δωμάτιο
to monokleeno dhomateeo

sink ο νεροχύτης *o nerokheetees*

sister η αδελφή *ee adhelfee*

to sit *(down)* κάθομαι *kathome*

site *(website)* το σάιτ *to saeet*

size *(of clothes, shoes)* το νούμερο
to noomero

ski το σκι *to skee*

to ski κάνω σκι *kano skee*

ski jacket το μπουφάν του σκι
to boofan too skee

ski pants το παντελόνι του σκι
to pandelonee too skee

ski pole το ραβδί του σκι *to ravdhee
too skee*

ski run η διαδρομή του σκι
ee dheeadhromee too skee

ski suit τα ρούχα του σκι *ta rookha
too skee*

skimmed milk το αποβουτυρωμένο
γάλα *to apovooteeromeno ghala*

skin το δέρμα to dherma

skin diving το υποβρύχιο κολύμπι to eepovreekheeo koleembee

skirt η φούστα ee foosta

sky ο ουρανός o ooranos

to sleep κοιμούμαι keemoome

sleeper το βαγκόν-λι to vagon-lee

sleeping bag το υπνόσακος o eepnosakos//το σλίπινμπάγκ to sleepeenbag

sleeping pill το υπνωτικό χάπι to eepnoteeko khapee

slice η φέτα ee feta

slide (photography) το σλάιντ to slide

slippery γλιστερός ghleesteros

slow σιγά seegha

small μικρός meekros

smaller (than) μικρότερος (από) meekroteros (apo)

smell η μυρωδιά ee meerodhya

smile το χαμόγελο to khamoyelo

to smile χαμογελώ khamoyelo

smoke ο καπνός o kapnos

to smoke καπνίζω kapneezo

smoked καπνιστός kapneestos

SMS message το μήνυμα SMS to meeneema esemes

snack bar το σνακ μπαρ to snack bar

snake το φίδι to feedhee

snorkel ο αναπνευστήρας o anapnevsteeras

snow το χιόνι to khyonee

snowed up αποκλεισμένος από το χιόνι apokleesmenos apo to khyonee

snowing: it's snowing χιονίζει khyoneezee

so (that's why) γι'αυτό yee afto
so much τόσο πολύ toso polee
so pretty τόσο ωραίος toso oreos
so that (in order to) για να ya na

soap το σαπούνι to sapoonee

soap powder το απορρυπαντικό to aporeepandeeko

sober ξεμέθυστος ksemetheestos

sock η κάλτσα ee kaltsa

socket (electrical) η πρίζα ee preeza

soda (water) η σόδα ee sodha

soft μαλακός malakos

soft drink το αναψυκτικό to anapseekteeko

some μερικοί mereekee

someone κάποιος kapyos

something κάτι katee

sometimes κάποτε kapote

son ο γιος o yos

song το τραγούδι to traghoodhee

soon σύντομα seendoma
as soon as possible
το συντομότερο to seendomotero
sooner νωρίτερα noreetera

sore: it's sore πονάει ponaee

sorry: I'm sorry (apology) συγγνώμη seeghnomee
(regret) λυπάμαι leepame

sort το είδος to eedhos

soup η σούπα ee soopa

south ο νότος o notos

souvenir το σουβενίρ to sooveneer

space (room) ο χώρος o khoros

spam (email) η ενοχλητική αλληλογραφία ee enokhleeteekee aleeloghrafeea

spanner το κλειδί to kleedhee

spare wheel η ρεζέρβα ee rezerva

spark plug το μπουζί *to boozee*

sparkling *(wine)* αφρώδης *afrodhees*

to speak μιλώ *meelo*

speaker *(loudspeaker)* το ηχείο
to eekheeo

special ειδικός *eedheekos*
special needs ειδικές ανάγκες
eedheekes anangkes
people with special needs άτομα
με ειδικές ανάγκες *atoma me
eedheekes anangkes*

speciality *(in restaurant)*
η σπεσιαλιτέ *ee spesyaleete*

speed η ταχύτητα *ee takheeteeta*

speed limit το όριο ταχύτητας
to oreeo takheeteetas

spell *(to write)* γράφω *ghrafo*
how do you spell it?
πώς γράφεται; *pos ghrafete*

SPF *(sun protection factor)*
αντιηλιακή προστασία δείκτης
*andee-eeleeakee prostaseea
dheektees*
SPF 30 δείκτης 30 *deektees 30*

spicy πικάντικος *peekandeekos*

spinach το σπανάκι *to spanakee*

spirits τα οινοπνευματώδη ποτά
ta eenopnevmatodhee pota

sponge το σφουγγάρι *to sfoongaree*

spoon το κουτάλι *to kootalee*

sport το σπορ *to spor*

spring *(season)* η άνοιξη *ee aneeksee*

square *(in town)* η πλατεία
ee plateea

squash *(sport)* το σκουός *to skoo-os*
orange squash η πορτοκαλάδα
ee portokaladha
lemon squash η λεμονάδα
ee lemonadha

squid το καλαμάρι *to kalamaree*

stadium το στάδιο *to stadheeo*

stairs η σκάλα *ee skala*

stalls *(in theatre)* η πλατεία *ee plateea*

stamp το γραμματόσημο
to ghramatoseemo

star *(in sky)* το άστρο *to astro*

to start αρχίζω *arkheezo*

starter *(in meal)* το ορεκτικό
to orekteeko

station ο σταθμός *o stathmos*

stationer's το χαρτοπωλείο
to khartopoleeo

to stay μένω *meno*

steak η μπριζόλα *ee breezola*

steep ανηφορικός *aneeforeekos*

sterling η αγγλική λίρα
ee angleekee leera

steward *(on a ship)* ο καμαρότος
o kamarotos
(on plane) ο αεροσυνοδός
o aeroseenodhos

stewardess *(on plane)*
η αεροσυνοδός *ee aeroseenodhos*

sticking plaster ο λευκοπλάστης
o lefkoplastees

still *(yet)* ακόμα *akoma*
(immobile) ακίνητος *akeeneetos*
(water) μη αεριούχο *mee aeryookho*

sting το τσίμπημα *to tseembeema*

stomach το στομάχι *to stomakhee*

stomach upset η στομαχική
διαταραχή *ee stomakheekee
dheeatarakhee*

to stop σταματώ *stamato*

storm *(thunder)* η καταιγίδα
ee kateyeedha

straight: straight on ευθεία *eftheea*

straw *(for drinking)* το καλαμάκι
to kalamakee

strawberry η φράουλα ee fraoola

street ο δρόμος o dhromos

street plan ο οδικός χάρτης
o odheekos khartees

string ο σπάγγος o spangos

striped ριγωτός reeghotos

strong δυνατός dheenatos

stuck (jammed) κολλημένος
koleemenos

student ο φοιτητής/η φοιτήτρια
o feeteetees/ee feeteetreea

stung: I've been stung by
something κάτι με τσίμπησε
katee me tseembeese

stupid ανόητος anoeetos

suddenly ξαφνικά ksafneeka

suede το καστόρι to kastoree

sugar η ζάχαρη ee zakharee

suit (man's) το κοστούμι
to kostoomee
(woman's) το ταγιέρ to ta-yer

suitcase η βαλίτσα ee valeetsa

summer το καλοκαίρι to kalokeree

sun ο ήλιος o eeleeos

to sunbathe κάνω ηλιοθεραπεία
kano eeleeotherapeea

sunbed η ξαπλώστρα ee ksaplostra

sun block το αντιηλιακό
to andee-eelyako

sunburn (painful) το κάψιμο από τον
ήλιο to kapseemo apo ton eeleeo

suncream η αντιηλιακή κρέμα
ee andee-eeleeakee krema

sunglasses τα γυαλιά του ήλιου
ta yalya too eeleeoo

sunny (weather) ηλιόλουστος
eelyoloostos

sunrise η ανατολή ee anatolee

sunset το ηλιοβασίλεμα
to eeleeovaseelema

sunshade η ομπρέλα ee ombrela

sunstroke η ηλίαση ee eeleeasee

suntan lotion το λάδι για τον ήλιο
to ladhee ya ton eeleeo

supermarket το σούπερμάρκετ
to supermarket

supper το δείπνο to dheepno

supplement το συμπλήρωμα
to seembleeroma

surcharge η επιβάρυνση
ee epeevareensee

surfboard η σανίδα σέρφινγκ
ee saneedha serfeeng

surfing το σέρφινγκ to serfeeng

surname το επώνυμο to eponeemo

surrounded by τριγυρισμένος από
treeyeereesmenos apo

suspension η ανάρτηση
ee anarteesee

to sweat ιδρώνω eedhrono

sweater το πουλόβερ to poolover

sweet adj (taste) γλυκός ghleekos

sweet n (dessert) το γλυκό
to ghleeko

sweets οι καραμέλες ee karameles

sweetener η ζαχαρίνη
ee zakhareenee

to swim κολυμπώ koleembo

swimming pool η πισίνα
ee peeseena

swimsuit το μαγιό to ma-yo

swing (for children) η κούνια
ee koonya

switch ο διακόπτης o dheeakoptees

to switch on ανάβω anavo

to switch off σβήνω sveeno

swollen *(ankle, etc.)* πρησμένος
preesmenos

synagogue η συναγωγή
ee seenaghoghee

T

table το τραπέζι *to trapezee*

tablecloth το τραπεζομάντηλο
to trapezomandeelo

tablespoon το κουτάλι *to kootalee*

tablet το χάπι *to khapee*

table tennis το πινγκ πονγκ
to ping pong

to take παίρνω *perno*

to take out βγάζω *vghazo*
(from bank account) αποσύρω
aposeero

to talk μιλώ *meelo*

tall ψηλός *pseelos*

tame *(animal)* ήμερος *eemeros*

tampons τα ταμπόν *ta tambon*

tap η βρύση *ee vreesee*

to taste δοκιμάζω *dhokeemazo*

taste *n* η γεύση *ee yefsee*

tax ο φόρος *o foros*

taxi το ταξί *to taksee*

taxi rank η πιάτσα για ταξί
ee pyatsa ya taksee

tea το τσάι *to tsaee*

tea bag το φακελλάκι τσαγιού
to fakelakee tsa-yoo

to teach διδάσκω *dheedhasko*

teacher ο δάσκαλος/η δασκάλα
o dhaskalos/ee dhaskala

teapot η τσαγιέρα *ee tsa-yera*

tear *(in eye)* το δάκρυ *to dhakree*
(in material) το σχίσιμο
to skheeseemo

teaspoon το κουταλάκι
to kootalakee

teat η ρώγα *ee rogha*

teeth τα δόντια *ta dhondeea*

telephone το τηλέφωνο
to teelefono

telephone box ο τηλεφωνικός
θάλαμος *o teelefoneekos thalamos*

telephone call το τηλεφώνημα
to teelefoneema

telephone directory
ο τηλεφωνικός κατάλογος
o teelefoneekos kataloghos

television η τηλεόραση
ee teeleorasee

telex το τέλεξ *to telex*

to tell λέγω *legho*
(story) διηγούμαι *dhee-eeghoome*

temperature η θερμοκρασία
ee thermokraseea
to have a temperature έχω
πυρετό *ekho peereto*

temple ο ναός *o naos*

temporary προσωρινός *prosoreenos*

tennis το τένις *to tenees*

tennis ball η μπάλα του τένις
ee bala too tenees

tennis court το γήπεδο του τένις
to yeepedho too tenees

tennis racket η ρακέτα του τένις
ee raketa too tenees

tent η σκηνή *ee skeenee*

tent peg ο πάσσαλος της σκηνής
o pasalos tees skeenees

terminus το τέρμα *to terma*

terrace η ταράτσα *ee taratsa*

to text στέλνω μήνυμα *stelno
meeneema*
I'll text you θα σου στείλω μήνυμα
tha soo steelo meeneema

thank you ευχαριστώ *efkhareesto*

that εκείνος *ekeenos*
  that book εκείνο το βιβλίο *ekeeno to veevleeo*
  that one εκείνο *ekeeno*

theatre το θέατρο *to theatro*

then τότε *tote*

there εκεί *ekee*
  there is υπάρχει *eeparkhee*
  there are υπάρχουν *eeparkhoon*

thermometer το θερμόμετρο *to thermometro*

these αυτοί/αυτές/αυτά *aftee* (masculine)/*aftes* (feminine)/*afta* (neuter)
  these books αυτά τα βιβλία *afta ta veevleea*

they αυτοί *aftee*

thick χοντρός *khontros*

thief ο κλέφτης *o kleftees*

thin λεπτός *leptos*

thing το πράγμα *to praghma*

third τρίτος *treetos*

thirsty: I'm thirsty διψάω *dheepsao*

this αυτός/αυτή/αυτό *aftos* (masculine)/*aftee* (feminine)/*afto* (neuter)
  this book αυτό το βιβλίο *afto to veevleeo*
  this one αυτό *afto*

those εκείνοι *ekeenee*
  those books εκείνα τα βιβλία *ekeena ta veevleea*

thread η κλωστή *ee klostee*

throat ο λαιμός *o lemos*

throat lozenges οι παστίλιες για το λαιμό *ee pasteelyes ya to lemo*

through διαμέσου *dheeamesoo*

thunder ο κεραυνός *o keravnos*

thunderstorm η θύελλα *ee theeela*

ticket το εισιτήριο *to eeseeteereeo*

ticket collector ο ελεγκτής *o elengtees*

ticket office η θυρίδα *ee theereedha*

tie η γραβάτα *ee ghravata*

tight σφιχτός *sfeekhtos*

tights το καλσόν *to kalson*

till (cash) το ταμείο *to tameeo*

till (until) μέχρι *mekhree*

time (by the clock) η ώρα *ee ora*
  what time is it? τι ώρα είναι; *tee ora eene*

timetable (buses, trains, etc) το δρομολόγιο *to dromoloyeeo* (school, shop opening hours etc) το ωράριο *to orareeo*

tin η κονσέρβα *ee konserva*

tinfoil το αλουμινόχαρτο *to aloomeenokharto*

tin-opener το ανοιχτήρι για κονσέρβες *to aneekhteeree ya konserves*

tip (to waiter, etc.) το πουρμπουάρ *to poorbooar*

tipped (cigarettes) με φίλτρο *me feeltro*

tired κουρασμένος *koorasmenos*

tissue το χαρτομάντηλο *to khartomandeelo*

to σε *se*
  to the στο/στη/στο *sto* (masculine) *stee* (feminine) *sto* (neuter)
  to Greece στην Ελλάδα *steen eladha*

toast η φρυγανιά *ee freeghanya*

tobacco ο καπνός *o kapnos*

tobacconists το καπνοπωλείο *to kapnopoleeo*

today σήμερα *seemera*

together μαζί *mazee*

toilet η τουαλέτα *ee tooaleta*

toilet paper το χαρτί υγείας
to khartee eeyeeas

toll τα διόδια *ta dheeodheea*

tomato η ντομάτα *ee domata*

tomato juice ο χυμός ντομάτας
o kheemos domatas

tomorrow αύριο *avreeo*

tongue η γλώσσα *ee ghlosa*

tonic water το τόνικ *to toneek*

tonight απόψε *apopse*

too (also) επίσης *epeesees*
(too much) πάρα πολύ *para polee*

tooth το δόντι *to dhondee*

toothache ο πονόδοντος
o ponodhondos

toothbrush η οδοντόβουρτσα
ee odhontovoortsa

toothpaste η οδοντόκρεμα
ee odhondokrema

top το πάνω μέρος *to pano meros*
(of mountain) η κορυφή
ee koreefee

torch ο φακός *o fakos*

torn σχισμένος *skheesmenos*

total το σύνολο *to seenolo*

tough (of meat) σκληρός *skleeros*

tour η εκδρομή *ee ekdhromee*

tourist ο τουρίστας/η τουρίστρια
o tooreestas/ee tooreestreea

tourist office το τουριστικό
γραφείο *to tooreesteeko ghrafeeo*

tourist ticket το τουριστικό
εισιτήριο *to tooreesteeko
eeseeteereeo*

to tow ρυμουλκώ *reemoolko*

towel η πετσέτα *ee petseta*

tower ο πύργος *o peerghos*

town η πόλη *ee polee*

town centre το κέντρο της πόλης
to kendro tees polees

town hall το δημαρχείο
to dheemarkheeo

town plan ο χάρτης της πόλης
o khartees tees polees

towrope το σχοινί ρυμούλκησης
to skheenee reemoolkeesees

toy το παιχνίδι *to pekhneedhee*

traditional παραδοσιακός
paradhosyakos

traffic η κυκλοφορία *ee
keekloforeea*

traffic lights τα φανάρια
(της τροχαίας) *ta fanareea
(tees trokheas)*

trailer το τρέιλερ *to trailer*

train το τρένο *to treno*

training shoes τα αθλητικά
παπούτσια *ta athleeteeka
papootsya*

tram το τραμ *to tram*

to translate μεταφράζω *metafrazo*

translation η μετάφραση *ee
metafrasee*

to travel ταξιδεύω *takseedhevo*

travel agent ο ταξιδιωτικός
πράκτορας *o takseedhyoteekos
praktoras*

travellers' cheques
τα ταξιδιωτικά τσεκ
ta takseedhyoteeka tsek

tray ο δίσκος *o dheeskos*

tree το δέντρο *to dhendro*

trim n (hair) το κόψιμο *to kopseemo*

trip η εκδρομή ee ekdhromee

trolley bus το τρόλεϊ to troley

trouble ο μπελάς o belas

trousers το παντελόνι to pandelonee

trout η πέστροφα ee pestrofa

true αληθινός aleetheenos

trunk το μπαούλο to baoolo

trunks το μαγιό to ma-yo

to try προσπαθώ prospatho

to try on δοκιμάζω dhokeemazo

T-shirt το μπλουζάκι to bloozakee

tuna ο τόνος o tonos

tunnel η σήραγγα ee seeranga

turkey η γαλοπούλα ee ghalopoola

to turn στρίβω streevo

turnip η ρέβα ee reva

to turn off (on a journey) στρίβω streevo
(radio, etc.) κλείνω kleeno
(engine, light) σβήνω sveeno

to turn on (radio, TV) ανοίγω aneegho
(engine, light) ανάβω anavo

TV η τηλεόραση ee teeleorasee

tweezers το τσιμπίδι to tseembeedhee

twice δύο φορές dheeo fores

twin ο δίδυμος o dheedheemos

twin-bedded το δίκλινο δωμάτιο to dheekleeno dhomateeo

to type δακτυλογραφώ dhakteeloghrafo

typical τυπικός teepeekos

tyre το λάστιχο to lasteekho

tyre pressure η πίεση στα λάστιχα ee peeyesee sta lasteekha

U

ugly άσχημος askheemos

umbrella η ομπρέλα ee ombrela

uncle ο θείος o theeos

uncomfortable άβολος avolos

unconscious αναίσθητος anestheetos

under κάτω από kato apo

underground (railway) το μετρό to metro

underpants see pants

underpass η υπόγεια διάβαση ee eepoyeea dheeavasee

to understand καταλαβαίνω katalaveno

underwear τα εσώρουχα ta esorookha

unemployed άνεργος anerghos

unfasten λύνω leeno

United States οι Ηνωμένες Πολιτείες ee eenomenes poleeteeyes

university το πανεπιστήμιο to panepeesteemeeo

unleaded petrol η αμόλυβδη βενζίνη ee amoleevdhee venzeenee

to unpack (case) αδειάζω adheeazo

until μέχρι/έως mekhree/eos

up (out of bed) ξύπνιος kseepneeos
to go up ανεβαίνω aneveno

upstairs πάνω pano

urgently επειγόντως epeeghondos

urine τα ούρα ta oora

urn ο αμφορέας o amforeas

to use χρησιμοποιώ khreeseemopyo

useful χρήσιμος khreeseemos

useful χρήσιμος khreeseemos

username το όνομα χρήστη to onoma khreestee

usually συνήθως seeneethos

V

vacancy (room) το διαθέσιμο δωμάτιο to dheeatheseemo dhomateeo

vacuum cleaner η ηλεκτρική σκούπα ee eelektreekee skoopa

valid έγκυρος engkeeros

valley η κοιλάδα ee keeladha

valuable πολύτιμος poleeteemos

valuables τα πολύτιμα αντικείμενα ta poleeteema andeekeemena

value η αξία ee akseea

van το φορτηγάκι to forteeghakee

vase το βάζο to vazo

VAT ο ΦΠΑ o fee pee a

veal το μοσχάρι to moskharee

vegetables τα λαχανικά ta lakhaneeka

vegetarian ο χορτοφάγος o khortofaghos

vein η φλέβα ee fleva

velvet το βελούδο to veloodho

ventilator ο εξαεριστήρας o eksa-ereesteeras

very πολύ polee

vest η φανέλα ee fanela

via μέσω meso

video το βίντεο to veedeo

video camera η βιντεοκάμερα ee veedeokamera

video recorder το βίντεο to veedeeo

view η θέα ee thea

villa η βίλλα ee veela

village το χωριό to khoryo

vine leaves τα κληματόφυλλα ta kleematofeela

vinegar το ξύδι to kseedhee

visa η βίζα ee veesa

to visit επισκέπτομαι epeeskeptome

visit επίσκεψη ee epeeskepsee

vitamin η βιταμίνη ee veetameenee

vodka η βότκα ee votka

voice η φωνή ee fonee

voicemail το φωνητικό ταχυδρομείο to foneeteeko takheedhromeeo

volleyball το βόλεϊ to voley

voltage η τάση ee tasee

W

wage ο μισθός o meesthos

waist η μέση ee mesee

to wait for περιμένω pereemeno

waiter το γκαρσόνι to garsonee

waiting room η αίθουσα αναμονής ee ethoosa anamonees

waitress η σερβιτόρα ee serveetora

Wales η Ουαλία ee ooaleea

walk ο περίπατος o pereepatos

to walk περπατώ perpato

walking stick το μπαστούνι to bastoonee

wall ο τοίχος o teekhos

wallet το πορτοφόλι to portofolee

walnut το καρύδι to kareedhee

to want θέλω thelo

war ο πόλεμος o polemos

wardrobe η γκαρνταρόμπα ee gardaroba

warm ζεστός zestos

warning triangle το τρίγωνο αυτοκινήτου to treeghono aftokeeneetoo

to wash (clothes) πλένω pleno (oneself) πλένομαι plenome

washbasin ο νιπτήρας
o neepteeras

washing machine το πλυντήριο
to pleendeereeo

washing powder το απορρυπαντικό
to aporeepandeeko

washing-up liquid το υγρό για τα
πιάτα to eeghro ya ta pyata

wasp η σφήκα ee sfeeka

waste bin το καλάθι των αχρήστων
to kalathee ton akhreeston

watch n το ρολόι to roloee

to watch (TV) βλέπω vlepo
(someone's luggage) προσέχω
prosekho

watchstrap το λουρί του ρολογιού
to looree too roloyoo

water το νερό to nero
fresh water το γλυκό νερό
to ghleeko nero
salt water το αλμυρό νερό
o almeero nero

waterfall ο καταρράκτης
o kataraktees

water heater ο θερμοσίφωνας
o thermoseefonas

water-skiing το θαλάσσιο σκι
to thalaseeo skee

watermelon το καρπούζι
to karpoozee

waterproof αδιάβροχος
adheeavrokhos

wave (on sea) το κύμα to keema

wax το κερί to keree

way (method) ο τρόπος o tropos
this way από 'δω apodho
that way από 'κει apokee

we εμείς emees

weak αδύνατος adheenatos

to wear φορώ foro

weather ο καιρός o keros

wedding ο γάμος o ghamos

week η εβδομάδα ee evdhomadha

weekday η καθημερινή ee
katheemereenee

weekend το σαββατοκύριακο
to savatokeereeako

weekly (rate, etc.) εβδομαδιαίος
evdhomadhyeos

weight το βάρος to varos

welcome καλώς ήλθατε kalos
eelthate

well (healthy) καλά kala

well done (steak) καλοψημένος
kalopseemenos

Welsh (person) ο Ουαλός/η Ουαλή
o ooalos/ee ooalee

west η δύση ee dheesee

wet (damp) βρεγμένος vreghmenos
(weather) βροχερός vrokheros

wetsuit η στολή για υποβρύχιο
ψάρεμα ee stolee ya eepovreekheeo
psarema

what τι tee
what is it? τι είναι; tee eene

wheel η ρόδα ee rodha

wheelchair η αναπηρική καρέκλα
ee anapeereekee karekla

when? πότε; pote

where? πού; poo

which? ποιος; pyos (masculine)
ποια; pya (feminine)
ποιο; pyo (neuter)
which is it? ποιο είναι; pyo eene

while ενώ eno

whisky το ουίσκυ to whisky

white άσπρος aspros

who? ποιος; pyos

whole όλος olos

wholemeal bread ψωμί ολικής αλέσεως *psomee oleekees aleseos*

whose: whose is it? ποιανού είναι; *pyanoo eene*

why? γιατί; *yatee*

wide πλατύς *platees*

wife η σύζυγος *ee seezeeghos*

wind ο αέρας *o a-eras*

window το παράθυρο *to paratheero*

windmill ο ανεμόμυλος *o anemomeelos*

windscreen το παρμπρίζ *to parbreez*

windsurfing το γουιντσέρφινγκ *to weendserfeeng*

wine το κρασί *to krasee*

wine list ο κατάλογος των κρασιών *o kataloghos ton krasyon*

wine shop η κάβα *ee kava*

winter ο χειμώνας *o kheemonas*

wireless internet το ασύρματο ίντερνετ *to aseermato eenternet*

with με *me*

without χωρίς *khorees*

woman η γυναίκα *ee yeeneka*

wood το ξύλο *to kseelo*

wool το μαλλί *to malee*

word η λέξη *ee leksee*

work η δουλειά *ee dhoolya*

to work (person) δουλεύω *dhoolevo* (machine) λειτουργεί *leetoorghee*

worried ανήσυχος *aneeseekhos*

worse χειρότερος *kheeroteros*

to wrap (up) τυλίγω *teeleegho*

wrapping paper το χαρτί περιτυλίγματος *to khartee pereeteeleeghmatos*

to write γράφω *ghrafo*

writing paper το χαρτί αλληλογραφίας *to khartee aleeloghrafeeas*

wrong λάθος *lathos* **you're wrong** κάνετε λάθος *kanete lathos*

Y

yacht το γιοτ *to yacht*

year ο χρόνος *o khronos*

yellow κίτρινος *keetreenos*

yes ναι *ne*

yesterday χτες *khtes*

yet ακόμα *akoma* **not yet** όχι ακόμα *okhee akoma*

yoghurt το γιαούρτι *to yaoortee*

you (singular/plural) εσύ/εσείς *esee/esees*

young νέος *neos*

youth hostel ο ξενώνας νεότητος *o ksenonas neoteetos*

Z

zero το μηδέν *to meedhen*

zip το φερμουάρ *to fermooar*

zone η ζώνη *ee zonee*

zoo ο ζωολογικός κήπος *o zo-ologheekos keepos*

νΝ ξΞ οO πΠ ρP σςΣ τT υY φΦ χX ψΨ ωΩ

α Α

άγαλμα (το) *aghalma* statue

αγάπη (η) *aghapee* love

αγαπώ *aghapo* to love

αγγελία (η) *angheleea* announcement

άγγελος (ο) *anghelos* angel

Αγγλία (η) *angleea* England

αγγλικός/ή/ό *angleekos/ee/o* English (thing)

Άγγλος/Αγγλίδα (ο/η) *anglos/angleedha* Englishman/-woman

αγγούρι (το) *angooree* cucumber

άγιος/α/ο *agheeos/a/o* holy ; saint
  Άγιον Όρος (το) *agheeon oros* Mount Athos (literally holy mountain)

αγκινάρα (η) *angheenara* artichoke

άγκυρα (η) *angheera* anchor

αγορά (η) *aghora* agora ; market

αγοράζω *aghorazo* to buy

αγοραστής (ο) *aghorastees* buyer

αγόρι (το) *aghoree* young boy

άδεια (η) *adheea* permit ; licence
  άδεια οδήγησης *adheea odheegheesees* driving licence

άδειος/α/ο *adheeos/a/o* empty

αδελφή (η) *adhelfee* sister

αδελφός (ο) *adhelfos* brother

αδιάβροχο (το) *adheeavrokho* raincoat

αδιέξοδο (το) *adhee-eksodho* cul-de-sac ; no through road

αδίκημα (το) *adheekeema* offence

αέρας (ο) *a-eras* wind

αερογραμμές (οι) *a-eroghrames* airways
  Βρετανικές Αερογραμμές *vretanekes a-eroghrames* British Airways
  Κυπριακές Αερογραμμές *keepreeakes a-eroghrames* Cyprus Airways

αεροδρόμιο (το) *a-erodhromeeo* airport

αεροπλάνο (το) *a-eroplano* aeroplane

αεροπορία (η) *aeroporeea* air force ; aviation

Ολυμπιακή Αεροπορία *oleempeeakee aeroporeea* Olympic Airways

αεροπορικό εισιτήριο (το) *a-eroporeeko eeseeteereeo* air ticket

αεροπορικώς *a-eroporeekos* by air

αζήτητος/η/ο *azeeteetos/ee/o* unclaimed

Αθήνα (η) *atheena* Athens

αθλητικό κέντρο (το) *athleeteeko kendro* sports centre

αθλητισμός (ο) *athleeteesmos* sports

Αιγαίο (το) *egheo* the Aegean Sea

αίθουσα (η) *ethoosa* room
  αίθουσα αναμονής *ethoosa anamonees* waiting room
  αίθουσα αναχωρήσεων *ethoosa anakhoreeseon* departure lounge

αιμορραγώ *emoragho* to bleed

αίμα (το) *ema* blood

αίτημα (το) *eteema* demand

αίτηση (η) *eteesee* application

ακάθαρτος/η/ο *akathartos/ee/o* dirty

-άκι *-akee* (as a suffix means little)
  e.g. **καφεδάκι** *kafedhakee* little coffee

ακουστικά (τα) *akoosteeka* earphones
  ακουστικό βαρυκοΐας *akoosteeko vareekoeeas* hearing aid

ακουστικό (το) *akoosteeko* receiver (telephone)

ακούω *akoo-o* to hear

άκρη (η) *akree* edge

Ακρόπολη (η) *akropolee* the Acropolis

ακτή (η) *aktee* beach ; shore

ακτινογραφία (η) *akteenoghrafeea* X-ray

ακυρώνω *akeerono* to cancel

αλάτι (το) *alatee* salt

αλεύρι (το) *alevree* flour

αλλαγή (η) *alaghee* change

αλλάζω *alazo* to change
  δεν αλλάζονται *dhen alazonte* goods will not be exchanged

αλληλογραφία (η) *aleelografeea* correspondence

αλληλογραφώ *aleelografo* to correspond

αλλοδαπός/ή alodhapos/ee foreign national
αστυνομία αλλοδαπών asteenomeea alodhapon immigration police
αλμυρός/ή/ό almeeros/ee/o salty
αλυσίδα (η) aleeseedha chain
αμάξι (το) amaksee car ; vehicle
αμερικάνικος/η/ο amereekaneekos/ee/o American (thing)
Αμερικανός/Αμερικανίδα amereekanos/amereekaneedha American (man/woman)
Αμερική (η) amereekee America
αμέσως amesos at once ; immediately
αμήν ameen amen
άμμος (η) amos sand
αμμουδιά (η) amoodheea sandy beach
αμοιβή (η) ameevee reward ; fare ; salary ; payment
αμπέλι (το) ambelee vine
αμύγδαλο (το) ameeghdhalo almond
αμφιθέατρο (το) amfeetheatro amphitheatre
αμφορέας (ο) amforeas jar ; amphora
αν an if
αναβολή (η) anavolee delay
ανάβω anavo to switch on
αναγγελία (η) anangheleea announcement
αναζήτηση (η) anazeeteesee search
ανάκριση (η) anakreesee interrogation
ανάκτορα (τα) anaktora palace
αναμονή (η) anamonee waiting
αίθουσα αναμονής ethoosa anamonees waiting room
ανανάς (ο) ananas pineapple
ανανεώνω ananeono to renew
ανάπηρος/η/ο anapeeros/ee/o handicapped ; disabled
αναπτήρας (ο) anapteeras cigarette lighter
ανασκαφή (η) anaskafee excavation
ανατολή (η) anatolee east ; sunrise
ανατολικός/ή/ό anatoleekos/ee/o eastern

ΑΝΑΧΩΡΗΣΕΙΣ anakhoreesees **DEPARTURES**

αναψυκτικό (το) anapseekteeko soft drink
αναψυχή (η) anapseekhee recreation ; pleasure
άνδρας (ο) andhras man ; male

ΑΝΔΡΩΝ andhron **GENTS**

ανδρική μόδα (η) andhreekee modha men's fashions
ανεμιστήρας (ο) anemeesteeras fan
άνθη (τα) anthee flowers (only on signs)
ανθοπωλείο (το) anthopoleeo florist's
άνθρωπος (ο) anthropos man ; person
ανοίγω aneegho to open

ΑΝΟΙΚΤΟ aneekto **OPEN**

άνοιξη (η) aneeksee spring (season)
ανταλλαγή (η) andalaghee exchange
ανταλλακτικά (τα) andalakteeka spare parts
αντιβιοτικά (τα) andeeveeoteeka antibiotics
αντίγραφο (το) andeeghrafo copy ; reproduction
αντίκες (οι) aneekes antiques
αντικλεπτικά (τα) andeeklepteeka anti-theft devices
αντίο andeeo goodbye
αντιπηκτικό (το) andeepeekteekho antifreeze
αντιπρόσωπος (ο) andeeprosopos representative
αντλία (η) andleea pump
αντλία βενζίνης andleea venzeenees petrol pump
ανώμαλος/η/ο anomalos/ee/o uneven ; rough
αξεσουάρ (τα) aksesooar accessories
αξεσουάρ αυτοκινήτου aksesooar aftokeeneetoo car accessories
αξία (η) akseea value
αξία διαδρομής akseea dheeadhromees fare

αξιοθέατα (τα) *akseeotheata*
the sights

απαγορεύω *apaghorevo* to forbid ;
no…

απαγορεύεται η αναμονή
apaghorevete ee anamonee
no waiting

απαγορεύεται η διάβαση
apaghorevete ee dheeavasee
keep off

απαγορεύεται η είσοδος
apaghorevete ee eesodhos
no entry

απαγορεύεται το κάπνισμα
apaghorevete to kapnesma
no smoking

απαγορεύεται η στάθμευση
apaghorevete ee stathmefsee
no parking

απαγορεύεται η φωτογράφηση
apaghorevete ee fotoghrafeesee
no photography

απαγορεύεται το κολύμπι
apaghorevete to koleembee
no swimming

απαγορεύεται η κατασκήνωση
apaghorevete ee kataskeenosee
no camping

απαγορεύονται τα σκυλιά
apaghorevonte ta skeeleea no dogs

απαίτηση (η) *apeteesee* claim

απάντηση (η) *apanteesee* answer

απέναντι *apenandee* opposite

απεργία (η) *apergheea* strike

απογείωση (η) *apogheeosee* takeoff

απόγευμα (το) *apoyevma* afternoon

απόδειξη (η) *apodheeksee* receipt

αποθήκη (η) *apotheekee* warehouse ;
store-room

αποκλειστικός/ή/ό
apokleesteekos/ee/o exclusive

απόκριες (οι) *apokree-es* carnival

αποσκευές (οι) *aposkeves* luggage
αναζήτηση αποσκευών
anazeeteesee aposkevon left-luggage
(office)

απόψε *apopse* tonight

ΑΠΡΙΛΙΟΣ *apreeleeos* APRIL

αργότερα *arghotera* later

αρέσω *areso* to please
μου αρέσει *moo aresee* I like
δεν μου αρέσει *dhen moo aresee*
I don't like
σου αρέσει *soo aresee* you like
δεν σου αρέσει *dhen soo aresee* you
don't like

αριθμός (ο) *areethmos* number
αριθμός διαβατηρίου *areethmos
dheevateereeoo* passport number
αριθμός πτήσεως *areethmos
pteeseos* flight number
αριθμός τηλεφώνου *areethmos
teelefonoo* telephone number

αριστερά *areestera* left *(opposite of right)*

αρνί (το) *arnee* lamb

αρρώστια (η) *arosteea* illness

άρρωστος/η/ο *arostos/ee/o* ill

αρτοποιείο (το) *artopee-eeo* bakery

αρχαιολογικός χώρος (ο)
arkheologheekos khoros archaeological
site

αρχαίος/α/ο *arkheos/a/o* ancient

αρχή (η) *arkhee* start ; beginning

αρχίζω *arkheezo* to begin ; to start

άρωμα (το) *aroma* perfume

ασανσέρ (το) *asanser* lift ; elevator

ασθενής (ο/η) *asthenees* patient

άσθμα (το) *asthma* asthma

άσκοπος/η/ο *askopos/ee/o* improper
άσκοπη χρήση *askopee khreesee*
improper use

ασπιρίνη (η) *aspeereenee* aspirin

άσπρος/η/ο *aspros/ee/o* white

αστακός (ο) *astakos* lobster

αστυνομία (η) *asteenomeea* police
αστυνομία αλλοδαπών *asteenomeea
alodhapon* immigration police
Ελληνική αστυνομία *eleeneekee*
Greek police

αστυνομική διάταξη (η)
asteenomeekee dheeatoksee police
notice

αστυνομικό τμήμα (το) *asteenomeeko
tmeema* police station

αστυνομικός σταθμός (o)
asteenomeekos stathmos police station

αστυνόμος (o) *asteenomos* policeman

αστυφύλακας (o) *asteefeelakas* town
policeman

ασφάλεια (η) *asfaleea* insurance ; fuse
ασφάλεια έναντι κλοπής *asfaleea
enandee klopees* theft insurance
ασφάλεια έναντι τρίτων *asfaleea
enandee treeton* third-party insurance
ασφάλεια ζωής *asfaleea zoees* life
insurance

ασφάλιση (η) *asfaleesee* insurance
πλήρης ασφάλιση *pleerees
asfaleesee* comprehensive insurance
ιατρική ασφάλιση *yatreekee
asfaleesee* medical insurance

ατομικός/ή/ό *atomeekos/ee/o* personal

άτομο (το) *atomo* person
άτομο τρίτης ηλικίας *atomo
treetees eeleekeeas* pensioner

ατύχημα (το) *ateekheema* accident

αυγή (η) *avghee* dawn

αυγό (το) *avgho* egg

ΑΥΓΟΥΣΤΟΣ *avgoostos* AUGUST

αυτοκίνητο (το) *aftokeeneeto* car
ενοικιάσεις αυτοκινήτων
eneekeeasees aftokeeneeton car hire

συνεργείο αυτοκινήτων *seenergheeon
aftokeeneeton* car repairs

αυτοκινητόδρομος (o)
aftokeeneetodhromos motorway

αυτόματος/η/ο *aftomatos/ee/o*
automatic

άφιξη (η) *afeeksee* arrival

ΑΦΙΞΕΙΣ *afeeksees* ARRIVALS

αφορολόγητα (τα) *aforologheeta* duty-
free goods

Αφροδίτη *afrodheetee* Aphrodite ;
Venus

αχλάδι (το) *akhladhee* pear

άχρηστα (τα) *akhreesta* waste

αψίδα (η) *apseedha* arch

β Β

βαγόνι (το) *vaghonee* carriage *(train)*

βάζω *vazo* to put

βαλβίδα (η) *valveedha* valve

βαλίτσα (η) *valeetsa* suitcase

βαμβακερός/ή/ό *vamvakeros/ee/o*
(made of) cotton

βαρέλι (το) *varelee* barrel
μπύρα από βαρέλι *beera apo varelee*
draught beer

βαρελίσιο κρασί (το) *vareleeseeo
krasee* house wine

βάρκα (η) *varka* boat

βάρος (το) *varos* weight

βαφή (η) *vafee* paint ; dye ; painting ;
dyeing

βάφω *vafo* to paint

βγάζω *vghazo* to take off

βγαίνω *vgheno* to go out

βελόνα (η) *velona* needle

βενζίνη (η) *venzeenee* petrol ;
gasoline

βήχας (o) *veekhas* cough

βιβλίο (το) *veevleeo* book

βιβλιοθήκη (η) *veevleeotheekee*
bookcase ; library
Δημοτική Βιβλιοθήκη
dheemoteekee veevleeotheekee
Public Library
Κεντρική Βιβλιοθήκη *khendreekee
veevleeotheekee* Central Library

βιβλιοπωλείο (το) *veevleeopoleeo*
bookshop

Βίβλος (η) *veevlos* the Bible

βίντεο (το) *veedeo* video

βιταμίνη (η) *veetameenee* vitamin

βιτρίνα (η) *veetreena* shop window

βλέπω *vlepo* to see

βοήθεια (η) *voeetheea* help
οδική βοήθεια *odheekee voeetheea*
breakdown service
πρώτες βοήθειες *protes voeethee-es*
casualty *(hospital)*

βόλτα (η) *volta* walk, drive, trip

βόμβα (η) *vomva* bomb

βόρειος/α/ο *voreeos/a/o* northern

βορράς (o) *voras* north

βουλή (η) *voolee* parliament
βουνό (το) *voono* mountain
βούρτσα (η) *voortsa* brush
βούτυρο (το) *vooteero* butter
βράδυ (το) *vradhee* evening
βραδινό (το) *vradheeno* evening meal
βράζω *vrazo* to boil
βραστός/ή/ό *vrastos/ee/o* boiled
Βρετανία (η) *vretaneea* Britain
βρετανικός/ή/ό *vretaneekos/ee/o*
British *(thing)*
Βρετανός/Βρετανίδα (ο/η)
vretanos/vretaneedha British
(man/woman)
βρέχει *vrekhee* it is raining
βρίσκω *vreesko* to find
βρόμικος/η/ο *vromeekos/ee/o* dirty
βροχή (η) *vrokhee* rain

γ Γ

γαϊδούρι *ghaeedhooree* donkey
γάλα (το) *ghala* milk
γαλάζιος/α/ο *ghalazeeos/a/o* blue ;
light blue
γαλακτοπωλείο (το) *ghalaktopoleeo*
dairy shop
Γαλλία (η) *ghaleea* France
γαλλικός/ή/ό *ghaleekos/ee/o* French
(thing)
Γάλλος/Γαλλίδα (ο/η)
ghalos/ghaleedha French *(man/woman)*
γαλοπούλα (η) *ghalopoola* turkey
γάμος (ο) *ghamos* wedding ; marriage
γαμήλια δεξίωση *ghameelya
dhekseeosee* wedding reception
γαρίδα (η) *ghareedha* shrimp ; prawn
γεια σας *ya sas* hello ; goodbye
(formal)
γειά σου *ya soo* hello ; goodbye
(informal)
γεμάτος/η/ο *yematos/ee/o* full
γενέθλια (τα) *yenethleea* birthday
γενικός/ή/ό *yeneekos/ee/o* general
Γενικό Νοσοκομείο *yeneeko
nosokomeeo* General Hospital
γέννηση (η) *yeneesee* birth

Γερμανία (η) *yermaneea* Germany
γερμανικός/ή/ό *yermaneekos/ee/o*
German *(thing)*
Γερμανός/Γερμανίδα (ο/η)
yermanos/yermaneedha German
(man/woman)
γεμιστός/ή/ό *yemeestos/ee/o* stuffed
γεύμα (το) *yevma* meal
γέφυρα (η) *yefeera* bridge
για *ya* for
γιαγιά (η) *yaya* grandmother
γιαούρτι (το) *yaoortee* yoghurt
γιασεμί (το) *yasemee* jasmine
γιατί; *yatee* why?
γιατρός (ο/η) *yatros* doctor
γίνομαι *yeenome* to become
γίνονται δεκτές πιστωτικές κάρτες
yeenonte dhektes peestoteekes kartes
we accept credit cards
γιορτή (η) *yortee* festival ; celebration
; name day
γιος (ο) *yos* son
γιοτ (το) *yot* yacht
γκάζι (το) *gazee* accelerator *(car)* ; gas
γκαλερί *galeree* art gallery ; art sales
γκαράζ (το) *garaz* garage
γκαρσόν (το)/γκαρσόνι (το)
garson/garsonee waiter
γλυκός/ιά/ό *ghleekos/eea/o* sweet
γλυκό (το)/γλυκά (τα)
ghleeko/ghleeka cakes and pastries ;
desserts
γλυκό ταψιού *ghleeko tapseeoo*
traditional pastries with syrup
γλύπτης/γλύπτρια (ο/η)
ghleeptees/ghleeptreea sculptor
γλυπτική (η) *ghleepteekee* sculpture
γλώσσα (η) *ghlosa* tongue ; language ;
sole *(fish)*
γονείς (οι) *ghonees* parents
γουιντσέρφινγκ (το) *weendserfeeng*
windsurfing
γράμμα (το) *ghrama* letter
γράμμα κατεπείγον *ghrama
katepeeghon* express letter
γράμμα συστημένο *ghrama
seesteemeno* recorded delivery
γραμμάριο (το) *ghramareeo* gram

αΑ βΒ γΓ δΔ εΕ ζΖ ηΗ θΘ ιΙ κΚ λΛ μΜ

γραμματοκιβώτιο (το) *ghramatokeevoteeo* letter box

γραμματόσημο (το) *ghramatoseemo* stamp

γραφείο (το) *ghrafeeo* office ; desk
Γραφείο Τουρισμού *ghrafeeo tooreesmoo* Tourist Office

γράφω *ghrafo* to write

γρήγορα *ghreegora* quickly

γρίπη (η) *ghreepee* influenza

γυαλί (το) *yalee* glass
γυαλιά (τα) *yalya* glasses
γυαλιά ηλίου *yalya eeleeoo* sunglasses

γυαλικός/ή/ό *yaleekos/ee/o* made of glass

γυμνάσιο (το) *yeemnaseeo* high school

γυμναστήριο (το) *yeemnasteereeo* gym

γυναίκα (η) *yeeneka* woman

γύρω *yeero* round ; about

γωνία (η) *ghoneea* corner

δ Δ

δακτυλίδι (το) *dhakteeleedee* ring *(for finger)*

δαμάσκηνο (το) *dhamaskeeno* plum

δαντέλα (η) *dhandela* lace

δασκάλα (η) *dhaskala* primary school teacher *(female)*

δάσκαλος (ο) *dhaskalos* primary school teacher *(male)*

δάσος (το) *dhasos* forest, wood

δείπνο (το) *dheepno* dinner

δέκα *dheka* ten

ΔΕΚΕΜΒΡΙΟΣ *dhekemvreeos* DECEMBER

δελτίο (το) *dhelteeo* card ; coupon
δελτίο αφίξεως *dhelteeo afeekseos* arrival card

δελφίνι (το) *dhelfeenee* dolphin
ιπτάμενο δελφίνι *eeptameno dhelfeenee* hydrofoil

Δελφοί (οι) *dhelfee* Delphi

δεν *dhen* not
δεν δίνεται ρέστα *dhen dheenete resta* no change given

ΔΕΝ ΛΕΙΤΟΥΡΓΕΙ *dhen leetoorghee* OUT OF ORDER

δεξιά *dhekseea* right *(opposite of left)*

δέρμα (το) *dherma* skin ; leather

δεσποινίς/δεσποινίδα (η) *dhespeenees/dhespeeneedha* Miss

ΔΕΥΤΕΡΑ *dheftera* MONDAY

δεύτερος/η/ο *dhefteros/ee/o* second

δηλητήριο (το) *dheeleeteereeo* poison

δήλωση (η) *dheelosee* announcement
δήλωση συναλλάγματος *dheelosee seenalaghmatos* currency declaration
είδη προς δήλωση *eedhee pros dheelosee* goods to declare
ουδέν προς δήλωση *oodhen pros dheelosee* nothing to declare

δημαρχείο (το) *dheemarkheeo* town hall

δημόσιος/α/ο *dheemoseeos* public/state
δημόσια έργα *dheemoseea ergha* road works
δημόσιος κήπος *dheemoseeos keepos* public gardens

δημοτικός/ή/ό *deemoteekos* public/municipal
Δημοτική Αγορά *dheemoteekee aghora* public market
Δημοτική Βιβλιοθήκη *dheemoteekee veevleeotheekee* Public Library

διάβαση (η) *dheeavasee* crossing
διάβαση πεζών *dheeavasee pezon* pedestrian crossing
υπόγεια διάβαση πεζών *eepoya dheeavasee pezon* pedestrian subway

διαβατήριο (το) *dheeavateereeo* passport
αριθμός διαβατηρίου *areethmos dheeavateereeoo* passport number
έλεγχος διαβατηρίων *elenghos dheeavateereeon* passport control

διαβήτης (ο) *dheeaveetees* diabetes

διαδρομή (η) dheeadhromee route

δίαιτα (η) dheeeta diet

διακεκριμένος/η/ο dheeakekreemenos distinguished
διακεκριμένη θέση dheeakekreemenee thesee business class

διακοπές (οι) dheeakopes holidays

διάλειμμα (το) dheealeema interval ; break

διαμέρισμα (το) dheeamereesma flat ; apartment

διανυχτερεύει dheeaneekhterevee open all night

διασκέδαση (η) dheeaskedhasee entertainment
κέντρο διασκεδάσεως kendro dheeaskedaseos nightclub

διασταύρωση (η) dheeastavrosee crossroads ; junction

διεθνής/ής/ές dhee-ethnees/ees/es international

διερμηνέας (ο/η) dhee-ermeeneas interpreter

διεύθυνση (η) dhee-eftheensee address

διευθυντής (ο) dhee-eftheentees manager

δικαστήριο (το) dheekasteereeo court

δικηγόρος (ο/η) dheekeeghoros lawyer

δίνω dheeno to give

δίπλα dheepla next to

διπλός/ή/ό dheeplos/ee/o double
διπλό δωμάτιο dheeplo domateeo double room
διπλό κρεβάτι dheeplo krevatee double bed

δισκοθήκη (η) dheeskotheekee disco (Cyprus) ; music collection

δίσκέτα (η) dheesketa floppy disk

δίχτυ (το) dheekhtee net

διψώ dheepso to be thirsty

δολάριο (το) dholareeo dollar

δόντι (το) dhondee tooth

δράμα (το) dhrama drama ; play

δραχμή (η) dhrakhmee drachma

δρομολόγιο (το) dhromologheeo timetable ; route

δρομολόγια εξωτερικού dhromologheea eksotereekoo international routes
δρομολόγια εσωτερικού dhromologheea esotereekoo domestic routes

δρόμος (ο) dhromos street ; way

δύση (η) dheesee west ; sunset

δυσκοιλιότητα (η) dheeskeeleeoteeta constipation

δύσκολος/η/ο dheeskolos/ee/o difficult

δυστύχημα (το) dheesteekheema accident ; mishap

δυτικός/ή/ό dheeteekos/ee/o western

Δωδεκάνησα (τα) dhodhekaneesa the Dodecanese

δωμάτιο (το) dhomateeo room

δωρεάν dhorean free of charge

δώρο (το) dhoro present ; gift

ε Ε

εβδομάδα (η) evdhomadha week

εγγραφή (η) engrafee registration

εγγύηση (η) engheeyeesee guarantee

έγχρωμος/η/ο enkhromos/ee/o coloured
έγχρωμες φωτογραφίες enkhromes fotoghrafee-es colour photographs

εδώ edho here

ΕΕ epseelon epseelon EU

εθνικός/ή/ό ethneekos/ee/o national
Εθνικό Θέατρο ethneeko theatro National Theatre
εθνική οδός ethneekee odhos motorway
Εθνικός Κήπος ethneekos keepos National Garden (in Athens)
εθνικός ύμνος ethneekos eemnos national anthem

έθνος (το) ethnos nation

εθνικότητα ethneekoteeta nationality

ειδικός/ή/ό eedheekos/ee/o special ; specialist

είδος (το) eedhos kind ; sort
είδη eedhee goods
είδη κήπου eedhee keepoo garden centre

είμαι eeme to be

εισιτήριο (το) *eeseeteereeo* ticket
  απλό εισιτήριο *aplo eeseeteereeo* single ticket
  εισιτήριο με επιστροφή *eeseeteereeo me epeestrofee* return ticket
  ατμοπλοϊκό εισιτήριο *atmoploeeko eeseeteereeo* boat ticket
  σιδηροδρομικό εισιτήριο *seedheerodromeeko eeseeteereeo* rail ticket
  φοιτητικό εισιτήριο *feeteeteeko eeseeteereeo* student ticket

ΕΙΣΟΔΟΣ *eesodhos* **ENTRANCE**

εκδόσεις εισιτηρίων *ekdhosees eeseeteereeon* ticket office

εκδοτήρια (τα) *ekdhoteereea* ticket machines

εκεί *ekee* there

έκθεση (η) *ekthesee* exhibition

εκθεσιακό κέντρο *ektheseeako kendro* exhibition centre

εκκλησία (η) *ekleeseea* church ; chapel

έκπτωση (η) *ekptosee* discount

ΕΚΠΤΩΣΕΙΣ *ekptosees* **SALE**

εκτελούνται έργα *ekteloonde ergha* road works

εκτός *ektos* except ; unless
  εκτός λειτουργίας *ektos leetoorgheeas* out of order

έλα! *ela* come on! (singular)

ελάτε! *elate* come on! (plural)

ελαιόλαδο (το) *eleoladho* olive oil

ελαττώνω *elatono* to reduce ; to decrease
  ελαττώσατε ταχύτητα *elatosate takheeteeta* reduce speed

έλεγχος (ο) *elenkhos* control
  έλεγχος διαβατηρίων *elenkhos dheeavateereeon* passport control
  έλεγχος εισιτηρίων *elenkhos eeseeteereeon* check-in
  έλεγχος ελαστικών *elenkhos elasteekon* tyre check

ελεύθερος/η/ο *eleftheros/ee/o* single ; unmarried ; free

ΕΛΕΥΘΕΡΟ *eleсtthero* **FREE**

ελιά (η) *elya* olive ; olive tree

έλκος (το) *elkos* ulcer

Ελλάδα (η) *eladha* Greece

Έλληνας/Ελληνίδα (ο/η) *eleenas/ eleeneedha* Greek (man/woman)

ελληνικά (τα) *eleeneeka* Greek (language)

ελληνικός/ή/ό *eleeneekos/ee/o* Greek (thing)
  Ελληνικά Ταχυδρομεία *eleeneeka takheedhromeea* Greek Post Office (ELTA)
  Ελληνική Δημοκρατία *eleeneekee dheemokrateea* Republic of Greece
  Ελληνικής κατασκευής *eleeneekees kataskevees* made in Greece
  Ελληνικός Οργανισμός Τουρισμού *eleeneekos orghaneesmos tooreesmoo* Greek Tourist Organisation (EOT)
  Ελληνικό προϊόν *eleeneeko proeeon* product of Greece

ΕΛΞΑΤΕ *elksate* (written only) **PULL**

εμπρός *embros* forward ; in front ; 'hello!' (on phone)

εμφανίζω *emfaneezo* to develop (film)

εμφάνιση (η) *emfaneesee* film developing

εναντίον *enandeeon* against

έναρξη (η) *enarksee* opening ; beginning

ένας/μία/ένα *enas/meea/ena* one

ένεση (η) *enesee* injection

ενήλικος (ο) *eneeleekos* adult

εννέα/εννιά *enea/enya* nine

ενοικιάζω *eneekeeazo* to rent ; to hire
  ενοικιάζεται *eneekeeazete* to let

ενοικιάσεις *eneekeeasees* for hire

ενοίκιο (το) *eneekeeo* rent

ενορία (η) *enoreea* parish

εντάξει *endaksee* all right ; OK

εντομοκτόνο (το) *endomoktono* insecticide

έντυπο (το) *endeepo* form (to fill in)

έξι *eksee* six

ΕΞΟΔΟΣ *eksodhos* **EXIT**

εξοχή (η) *eksokhee* countryside

εξυπηρέτηση (η) *ekseepeereteesee* service

εξυπηρετώ *ekseepeereto* to serve

έξω *ekso* out ; outside

εξώστης (ο) *eksostees* balcony *(theatre)*

εξωτερικός/ή/ό *eksotereekos/ee/o* external

το εξωτερικό *to eksotereeko* abroad
εξωτερικού *eksotereekoo* letters abroad *(on postbox)*
πτήσεις εξωτερικού *pteesees eksotereekoo* international flights

ΕΟΚ *e-ok* EU

ΕΟΤ *e-ot* Greek Tourist Organization

επάγγελμα (το) *epanghelma* occupation ; profession

επείγον/επείγουσα *epeeghon/ epeeghoosa* urgent ; express
επείγοντα περιστατικά *epeeghonta pereestateeka* casualty department

επιβάτης/τρια (ο/η) *epeevatees/treea* passenger
διερχόμενοι επιβάτες *dhee- erkhomenee epeevates* passengers in transit

επιβεβαιώνω *epeeveveono* to confirm

επιβίβαση (η) *epeeveevasee* boarding
κάρτα επιβιβάσεως *karta epeeveevaseos* boarding card

επειδή *epeedhee* because

επιδόρπιο (το) *epeedhorpeeo* dessert

επικίνδυνος/η/ο *epeekeendeenos/ee/o* dangerous

επίσης *epeesees* also ; the same to you

επισκεπτήριο (το) *epeeskepteereeo* visiting hours

επισκέπτης (ο) *epeeskeptees* visitor

επισκευή (η) *epeeskevee* repair
επισκευές *epeeskeves* repairs

επίσκεψη (η) *epeeskepsee* visit
ώρες επισκέψεων *ores epeeskepseon* visiting hours

επιστροφή (η) *epeestrofee* return ; return ticket
επιστροφή νομισμάτων *epeestrofee nomeesmaton* returned coins

επιστροφές *epeestrofes* returned goods ; refunds

επιταγή (η) *epeetaghee* cheque ; invoice
ταχυδρομική επιταγή *takheedhromeekee epeetaghee* postal order

επόμενος/η/ο *epomenos/ee/o* next

εποχή (η) *epokhee* season

επτά/εφτά *epta/efta* seven

Επτάνησα (τα) *eptaneesa* Ionian Islands

επώνυμο (το) *eponeemo* surname ; last name

έργα (τα) *ergha* works

εργαλείο (το) *erghaleeo* tool

έργο *ergo* film ; play ; TV program

εργοστάσιο (το) *erghostaseeo* factory

έργο τέχνης (το) *ergho tekhnees* artwork

έρχομαι *erkhome* to come

ερώτηση (η) *eroteesee* question

εστιατόριο (το) *esteeatoreeo* restaurant

εσώρουχα (τα) *esorookha* underwear ; lingerie

εσωτερικός/ή/ό *esotereekos/ee/o* internal
εσωτερικού *esotereekoo* inland *(on post boxes)* ; domestic
πτήσεις εσωτερικού *pteesees esotereekoo* domestic flights

εταιρ(ε)ία (η) *etereea* company ; firm

έτος (το) *etos* year

έτσι *etsee* so ; like this

ευθεία (η) *eftheea* straight
κατ' ευθείαν *kat' eftheean* straight on

ευθύνη (η) *eftheenee* responsibility

ευκαιρία (η) *efkereea* opportunity ; bargain

ευκολία (η) *efkoleea* ease ; convenience
ευκολίες πληρωμής *efkoleees pleeromees* credit terms

εύκολος/η/ο *efkolos/ee/o* easy

ευρωπαϊκός/ή/ό *evropaeekos/ee/o* European

Ευρώπη (η) *evropee* Europe

ευχαριστώ *efkhareesto* thank you
εύκολος/η/ο *efkolos/ee/o* easy
εφημερίδα (η) *efeemereedha*
newspaper
έχω *ekho* to have

ζ Z

ζάλη (η) *zalee* dizziness
ζαμπόν (το) *zambon* ham
ζάχαρη (η) *zakharee* sugar
ζαχαροπλαστείο (το) *zakharoplasteeo*
patisserie
ζέστη (η) *zestee* heat
  κάνει ζέστη *kanee zestee* it's hot
ζευγάρι (το) *zevgharee* couple
ζημιά (η) *zeemya* damage
  πάσα ζημιά τιμωρείται *pasa zeemya*
  teemoreete anyone causing damage
  will be prosecuted
ζητώ *zeeto* to ask ; to seek
ζυγαριά (η) *zeeghareea* scales
  (for weighing)
ζυμαρικά (τα) *zeemareekha* pasta
products
ζωγραφιά (η) *zografya* picture ;
painting
ζώνη (η) *zonee* belt
  ζώνη ασφαλείας *zonee asfaleeas*
  safety belt ; seat belt
ζώο (το) *zo-o* animal
ζωολογικός κήπος (ο)
  zo-ologheekos keepos zoo

η H

η *ee* the (with feminine nouns)
ή *ee* or
ηλεκτρικός/ή/ό *eelektreekos/ee/o*
electrical
ηλεκτρισμός (ο) *eelektreesmos*
electricity
ηλεκτρονικός/ή/ό *eelektroneekos/ee/o*
electronic
ηλιακός/ή/ό *eeleeakos/ee/o* solar
ηλίαση (η) *eeleeasee* sunstroke
ηλικία (η) *eeleekeea* age
ηλιοβασίλεμα (το) *eeleeovaseelema*
sunset

ηλιοθεραπεία (η) *eeleeotherapeea*
sunbathing
ήλιος (ο) *eeleeos* sun
ημέρα (η) *eemera* day
ημερήσιος/α/ο *eemereeseeos/a/o* daily

ΗΜΕΡΟΜΗΝΙΑ *eemeromeeneea*
DATE

ημερομηνία αναχωρήσεως
  eemeromeeneea anakhoreeseos
  date of departure
ημερομηνία αφίξεως
  eemeromeeneea afeekseos
  date of arrival
ημερομηνία γεννήσεως
  eemeromeeneea yeneeseos
  date of birth
ημερομηνία λήξης *eemeromeeneea*
  leeksees expiry date
ημιδιατροφή (η) *eemeedheeatrofee*
half board
Ηνωμένο Βασίλειο (το) *eenomeno*
  vaseeleeo United Kingdom (UK)
ΗΠΑ USA
Ηνωμένες Πολιτείες της Αμερικής
  eenomenes poleeteees tees amereekees
  United States of America
ησυχία (η) *eesekheea* calm ; quiet
ήσυχος/η/ο *eeseekhos* calm ; quiet

θ Θ

θάλασσα (η) *thalasa* sea
θαλάσσιος/α/ο *thalaseeos/a/o*
  of the sea
  θαλάσσιο αλεξίπτωτο *thalaseeo*
  alekseeptoto paragliding
  θαλάσσιο σκι *thalaseeo skee*
  water-skiing
θέατρο (το) *theatro* theatre
θέλω *thelo* to want
Θεός (ο) *theos* God
θεός/θεά (ο/η) *theos/thea* god ;
  goddess
θεραπεία (η) *therapeea* treatment
θέρμανση (η) *thermansee* heating
θερμίδα (η) *thermeedha* calorie
θερμοστάτης (ο) *thermostatees*
  thermostat

θέση (η) thesee place ; seat
διακεκριμένη θέση
dheeakekreemenee thesee business
class
κράτηση θέσης krateesee thesees
seat reservation
οικονομική θέση eekonomeekee
thesee economy class
πρώτη θέση protee first class
Θεσσαλονίκη (η) thesaloneekee
Salonica/Thessaloniki
θύελλα (η) thee-ela storm
θύρα (η) theera gate (airport)
θυρίδα (η) theereedha ticket window

ι I

ΙΑΝΟΥΑΡΙΟΣ eeanooareeos
JANUARY

ιατρική περίθαλψη (η) yatreekee
pereethalpsee medical treatment
ιατρός (ο/η) yatros doctor
ιδιοκτήτης/τρια (ο/η)
eedheeokteetees/treea owner

ΙΔΙΩΤΙΚΟΣ ΧΩΡΟΣ
eedheeoteekos khoros PRIVATE

ίντερνετ (το) eenternet internet
Ιόνιο Πέλαγος (το) eeoneeo pelaghos
Ionian sea

ΙΟΥΛΙΟΣ eeooleeos JULY

ΙΟΥΝΙΟΣ eeooneeos JUNE

ιππασία (η) eepaseea horse riding
ιππόκαμπος (ο) eepokampos sea-horse
ιπτάμενο δελφίνι eeptameno
dhelfeenee hydrofoil (flying dolphin)
Ισθμός της Κορίνθου eesthmos tees
koreenthoo Corinth canal

ΙΣΟΓΕΙΟ eesoyeeo
GROUND FLOOR

ισοτιμία (η) eesoteemeea exchange
rate
Ισπανία (η) eespaneea Spain
ισπανικός/ή/ό eespaneekos/ee/o
Spanish (thing)

Ισπανός/ίδα (ο/η) eespanos/eedha
Spaniard (man/woman)
ιστιοπλοΐα (η) eesteeoploeea sailing
Ιταλία (η) eetaleea Italy
ιταλικός/ή/ό eetaleekos/ee/o Italian
(thing)
Ιταλός/ίδα (ο/η) eetalos/eedha Italian
(man/woman)
ιχθυοπωλείο (το) eekhtheeopoleeo
fishmonger's

κ K

κάβα (η) kava wine merchant;
off-licence
κάβουρας (ο) kavooras crab
καζίνο (το) kazeeno casino
καθαριστήριο (το) kathareesteereeo
dry-cleaner's
καθαρίστρια (η) kathareestreea
cleaner
καθαρός/ή/ό katharos/ee/o clean
κάθε kathe every ; each
κάθε μέρα kathe mera every day
καθεδρικός ναός (ο) kathedhreekos
naos cathedral
καθημερινός/ή/ό katheemereenos/ee/o
daily
καθημερινά δρομολόγια
katheemereena dhromologheea daily
departures
κάθισμα (το) katheesma seat
καθολικός/ή/ό katholeekos/ee/o
Catholic ; total
καθυστέρηση (η) katheestereesee
delay
και ke and
καιρός (ο) keros weather ; time
κακάο (το) kakao cocoa ; chocolate
flavour
κακός/ή/ό kakos/ee/o bad
καλά kalathee well ; all right
καλάθι (το) kalathee basket
καλαμάρι (το) kalamaree squid ;
calamari
καλημέρα kaleemera good morning
καληνύχτα kaleeneekhta good night
καλησπέρα kaleespera good evening

καλοκαίρι (το) kalok*ee*ree summer

καλοριφέρ (το) kaloree*fer* central
heating ; radiator

καλοψημένο kalopseem*e*no
well done *(meat)*

καλσόν (το) kals*on* tights

κάλτσα (η) k*a*ltsa sock ; stocking

καμαριέρα (η) kamaree-*e*ra
chambermaid

κάμερα (η) k*a*mera camcorder

καμπίνα (η) kamb*ee*na cabin

κανάλι (το) kan*a*lee canal ; channel
(TV)

κανέλα (η) kan*e*la cinnamon

κανένας kan*e*nas no-one

καντίνα (η) kant*ee*na mobile roadside
cafe

κάνω k*a*no to do

καπέλο (το) kap*e*lo hat

καπετάνιος (ο) kapet*a*neeos captain
(of ship)

καπνίζω kapn*ee*zo to smoke
μην καπνίζετε meen kapn*ee*zete
no smoking

καπνιστός/ή/ό kapneest*os/ee/o*
smoked
καπνιστός σολομός kapneest*os*
solom*os* smoked salmon
καπνιστό χοιρινό kapneest*o*
kheereen*o* smoked ham
καπνιστό ψάρι kapneest*o* ps*a*ree
smoked fish
καπνιστό τυρί kapneest*o* teer*ee*
smoked cheese

κάπνισμα (το) k*a*pneesma smoking
απαγορεύεται το κάπνισμα
apaghor*e*vete to k*a*pneesma
no smoking

καπνιστής (ο) kapneest*ees* smoker

καπνοπωλείο (το) kapnopol*ee*o
tobacconist

καπνός (ο) kapn*os* smoke

κάποτε k*a*pote sometimes ; one time

καράβι (το) kar*a*vee boat ; ship

καραμέλα (η) karam*e*la sweet

κάρβουνο (το) k*a*rvoono coal ;
charcoal
στα κάρβουνα sta k*a*rvoona charcoal-
grilled

καρδιά (η) kardh*ee*a heart

καρναβάλι (το) karnav*a*lee carnival

καροτσάκι (το) karots*a*kee pushchair
καροτσάκι αναπηρικό karots*a*kee
anapeer*ee*ko wheelchair

καρπούζι (το) karp*oo*zee watermelon

κάρτα (η) k*a*rta card ; postcard
κάρτα απεριόριστων διαδρομών
k*a*rta apeere*o*reeston dheeadhrom*on*
rail card for unlimited monthly travel
κάρτα επιβιβάσεως k*a*rta
epeeveev*a*seos boarding card
επαγγελματική κάρτα
epanghelmateek*ee* k*a*rta business card
μόνο με κάρτα m*o*no me k*a*rta
cardholders only
πιστωτική κάρτα peestoteek*ee* k*a*rta
credit card
κάρτα αναλήψεως k*a*rta anal*ee*pseos
ATM card ; cash card

καρτοτηλέφωνο (το) kartoteel*e*fono
card phone

καρτποστάλ (το) kartpost*a*l postcard

καρύδα (η) kar*ee*dha coconut

καρύδι (το) kar*ee*dhee walnut

καρχαρίας (ο) karkhar*ee*as shark

κασέτα (η) kas*e*ta tape ; cassette
(for recording)
CD (το) s*ee*dee CD

κασετόφωνο (το) kaset*o*fono
tape recorder

κάστανο (το) k*a*stano chestnut

κάστρο (το) k*a*stro castle ; fortress

κατάθεση (η) kat*a*thesee deposit ;
statement to police

καταιγίδα (η) kateegh*ee*dha storm

καταλαβαίνω katalav*e*no to understand
καταλαβαίνεις; katalav*e*nees
do you understand? *(familiar form)*
καταλαβαίνετε; katalav*e*nete do you
understand? *(polite form)*

κατάλογος (ο) kat*a*loghos list ;
menu ; directory
τηλεφωνικός κατάλογος
teelefoneek*os* katal*o*ghos telephone
directory

καταπραϋντικό (το) katapra*ee*nteeko
tranquillizer

κατασκήνωση (η) katask*ee*nosee
camping

κατάσταση (η) katastasee condition ; situation

κατάστημα (το) katasteema shop

κατάστρωμα (το) katastroma deck

κατεπείγον/κατεπείγουσα katepeeghon/katepeeghoosa urgent ; express

κατεψυγμένος/η/ο katepseeghmenos/ee/o frozen

κατηγορία (η) kateghoreea class (of hotel)

κατσαρόλα (η) katsarola saucepan ; pot

κατσίκα (η) katseeka goat

κατσικάκι (το) katseekakee kid (young goat)

κάτω kato under ; lower ; down

καύσιμα (τα) kafseema fuel

καφέ kafe brown

καφενείο (το) kafeneeo coffee house

καφές (ο) kafes coffee (usually Greek)
καφές γλυκός kafes ghleekos sweet coffee
καφές μέτριος kafes metreeos medium sweet coffee
καφές σκέτος kafes sketos strong black coffee
καφές στιγμιαίος kafes steeghmeeeos instant coffee (Nescafé)
καφές φραπέ kapes frape iced coffee (Nescafé)

καφετέρια (η) kafetereea cafeteria

καφετιέρα (η) kafetee-era coffee maker

κέικ (το) ke-eek cake

κεντρικός/ή/ό kendreekos/ee/o central

κέντρο (το) kendro centre
κέντρο αλλοδαπών kendro allodhapon immigration office
κέντρο διασκεδάσεως kendro dheeaskedhaseos nightclub
κέντρο εκδώσεως kendro ekdhoseos ticket office
κέντρο υγείας kendro eegheeas health centre
αθλητικό κέντρο athleeteeko kendro sports centre
τηλεφωνικό κέντρο teelefoneeko kendro telephone exchange

κεράσι (το) kerasee cherry

Κέρκυρα (η) kerkeera Corfu

κέρμα (το) kerma coin

κερνώ kerno to buy a drink
να κεράσω na keraso can I buy (you) a drink… ?

κεφάλι (το) kefalee head

κεφτέδες (οι) keftedhes meatballs

κήπος (ο) keepos garden
δημόσιος κήπος dheemoseeos keepos public garden
ζωολογικός κήπος zo-ologheekos keepos zoo

κιβώτιο (το) keevoteeo large box
κιβώτιο ταχυτήτων keevoteeo takheeteeton gearbox

κιλό (το) keelo kilo

κίνδυνος (ο) keendheenos danger
κίνδυνος θανάτου keendheenos thanatoo extreme danger

κινητό (το) keeneeto mobile phone

κίτρινος/η/ο keetreenos/ee/o yellow

κλαμπ (το) klab club

κλειδί (το) kleedhee key ; spanner

κλείνω kleeno to close

ΚΛΕΙΣΤΟ kleesto CLOSED

κλέφτης (ο) kleftees thief

κλέφτικο (το) klefteeko lamb dish

κλήση (η) kleesee summons

κλήση τροχαίας (η) kleesee trokheas traffic ticket

κλίμα (το) kleema climate

κλινική (η) kleeneekee clinic ; hospital ; ward

κοιμάμαι keemame to sleep

κοινωνικός/ή/ό keenoneekos/ee/o social
κοινωνικές ασφαλίσεις keenoneekes asfaleesees national insurance

κόκκινος/η/ο kokeenos/ee/o red

κολοκυθάκι (το) kolokeethakee courgette

κολοκύθι (το) kolokeethee marrow

κόλπος (ο) kolpos gulf ; vagina

κολύμπι (το) koleembee swimming

κολυμπώ koleembo to swim

κολώνα (η) kolona pillar ; column

κομμωτήριο (το) *komoteereeo* hairdresser's

κομμωτής/μώτρια (ο/η) *komotees/komotreea* hairstylist

κομπιούτερ (το) *kompyooter* computer

κομπιουτεράκι (το) *kompyooterakee* calculator

κονιάκ (το) *konyak* cognac ; brandy

κονσέρβα (η) *konserva* tinned food

κονσέρτο (το) *konserto* concert

κοντά *konda* near

κόρη (η) *koree* daughter

κορίτσι (το) *koreetsee* young girl

κόρνα (η) *korna* horn *(in car)*

κοσμήματα (τα) *kosmeemata* jewellery

κοσμηματαπωλείο (το) *kosmeematapoleeo* jewellery shop

κοστούμι (το) *kostoomee* man's suit

κότα (η) *kota* hen

κοτολέτα (η) *kotoleta* chop

κοτόπουλο (το) *kotopoolo* chicken

κουβέρ (το) *koover* cover-charge

κουβέρτα (η) *kooverta* blanket ; cover

κουζίνα (η) *koozeena* kitchen ; cuisine
  ελληνική κουζίνα *eleeneekee koozeena* Greek cuisine

κουμπί (το) *koombee* button

κουνέλι (το) *koonelee* rabbit

κουνούπι (το) *koonoopee* mosquito

κουνουπίδι (το) *koonoopeedhee* cauliflower

κουπί (το) *koopee* oar

κουρείο (το) *kooreeo* barber's shop

κουταλάκι (το) *kootalakee* teaspoon

κουτάλι (το) *kootalee* dessertspoon

κουτί (το) *kootee* box

κραγιόν (το) *kra-yon* lipstick

κρασί (το) *krasee* wine
  κρασί γλυκό *krasee ghleeko* sweet wine
  κρασί ξηρό *krasee kseero* dry wine
  κρασί κόκκινο *krasee kokeeno* red wine
  κρασί λευκό *krasee lefko* white wine
  κρασί ροζέ *krasee roze* rosé wine

κρατήσεις (οι) *krateesees* bookings ; reservations

κρατήσεις ξενοδοχείων *krateesees ksenodhokheeon* hotel bookings

κράτηση (η) *krateesee* reservation
  κράτηση θέσης *krateesee thesees* seat reservation

κρέας (το) *kreas* meat
  κρέας αρνίσιο *kreas arneeseeo* lamb
  κρέας μοσχαρίσιο *kreas moskhareeseeo* beef
  κρέας χοιρινό *kreas kheereeno* pork

κρεβάτι (το) *krevatee* bed

κρεβατοκάμαρα (η) *krevatokamara* bedroom

κρέμα (η) *krema* cream

κρεμμύδι (το) *kremeedhee* onion

κρεοπωλείο (το) *kreopoleeo* butcher's shop

Κρήτη (η) *kreetee* Crete

κρουαζιέρα (η) *krooazyera* cruise

κρύος/α/ο *kreeos/a/o* cold

κτηνιατρείο (το) *kteenyatreeo* veterinary surgery

κωμωδία (η) *komodeea* comedy

κυβέρνηση (η) *keeverneesee* government

κυβερνήτης (ο) *keeverneetees* captain *(of aircraft)*

Κυκλάδες (οι) *keekladhes* Cyclades *(islands)*

κύκλος (ο) *keeklos* circle

κυκλοφορία (η) *keekloforeea* traffic ; circulation

κυλικείο (το) *keeleekeeo* canteen ; cafeteria

Κύπρος (η) *keepros* Cyprus

Κύπριος/Κυπρία (ο/η) *keepreeos/keepreea* from Cyprus ; Cypriot *(man/woman)*

κυρία (η) *keereea* Mrs ; lady

ΚΥΡΙΑΚΗ *keereeakee* SUNDAY

κύριος (ο) *keereeos* Mr ; gentleman

κωδικός (ο) *kodheekos* code
  ταχυδρομικός κωδικός *takheedhromeekos kodheekos* postcode
  τηλεφωνικός κωδικός *teelefoneekos kodheekos* dialling code ; area code

κωμωδία (η) *komodheea* comedy

λ Λ

λάδι (το) ladhee oil
 λάδι ελιάς ladhee elyas olive oil
λαϊκός/ή/ό laeekos/ee/o popular ; folk
 λαϊκή αγορά laeekee aghora market
 λαϊκή μουσική laeekee mooseekee
 popular music
 λαϊκή τέχνη laeekee tekhnee folk art
λάστιχο (το) lasteekho tyre ; rubber ;
 elastic
λαχανικά (τα) lakhaneeka vegetables
λαχείο (το) lakheeo lottery ticket
λεμονάδα (η) lemonadha lemonade
λεμόνι (το) lemonee lemon
 χυμός λεμονιού kheemos lemoneeoo
 lemon juice
λεξικό (το) lekseeko dictionary
λεπτό (το) lepto minute
λεπτός/ή/ό leptos/ee/o thin ; slim
λευκός/ή/ό lefkos/ee/o white
λεφτά (τα) lefta money
λέω leo to say
λεωφορείο (το) leoforeeo bus
λεωφόρος (η) leoforos avenue
λήξη (η) leeksee expiry
λιανικός/ή/ό leeaneekos/ee/o retail
 λιανική πώληση leeaneekee
 poleesee retail sale
λίγος/η/ο leeghos/ee/o a few ; a little
 λίγο ψημένο leegho pseemeno rare
 (meat)
λικέρ (το) leeker liqueur
λιμάνι (το) leemanee port ; harbour
Λιμενικό Σώμα (το) leemeneeko soma
 coastguard ; Port Police
λίμνη (η) leemnee lake
λίρα (η) leera pound
λίτρο (το) leetro litre
λογαριασμός (ο) loghareeasmos bill
λουκάνικο (το) lookaneeko sausage
λουκανικόπιτα (η) lookaneekopeeta
 sausage pie
λουκούμι (το) lookoomee Turkish
 delight
λουλούδι (το) looloodhee flower
λύσσα (η) leesa rabies

μ M

μαγαζί (το) maghazee shop
μαγειρεύω magheerevo to cook
μαγιό (το) ma-yo swimsuit
μαϊντανός (ο) maeendanos parsley

ΜΑΙΟΣ maeeos **MAY**

μακαρόνια (τα) makaroneea spaghetti,
 pasta
μάλιστα maleesta yes ; of course
μαλλί (το) malee wool
μαλλιά (τα) malya hair
μάλλινος/η/ο maleenos/ee/o woollen
μαμά (η) mama mum
μανιτάρια (τα) maneetareea
 mushrooms
μανταρίνι (το) mandareenee mandarin
 orange ; tangerine
μαντήλι (το) mandeelee handkerchief
μαξιλάρι (το) makseelaree
 pillow ; cushion
μαργαρίνη (η) marghareenee
 margarine
μαργαριτάρι (το) marghareetaree pearl
μάρμαρο (το) marmaro marble
μαρμελάδα (η) marmeladha jam
μαρούλι (το) maroolee lettuce

ΜΑΡΤΙΟΣ marteeos **MARCH**

μαύρος/η/ο mavros/ee/o black
μαχαίρι (το) makheree knife
μαχαιροπήρουνα (τα)
 makheropeeroona cutlery
με me with
μεγάλος/η/ο meghalos/ee/o large ; big
μέγαρο (το) megharo hall ; palace ;
 block of apartments
 μέγαρο μουσικής megharo
 mooseekees concert hall
μέγεθος (το) meghethos size
μεζές mezes (plural **μεζέδες** mezedhes)
 small snacks served free of charge with
 ouzo or retsina ; assortment of mini-
 portions of various dishes, available
 on the menu (or on request) at some
 restaurants.
μέλι (το) melee honey

μελιτζάνα (η) *meleetzana* aubergine ; eggplant

μέλος (το) *melos* member

μενού (το) *menoo* menu

μέρα (η) *mera* day

μερίδα (η) *mereedha* portion

μέσα *mesa* in ; inside

μεσάνυχτα (τα) *mesaneekhta* midnight

μεσημέρι (το) *meseemeree* midday

μεσημεριανό (το) *meseemereeano* midday meal

Μεσόγειος (η) *mesoyeeos* Mediterranean Sea

μέσω *meso* via

μετά *meta* after

μετάξι (το) *metaksee* silk

μεταξύ *metaksee* between ; among
εν τω μεταξύ *en to metaksee* meanwhile

μεταφράζω *metafrazo* to translate

μεταχειρισμένος/η/ο
metakheereesmenos/ee/o used ; second-hand

μετεωρολογικό δελτίο (το)
meteorologheeko dhelteeo weather forecast

μετρητά (τα) *metreeta* cash

μετρό (το) *metro* underground (railway)

μη... *mee* do not...
μη καπνίζετε *mee kapneezete* no smoking
μην κόπτετε άνθη *meen koptete anthee* do not pick flowers
μην πατάτε το πράσινο *meen patate to praseeno* keep off the grass
μη ρίπτετε σκουπίδια *mee reeptete skoopeedheea* no dumping (rubbish)
μη σταθμεύετε *me stathmevete* no parking

μηδέν *meedhen* zero

μήλο (το) *meelo* apple

μηλόπιτα (η) *meelopeeta* apple pie

μήνας (ο) *meenas* month
μήνας του μέλιτος *meenas too meleetos* honeymoon

μητέρα (η) *meetera* mother

μηχανάκι (το) *meekhanakee* moped ; motorbike

μηχανή (η) *meekhanee* machine ; engine

μηχάνημα (το) *meekhaneema* machine (general)

μηχανικός (ο) *meekhaneekos* mechanic ; engineer

μία *meea* a(n) ; one (with feminine nouns)

μικρός/ή/ό *meekros/ee/o* small

μιλάω/μιλώ *meelao/meelo* to speak

μόδα (η) *modha* fashion

μολύβι (το) *moleevee* pencil

μόλυνση (η) *moleensee* infection ; pollution

μοναστήρι (το) *monasteeree* monastery

μονόδρομος (ο) *monodhromos* one-way street

μονοπάτι (το) *monopatee* path

μόνος/η/ο *monos/ee/o* alone ; only
μόνο είσοδος/έξοδος *mono eesodhos/eksodhos* entrance/exit only

μοσχάρι (το) *moskharee* calf ; beef

μοτοσυκλέτα (η) *motoseekleta* motorcycle

ΜΟΥΣΕΙΟ *mooseeo* MUSEUM

Αρχαιολογικό Μουσείο
arkheologheeko mooseeo Archaeological Museum
Μουσείο Λαϊκής Τέχνης *mooseeo laeekees tekhnees* Folk Museum

μουσική (η) *mooseekee* music

μουστάρδα (η) *moostardha* mustard

μπακάλης (ο) *bakalees* grocer

μπαμπάς (ο) *babas* dad

μπανάνα (η) *banana* banana

μπάνιο (το) *banyo* bathroom ; bath

μπαρμπούνι (το) *barboonee* red mullet

μπαταρία (η) *batareea* battery

μπέικον (το) *beeekon* bacon

μπιζέλια (τα) *beezelya* peas

μπισκότο (το) *beeskoto* biscuit

μπλε *ble* blue

μπλούζα (η) *blooza* jumper, sweatshirt

μπογιά (η) *bo-ya* paint (for decorating houses)

νΝ ξΞ οΟ πΠ ρΡ σςΣ τΤ υΥ φΦ χΧ ψΨ ωΩ

μπουζούκι (το) boozookee bouzouki

μπουκάλι (το) bookalee bottle
μεγάλο μπουκάλι meghalo bookalee large bottle
μικρό μπουκάλι meekro bookalee half-bottle

μπουρνούζι (το) boornoozee bathrobe

μπριζόλα (η) breezola chop ; steak

μπύρα (η) beera beer

Μυκήνες meekeenes Mycenae

Μυκηναϊκός πολιτισμός (ο) meekeenaeekos poleeteesmos Mycenean civilization

μύτη (η) meetee nose

μωρό (το) moro baby
για μωρά ya mora for babies

μωσαϊκό (το) mosaeeko mosaic

ν N

ναι ne yes

ναός (ο) naos temple ; church

νάιλον (το) naeelon nylon

ναυλωμένος/η/ο navlomenos/ee/o chartered
ναυλωμένη πτήση navlomenee pteesee charter flight

ναυτία (η) nafteea travel sickness

ναυτικός όμιλος (ο) nafteekos omeelos sailing club

νεκροταφείο (το) nekrotafeeo cemetery

νεοελληνικά (τα) neoeleeneeka Modern Greek

νερό (το) nero water
μεταλλικό νερό metaleeko nero mineral water
πόσιμο νερό poseemo nero drinking water

νες, νεσκαφέ (το) nes, neskafe instant coffee

νεφρό (το) nefro kidney

νηπιαγωγείο (το) neepeeaghogheeo nursery school

νησί (το) neesee island

νησίδα (η) neeseedha traffic island

νίκη (η) neekee victory

ΝΟΕΜΒΡΙΟΣ noemvreeos
NOVEMBER

νοίκι (το) neekee rent

νομίζω nomeezo to think

νόμισμα (το) nomeesma coin ; currency

νοσοκομείο (το) nosokomeeo hospital

νοσοκόμος/α (ο/η) nosokomos/a nurse

νότιος/α/ο noteeos/a/o southern

νότος (ο) notos south

νούμερο (το) noomero number

ντομάτα (η) domata tomato

ντουζίνα (η) doozeena dozen

ντους (το) doos shower (in bath)

νυκτερινός/ή/ό neektereenos/ee/o all-night (chemists, etc)

νύχτα (η) neekhta night

ξ Ξ

ξεκουράζω ksekoorazo to have a rest ; to relax

ξεναγός (ο/η) ksenaghos guide

ξενοδοχείο (το) ksenodhokheeo hotel
κρατήσεις ξενοδοχείων krateesees ksenodhokheeon hotel reservations

ξένος/η/ο ksenos/ee/o foreign
ξένος/η (ο/η) ksenos/ee foreigner ; visitor

ξενώνας (ο) ksenonas guesthouse

ξέρω ksero to know

ξεχνώ ksekhno to forget

ξηρός/ή/ό kseeros/ee/o dry
ξηροί καρποί kseeree karpee dried fruit and nuts

ξιφίας (ο) kseefeeas swordfish

ξύδι (το) kseedhee vinegar

ξύλο (το) kseelo wood

ξυριστική μηχανή (η) kseereesteekee meekhanee safety razor

ο Ο

οδηγία (η) odheegheea instruction
οδηγίες χρήσεως odheeghees khreeseos instructions for use

οδηγός (ο) odheeghos driver ; guidebook

οδηγώ *odheegho* to drive
οδική βοήθεια (η) *odheekee voeetheea* breakdown service
οδοντιατρείο (το) *odhondeeatreeo* dental surgery
οδοντίατρος (ο/η) *odhondeeatros* dentist
οδοντόβουρτσα (η) *odhondovoortsa* toothbrush
οδοντόκρεμα (η) *odhondokrema* toothpaste
οδοντοστοιχία (η) *odhondosteekheea* denture(s)
οδός (η) *odhos* road ; street
οικογένεια (η) *eekoyenya* family
οικονομική θέση (η) *eekonomeekee thesee* economy class
οινοπνευματώδη ποτά (τα) *eenopnevmatodhee pota* spirits
οκτώ/οχτώ *okto/okhto* eight

ΟΚΤΩΒΡΙΟΣ *oktovreeos*
OCTOBER

ολισθηρόν οδόστρωμα (το) *oleestheeron odhostroma* slippery road surface
όλος/η/ο *olos/ee/o* all of
Ολυμπία (η) *oleempeea* Olympia
ολυμπιακός/ή/ό *oleempeeakos/ee/o* Olympic
  Ολυμπιακή Αεροπορία *oleempeeakee aeroporeea* Olympic Airways
  Ολυμπιακό Στάδιο *oleempeeako stadheeo* Olympic stadium
  Ολυμπιακοί Αγώνες *oleempeeakee aghones* Olympic games
Όλυμπος (ο) *oleempos* Mount Olympus
ομελέτα (η) *omeleta* omelette
όμιλος (ο) *omeelos* club
  ναυτικός όμιλος *nafteekos omeelos* sailing club
ομπρέλα (η) *ombrela* umbrella
όνομα (το) *onoma* name
ονοματεπώνυμο (το) *onomateponeemo* full name
όπερα (η) *opera* opera
οπτικός (ο) *opteekos* optician

οργανισμός (ο) *orghaneesmos* organization
  Οργανισμός Σιδηροδρόμων Ελλάδος (ΟΣΕ) *orghaneesmos seedheerodhromon eladhos (O.S.E.)* Greek Railways
οργανωμένος/η/ο *orghanomenos/ee/o* organized
  οργανωμένα ταξίδια *orghanomena takseedheea* organized tours
ορειβασία (η) *oreevaseea* mountaineering
ορεκτικό (το) *orekteeko* starter ; appetizer
όρεξη (η) *oreksee* appetite
  καλή όρεξη *kalee oreksee* enjoy your meal!
ορθόδοξος/η/ο *orthodhoksos/ee/o* orthodox
όρος (ο) *oros* condition
  όροι ενοικιάσεως *oree eneekeeaseos* conditions of hire
όροφος (ο) *orofos* floor ; storey
ΟΣΕ *ose* Greek Railways
ΟΤΕ *ote* Greek Telecom
ούζο (το) *oozo* ouzo
ουρά (η) *oora* tail ; queue
όχι *okhee* no

π Π

παγάκι (το) *paghakee* ice cube
παϊδάκι (το) *paeedhakee* lamb chop
πάγος (ο) *paghos* ice
παίρνω *perno* to take
παγωμένος/η/ο *paghomenos/ee/o* frozen
παγωτό (το) *paghoto* ice cream
παιδικός/ή/ό *pedheekos/ee/o* for children
  παιδικά *pedeeka* children's wear
  παιδικός σταθμός *pedheekos stathmos* crèche
πακέτο (το) *paketo* parcel ; packet
παλτό (το) *palto* coat
πάνα (η) *pana* nappy
Παναγία (η) *panagheea* the Virgin Mary
πανεπιστήμιο (το) *panepeesteemeeo* university

νΝ ξΞ οΟ πΠ ρΡ σςΣ τΤ υΥ φΦ χΧ ψΨ ωΩ

πανηγυρι (το) *panee-yeeree* festival

πανσιόν (η) *panseeon* guesthouse

πάντα/πάντοτε *panda/pandote* always

παντελόνι (το) *pandelonee* trousers

παντοπωλείο (το) *pandopoleeo* grocer's

παντρεμένος/η/ο *pantremenos/ee/o* married

παντρεύω *pantrevo* to marry

πάνω *pano* up ; on ; above

παπάς (ο) *papas* priest

πάπλωμα (το) *paploma* duvet

παππούς (ο) *papoos* grandfather

παπούτσι (το) *papootsee* shoe

παραγγελία (η) *parangheleea* order

παραγγέλνω *paranghelno* to order

παραγωγή (η) *paraghoghee* production
Ελληνικής παραγωγής *eleeneekees paraghoghees* produce of Greece

παράθυρο (το) *paratheero* window

παρακαλώ *parakalo* please

παρακαμπτήριος (ο) *parakampteereeos* by-pass

παραλία (η) *paraleea* seashore ; beach

παράξενος/η/ο *paraksenos/ee/o* strange

ΠΑΡΑΣΚΕΥΗ *paraskevee* FRIDAY

παράσταση (η) *parastasee* performance

παρέα (η) *parea* company ; group

Παρθενώνας (ο) *parthenonas* the Parthenon

πάρκο (το) *parko* park

παρμπρίζ (το) *parbreez* windscreen

πάστα (η) *pasta* pastry ; cake

παστέλι (το) *pastelee* honey and sesame seed bar

Πάσχα (το) *paskha* Easter

πατάτα (η) *patata* potato
πατάτες πουρέ *patates poore* creamed/mashed potatoes
πατάτες τηγανητές *patates teeghaneetes* chips
πατάτες φούρνου *patates foornoo* roast potatoes

πατέρας (ο) *pateras* father

παυσίπονο (το) *pafseepono* painkiller

πάω *pao* to go

πεζοδρόμιο (το) *pezodhromeeo* pavement

ΠΕΖΟΔΡΟΜΟΣ *pezodhromos* PEDESTRIAN AREA

πεζός (ο) *pezos* pedestrian

πεθαμένος/η/ο *pethamenos/ee/o* dead

Πειραιάς (ο) *peereeas* Piraeus

πελάτης/πελάτισσα (ο/η) *pelatees/pelateesa* customer

Πελοπόννησος (η) *peloponeesos* Peloponnese

ΠΕΜΠΤΗ *pemptee* THURSDAY

πεπόνι (το) *peponee* melon

περιοδικό (το) *pereeodheeko* magazine

περιοχή (η) *pereeokhee* area

περίπατος *n* (ο) *pereepatos* walk

περίπτερο (το) *pereeptero* kiosk

περιστέρι (το) *pereesteree* pigeon ; dove

πέτρα (η) *petra* stone

πετρέλαιο (το) *petreleo* diesel fuel

πέτρινος/η/ο *petreenos/ee/o* made of stone

πετσέτα (η) *petseta* towel

πεύκο (το) *pefko* pine tree

πηγαίνω *peegheno* to go

πιάτο (το) *pyato* plate ; dish

ΠΙΕΣΑΤΕ *pyesate* PUSH

πίεση (η) *peeyesee* pressure
πίεση αίματος *peeyesee ematos* blood pressure

πιλότος (ο) *peelotos* pilot

πινακίδα (η) *peenakeedha* sign ; number plate
πινακίδα κυκλοφορίας *peenakeedha keekloforeeas* number plate

πινακοθήκη (η) *peenakotheekee* art gallery ; collection of paintings

πίνω *peeno* to drink

πίπα (η) *peepa* pipe *(for smoking)*

πιπέρι (το) *peeperee* ground pepper
πιπεριά (η) *peeperya* pepper (vegetable)
πιπεριές γεμιστές *peeperyes yemeestes* stuffed peppers

πισίνα (η) *peeseena* swimming pool

πιστοποιητικό (το) *peestopyeeteeko* certificate

πιστωτική κάρτα (η) *peestoteekee karta* credit card

πίσω *peeso* behind ; back

πίτα (η) *peeta* pie, pitta bread

πιζάμα (η) *peezama* pyjamas

πίτσα (η) *peetsa* pizza

πιτσαρία (η) *peetsareea* pizzeria

πλαζ (η) *plaz* beach

πλάι *plaee* next to

πλατεία (η) *plateea* square

πλατίνες (οι) *plateenes* points (in car)

πλεκτά (τα) *plekta* knitwear

ΠΛΗΡΟΦΟΡΙΕΣ *pleeforeeyes* INFORMATION

πληροφορίες δρομολογίων *pleeroforeeyes dhromologheeon* travel information

πλήρωμα (το) *pleeroma* crew
τα μέλη του πληρώματος *ta melee too pleeromatos* crew members

πληρωμή (η) *pleeromee* payment
ευκολίες πληρωμής *efkoleeyes pleeromees* credit facilities
προς πληρωμή *pros pleeromee* insert money

πληρώνω *pleerono* to pay

πλοίο (το) *pleeo* ship

πλυντήριο (το) *pleenteereeo* washing machine
πλυντήριο αυτοκινήτων *pleenteereeo aftokeeneeton* car wash
πλυντήριο πιάτων *pleenteereeo pyaton* dish washer

ποδηλάτης (ο) *podheelatees* cyclist

ποδήλατο (το) *podheelato* bicycle
ποδήλατο της θάλασσας *podheelato tees thalasas* pedalo

πόδι (το) *podhee* foot ; leg

ποδόσφαιρο (το) *podhosfero* football

ποιος/ποια/ποιο *pyos/pya/pyo* who ; which

ποιότητα (η) *peeoteeta* quality

πόλη (η) *polee* town ; city

πολίτης (ο) *poleetees* citizen

πολιτική (η) *poleeteekee* politics

πολυκατάστημα (το) *poleekatasteema* department store

πολυκατοικία (η) *poleekateekeea* block of flats

πολύς/πολλή/πολύ *polees/polee/polee* much ; many

πονόδοντος (ο) *ponodhontos* toothache

πονοκέφαλος (ο) *ponokefalos* headache

πονόλαιμος (ο) *ponolemos* sore throat

πόνος (ο) *ponos* pain

πόρτα (η) *porta* door

πορτοκαλάδα (η) *portokaladha* orangeade

πορτοκάλι (το) *portokalee* orange
χυμός πορτοκαλιού *kheemos portokalyoo* orange juice

πορτοφόλι (το) *portofolee* wallet

πόσα; *posa* how many?

πόσο; *poso* how much?
πόσο κάνει; *poso kanee* how much is it?
πόσο κοστίζει; *poso kosteezee* how much does it cost?

ποσοστό (το) *pososto* rate ; percentage
ποσοστό υπηρεσίας *pososto eepeereseeas* service charge
συμπεριλαμβανομένου ποσοστού υπηρεσίας *seempereelamvanomenoo posostoo eepeereseeas* service included

ποσότητα (η) *posoteeta* quantity

ποτάμι (το) *potamee* river

πότε; *pote* when?

ποτέ *pote* never

ποτήρι (το) *poteeree* glass (for drinking)

ποτό (το) *poto* drink

πού; *poo* where?

πουκάμισο (το) *pookameeso* shirt

πούλμαν (το) *poolman* coach

πουλώ *poolo* to sell

πουρμπουάρ (το) *poorbwar* tip
(to waiter, etc)

πούρο (το) *pooro* cigar

πράκτορας (ο) *praktoras* agent

πρακτορείο (το) *praktoreeo* agency

πράσινος/η/ο *praseenos/ee/o* green

πρατήριο (το) *prateereeo* specialist
shop
πρατήριο βενζίνης *prateereeo
venzeenees* petrol station
πρατήριο άρτου *prateereeo artoo*
baker's

πρεσβεία (η) *presveea* embassy

πρίζα (η) *preeza* socket

πριν *preen* before

πρόγραμμα (το) *proghrama*
programme

πρόεδρος (ο) *proedhros* president
προεδρικό μέγαρο *proedhreeko
megharo* presidential palace

προειδοποίηση (η) *proeedhopee-
eesee* warning

προϊόν (το) *proeeon* product
Ελληνικό προϊόν *eleeneeko proeeon*
product of Greece

προκαταβολή (η) *prokatavolee*
deposit

προκρατήσεις (οι) *prokrateesees*
advance bookings

προορισμός (ο) *pro-oreesmos*
destination

προπληρώνω *propleerono* to pay
in advance

Προ-πο (το) *propo* Greek football pools

προσγείωση (η) *prosgheeosee* landing

προσδεθείτε *prosdhetheete* fasten
safety belts

πρόσκληση (η) *proskleesee* invitation

προσοχή (η) *prosokhee* attention

προτεστάντης (ο) *protestantees*
protestant

πρόστιμο (το) *prosteemo* fine

πρόχειρος/η/ο *prokheeros/ee/o*
impromptu ; rough
πρόχειρο φαγητό *prokheero
fa-yeeto* snack

πρωί *n* (το) *proee* morning

πρωινός/ή/ό adj *proeenos/ee/o*
morning

πρωινό (το) *proeeno* breakfast

πρωτεύουσα (η) *protevoosa* capital city

πρωτομαγιά (η) *protoma-ya*
May Day

πρώτος/η/ο *protos* first
πρώτες βοήθειες *protes voeethee-es*
first aid
πρώτη θέση *protee thesee* first class

πρωτοχρονιά (η) *protokhronya*
New Years Day

πτήση (η) *pteesee* flight
πτήσεις εξωτερικού *pteesees
eksotereekoo* international flights
πτήσεις εσωτερικού *pteesees
esotereekoo* domestic flights
αριθμός πτήσης *areethmos pteesees*
flight number
τακτικές πτήσεις *takteekes pteesees*
scheduled flights

πυροσβεστήρας (ο) *peerosvesteeras*
fire extinguisher

πυροσβέστης (ο) *peerosvestees*
fireman

πυροσβεστική (η) *peerosvesteekee*
fire brigade
πυροσβεστική υπηρεσία
peerosvesteekee eepereseea
fire brigade
πυροσβεστικός σταθμός
peerosvesteekos stathmos fire station

πώληση (η) *poleesee* sale
λιανική πώληση *leeaneekee
poleesee* retail sale
χονδρική πώληση *khondreekee
poleesee* wholesale

πωλητής/ήτρια(ο/η) *poleetees/
eetreea* sales assistant

ΠΩΛΕΙΤΑΙ *poleete* FOR SALE

πώς; *pos* how?

ρ P

ρεζέρβα (η) *rezerva* spare wheel

ρεσεψιόν (η) *resepsyon* reception
(desk)

ρέστα (τα) *resta* change (money)

ρετσίνα (η) *retseena* retsina

ρεύμα (το) *revma* current ; electricity
ρόδα (η) *rodha* wheel
ροδάκινο (το) *rodhakeeno* peach
ρόδι (το) *rodhee* pomegranate
Ρόδος (η) *rodhos* Rhodes (island)
ρολόι (το) *roloee* watch ; clock
ρούμι (το) *roomee* rum
ρούχα (τα) *rookha* clothes
ρύζι (το) *reezee* rice
ρυμουλκώ *reemoolko* to tow

σς Σ

ΣΑΒΒΑΤΟ *savato* **SATURDAY**

Σαββατοκύριακο (το) *savatokeereeako* weekend
σακάκι (το) *sakakee* jacket (menswear)
σαλάμι (το) *salamee* salami
σαλάτα (η) *salata* salad
σαλιγκάρι (το) *saleengkaree* snail
σάλτσα (η) *saltsa* sauce
σαμπάνια (η) *sambanya* champagne
σαμπουάν (το) *sambooan* shampoo
σάντουιτς (το) *sandweets* sandwich
σαπούνι (το) *sapoonee* soap
σβήνω *sveeno* to extinguish ; to rub out
  σβήσατε τα τσιγάρα σας *sveesate ta tseeghara sas* extinguish cigarettes

ΣΕΠΤΕΜΒΡΙΟΣ *septemvreeos* **SEPTEMBER**

σέρβις (το) *servees* service (of car etc)
σεφ (ο) *sef* chef
σήμα (το) *seema* sign ; signal
  σήμα κατατεθέν *seema katatethen* trademark
  σήμα κινδύνου *seema keendheenoo* emergency signal
σήμερα *seemera* today
σιγά *seegha* slowly
σιδηρόδρομος (ο) *seedheerodhromos* railway
  σιδηροδρομικός σταθμός *seedheerodhromeekos stathmos* railway station

σιδηροδρομικώς *seedheerodhromeekos* by rail
σινεμά (το) *seenema* cinema
σκάλα (η) *skala* ladder ; staircase
σκαλοπάτι (το) *skalopatee* step
σκέτος/η/ο *sketos* plain
  καφές σκέτος *kafes sketos* black coffee
σκηνή (η) *skeenee* tent ; stage
σκι (το) *skee* ski
  θαλάσσιο σκι *thalaseeo skee* water-skiing
σκοινί (το) *skeenee* rope
σκορδαλιά (η) *skordhalya* garlic and potato mash
σκόρδο (ο) *skordho* garlic
σκουπίδια (τα) *skoopeedheea* rubbish ; refuse
σκυλί (το) *skeelee* dog
Σκωτία (η) *skoteea* Scotland
σκωτσέζικος/η/ο *skotsezeekos/ee/o* Scottish (thing)
Σκωτσέζος/Σκωτσέζα (ο/η) *skotsezos/skotseza* Scotsman/Scotswoman
σόδα (η) *sodha* soda
σοκολάτα (η) *sokolata* chocolate
σολομός (ο) *solomos* salmon
σόμπα (η) *soba* stove ; heater
σούβλα (η) *soovla* skewer
σουβλάκι (το) *soovlakee* meat cooked on skewer
σούπα (η) *soopa* soup
σπανάκι (το) *spanakee* spinach
σπανακόπιτα (η) *spanakopeeta* spinach pie
σπαράγγι (το) *sparang-ee* asparagus
σπεσιαλιτέ της κουζίνας *speseealeete tees koozeenas* today's special dish
σπίρτο (το) *speerto* match
σπίτι (το) *speetee* house ; home
σπιτικός/ή/ο *speeteekos/ee/o* homemade
σπορ (τα) *spor* sports
Σποράδες (οι) *sporadhes* the Sporades
στάδιο (το) *stadheeo* stadium ; stage

σταθμεύω stathmevo to park
απαγορεύεται η στάθμευση
apaghorevete ee stathmevsee no parking
μη σταθμεύετε mee stathmevete
no parking
χώρος σταθμεύσεως khoros
stathmevseos parking area

σταθμός (ο) stathmos station
πυροσβεστικός σταθμός
peerosvesteekos stathmos fire station
σιδηροδρομικός σταθμός
seedheerodhromeekos stathmos
railway station
σταθμός υπεραστικών λεωφορείων
stathmos eeperasteekon leoforeeon
bus station (intercity)

σταμάτα! stamata stop!

στάση n **(η)** stasee stop
στάση εργασίας stasee erghaseeas
strike
στάση ΗΛΠΑΠ stasee eelpap
trolley bus stop
στάση λεωφορείου stasee leoforeeoo
bus stop

σταυροδρόμι (το) stavrodhromee
crossroads

σταφίδα (η) stafeedha raisin

σταφύλι (το) stafeelee grape

στεγνοκαθαριστήριο (το)
steghnokathareesteereeo dry-cleaner's

στιγμή (η) steeghmee moment

στοά (η) stoa arcade

στροφή (η) strofee turn ; bend

στρώμα (το) stroma mattress

στυλό (το) steelo pen

συγγνώμη seeghnomee sorry ;
excuse me

συγχαρητήρια seenkhareeteereea
congratulations

συγχωρώ seenkhoro to excuse
με συγχωρείτε me seenkhoreete
excuse me

σύζυγος (ο/η) seezeeghos husband/wife

σύκο (το) seeko fig

συκώτι (το) seekotee liver

συλλυπητήρια (τα) seeleepeeteereea
condolences

συμπεριλαμβάνω seempereelamvano
to include

συμπλέκτης (ο) seemplektees clutch
(of car)

συμπληρώνω seempleerono to fill in

σύμπτωμα (το) seemptoma symptom

συμφωνία (η) seemfoneea agreement

συμφωνώ seemfono to agree

συνάλλαγμα (το) seenalaghma foreign
exchange
δήλωση συναλλάγματος dheelosee
seenalaghmatos currency declaration
η τιμή του συναλλάγματος
ee teemee too seenalaghmatos
exchange rate

συνάντηση (η) seenandeesee meeting

συναντώ seenando to meet

συναυλία (η) seenavleea concert

συνεργείο (το) seenergheeo workshop ;
garage for car repairs
συνεργείο αυτοκινήτων
seenergheeo aftokeeneeton
car repairs

σύνολο (το) seenolo total

σύνορα (τα) seenora border ; frontier

συνταγή (η) seendaghee prescription ;
recipe

ΣΥΡΑΤΕ seerate PULL

σύστημα κλιματισμού (το) seesteema
kleemateesmoo air conditioning

συστημένη επιστολή (η)
seesteemenee epeestolee recorded
delivery

συχνά seekhna often

σφράγισμα (το) sfragheesma filling
(in tooth)

σχολείο (το) skholeeo school (primary)

σχολή (η) skholee school
σχολή οδηγών skholee odheeghon
driving school
σχολή σκι skholee skee ski school

σώζω sozo to save ; to rescue

σώμα (το) soma body

σωσίβιο (το) soseeveeo life jacket

τ T

ταβέρνα (η) taverna tavern with
traditional food and wine

ταινία (η) teneea film ; strip ; tape

ΤΑΜΕΙΟ *tameeo* **CASH DESK**

ταμίας (ο/η) *tameeas* cashier

ταμιευτήριο (το) *tamee-efteereeo*
savings bank

ταξί (το) *taksee* taxi
αγοραίο ταξί *aghoreo taksee* minicab
(no meter)
γραφείο ταξί *ghrafeeo taksee* taxi office
ράδιο ταξί *radheeo taksee* radio taxi

ταξίδι (το) *takseedhee* journey ; tour
καλό ταξίδι *kalo takseedhee* have
a good trip
ταξιδιωτικό γραφείο
takseedheeoteeko ghrafeeo travel agent
οργανωμένα ταξίδια *orghanomena*
takseedeea organized tours

ταραμοσαλάτα (η) *taramosalata*
taramosalata

ταυτότητα (η) *taftoteeta* identity ;
identity card

ταχεία (η) *takheea* express train

ταχυδρομείο (το) *takheedhromeeo*
post office
Ελληνικά Ταχυδρομεία (ΕΛΤΑ)
eleeneeka takheedhromeea Greek
Post Office

ταχυδρομικά τέλη *takheedhromeeka*
telee postage
ταχυδρομικές επιταγές
takheedhromeekes epeetaghes postal
orders
ταχυδρομικός κώδικας
takheedhromeekos kodheekas postcode
ταχυδρομικώς *takheedhromeekos*
by post

ταχύμετρο (το) *takheemetro*
speedometer

ταχύτητα/ταχύτης (η)
takheeteeta/takheetees speed
κιβώτιο ταχύτητων *keevoteeo*
takheeteeton gearbox

τελευταίος/α/ο *telefteos* last

τέλος (το) *telos* end ; tax ; duty
οδικά τέλη *odheeka telee* road tax
τέλος πάντων *telos pandon*
well ; anyway *(to start sentence)*

τελωνείο (το) *teloneeo* customs

τένις (το) *tenees* tennis

τέντα (η) *tenda* awning

τέρμα (το) *terma* terminus ; end of route

ΤΕΤΑΡΤΗ *tetartee* **WEDNESDAY**

τέχνη (η) *tekhnee* art
λαϊκή τέχνη *laeekee tekhnee* folk art

τζαμί (το) *dzamee* mosque

τζάμι (το) *dzamee* glass *(of window)*

τζατζίκι (το) *tzatzeekee* tsatsiki
(yoghurt, cucumber and garlic)

τηγανίτα (η) *teeghaneeta* pancake

τηλεκάρτα (η) *teelekarta* phonecard

τηλεόραση (η) *teeleorasee* television

τηλεπικοινωνίες (οι)
teelepeekeenonee-yes
telecommunications

τηλεφώνημα (το) *teelefoneema*
telephone call

ΤΗΛΕΦΩΝΟ *teelefono*
TELEPHONE

τηλεφωνικός θάλαμος *teelefoneekos*
thalamos phone box
τηλεφωνικός κατάλογος
teelefoneekos kataloghos telephone
directory
τηλεφωνικός κωδικός *teelefoneekos*
kodheekos dialling code ; area code

τι; *tee* what?
τι είναι; *tee eenee* what is it?

τιμή (η) *teemee* price ; honour
τιμή εισιτηρίου *teemee*
eeseeteereeoo price of ticket ; fare

τιμοκατάλογος (ο) *teemokataloghos*
price list

τιμολόγιο (το) *teemologheeo* invoice

τιμόνι (το) *teemonee* steering wheel

τιμωρώ *teemoro* to punish

τίποτα *teepota* nothing
έχετε τίποτα να δηλώσετε
ekhete teepota na dheelosete
have you anything to declare

τμήμα (το) *tmeema* department ;
police station

το *to* it ; the *(with neuter nouns)*

τοιχοκόλληση (η) *teekhokoleesee*
bill posting

τόκος (ο) *tokos* interest *(bank)*

τόνος (ο) *tonos* ton ; tuna fish

τοστ (το) *tost* toasted sandwich

νΝ ξΞ οΟ πΠ ρΡ σςΣ τΤ υΥ φΦ χΧ ψΨ ωΩ

ΤΟΥΑΛΕΤΕΣ *tooaletes* TOILETS

τουρισμός (ο) *tooreesmos* tourism

τουρίστας/στρια (ο/η)
tooreestas/streea tourist

τουριστικός/ή/ό *tooreesteekos/ee/o*
tourist
τουριστικά είδη *tooreesteeka eedhee*
souvenirs
τουριστική αστυνομία *tooreesteekee*
asteenomeea Tourist Police

Τουρκία (η) *toorkeea* Turkey

τραγούδι (το) *traghoodhee* song

τραγωδία (η) *traghodheea* tragedy

τράπεζα (η) *trapeza* bank

τραπεζαρία (η) *trapezareea* dining
room

τραπέζι (το) *trapezee* table

τρένο (το) *treno* train

ΤΡΙΤΗ *treetee* TUESDAY

τρόλεϋ (το) *troley* trolley bus

τροχαία (η) *trokhea* traffic police

τροχόσπιτο (το) *trokhospeeto* caravan ;
mobile home

τρώγω/τρώω *trogho/troo* to eat

τσάι (το) *tsaee* tea

τσάντα (η) *tsanda* bag

τσάρτερ (το) *tsarter* charter flight

τσιγάρο (το) *tseegharo* cigarette

τυρί (το) *teeree* cheese

τυρόπιτα (η) *teeropeeta* cheese pie

τυφλός/ή/ό *teeflos/ee/o* blind

τώρα *tora* now

υ Υ

υγεία (η) *eegheea* health
στην υγειά σας *steen eeyeea sas*
your health ; cheers

υγειονομικός έλεγχος (ο)
eegheeonomeekos elenkhos health
inspection

Ύδρα (η) *eedhra* Hydra (island)

Υμηττός (ο) *eemeetos* Mount
Hymettos

υπεραγορά (η) *eeperaghora*
supermarket

υπεραστικό λεωφορείο (το)
eeperasteeko leoforeeo long-distance
coach

υπερωκεάνιο (το) *eeperokeaneeo* liner

υπηρεσία (η) *eepeereseea* service
ποσοστό υπηρεσίας *pososto*
eepeereseeas service charge

υπηρέτης (ο) *eepeeretees* servant

υπηρέτρια (η) *eepeeretreea* maid

υπόγειος/α/ο *eepoyeeos/a/o*
underground
υπόγεια διάβαση πεζών *eepoyeea*
dheeavasee pezon pedestrian subway
υπόγειος σιδηρόδρομος *eepoyeeos*
seedheerodhromos underground
(railway)

υπολογιστής (ο) *eepologheestees*
computer

υπουργείο (το) *eepoorgheeo* ministry

υψηλός/ή/ό *eepseelos/ee/o* high
υψηλή τάση *eepseelee tasee* high
voltage

ύφασμα (το) *eefasma* fabric ; cloth
υφάσματα *eefasmata* textiles
υφάσματα επιπλώσεων *eefasmata*
epeeploseon upholstery fabrics

ύψος (το) *eepsos* height
ύψος περιορισμένο *eepsos*
pereeoreesmeno height limit

φ Φ

φαγητό (το) *fa-yeeto* food ; meal

φαΐ (το) *fay-ee* food

φακός (ο) *fakos* lens ; torch
φακοί επαφής *fakee epafees*
contact lenses

φακές (οι) *fakes* lentils

φανάρι (το) *fanaree* traffic light ;
lantern

φαξ (το) *faks* fax

φαρμακείο (το) *farmakeeo* chemist's

φάρμακο (το) *farmako* medicine

φάρος (ο) *faros* lighthouse

φασολάκι (το) *fasolakee* green bean

φασόλι (το) *fasolee* haricot bean

φάω *fao* to eat

ΦΕΒΡΟΥΑΡΙΟΣ *fevrooareeos*
FEBRUARY

φεριμπότ (το) *fereebot* ferry boat

φεστιβάλ (το) *festeeval* festival

φέτα (η) *feta* feta cheese ; slice

φιλενάδα (η) *feelenadha* girlfriend

φιλέτο (το) *feeleto* fillet of meat

φιλμ (το) *feelm* film
  εμφανίσεις φιλμ *emfaneesees feelm*
  film developing

φίλος/η (ο/η) *feelos/ee* friend

φίλτρο (το) *feeltro* filter
  φίλτρο αέρος *feeltro aeros* air filter
  φίλτρο λαδιού *feeltro ladheeoo*
  oil filter
  καφές φίλτρου *kafes feeltroo* filter
  coffee

φις (το) *fees* plug (electric)

φλας (το) *flas* flash (camera) ; indicators
  (on car)

φοιτητής/φοιτήτρια (ο/η)
  feeteetees/feeteetreea student

φοιτητικό εισιτήριο (το) *feeteeteeko*
  eeseeteereeo student fare

φόρεμα (το) *forema* dress

φόρος (ο) *foros* tax

φουντούκι (το) *foondookee* hazelnut

φούρνος (ο) *foornos* oven ; bakery

φουσκωτά σκάφη (τα) *fooskota skafee*
  inflatable boats

ΦΠΑ (ο) *feepeea* VAT

φράουλα (η) *fraoola* strawberry

φρένο (το) *freno* brake (in car)

φρέσκος/ια/ο *freskos/eea/o* fresh

φρούτο (το) *frooto* fruit

φρουτοσαλάτα (η) *frootosalata* fruit
  salad

φύλακας (ο) *feelakas* guard

φύλαξη αποσκευών (η) *feelaksee*
  aposkevon left-luggage office

φυστίκι (το) *feesteekee* peanut
  φυστίκια Αιγίνης *feesteekeea*
  e-yeenees pistachio nuts

φυτό (το) *feeto* plant

φως (το) *fos* light

φωτιά (η) *fotya* fire

φωτογραφία (η) *fotoghrafeea*
  photograph
  έγχρωμες φωτογραφίες *enkhromes*
  fotoghrafeees colour photographs

φωτογραφίζω *fotoghrafeezo*
  to take photographs
  μη φωτογραφίζετε *me*
  fotoghrafeezete no photographs

φωτογραφική μηχανή (η)
  fotoghrafeekee meekhanee camera

φωτοτυπία (η) *fototeepeea* photocopy

χ Χ

χαίρετε *kherete* hello (polite)

χάπι (το) *khapee* pill

χάρτης (ο) *khartees* map
  οδικός χάρτης *odheekos khartees*
  road map

χαρτί (το) *khartee* paper
  χαρτί κουζίνας *khartee koozeenas*
  kitchen paper

χαρτικά (τα) *kharteeka* stationery

χαρτομάντηλο (το) *khartomandeelo*
  tissue

χαρτονόμισμα (το) *khartonomeesma*
  banknote

χαρτοπωλείο (το) *khartopoleeo*
  stationer's shop

χειροποίητος/η/ο *kheeropee-*
  eetos/ee/o handmade

χειροτεχνία (η) *kheerotekhneea*
  handicraft

χειρούργος (ο) *kheeroorghos* surgeon

χειρόφρενο (το) *kheerofreno*
  handbrake

χέρι (το) *kheree* hand ; arm

χιλιόμετρο (το) *kheeleeometro*
  kilometre

χιόνι (το) *kheeonee* snow

χοιρινό (το) *kheereeno* pork

χορός (ο) *khoros* dance

χορτοφάγος (ο/η) *khortofaghos*
  vegetarian

χορωδία (η) *khorodheea* choir

χουρμάς (ο) *khoormas* date (fruit)

χρειάζομαι *khreeazome* to need

χρήματα (τα) *khreemata* money

χρηματοκιβώτιο (το)
  khreematokeevoteeo safe (for valuables)

χρήση (η) khreesee use
  οδηγίες χρήσεως odheegheees
  khreeseos instructions for use

χρήσιμος/η/ο khreeseemos/ee/o useful

χρησιμοποιώ khreeseemopyo to use

χριστιανός/ή khreesteeanos/ee
  Christian

Χριστούγεννα (τα) khreestooyena
  Christmas
  Καλά Χριστούγεννα kala
  khreestooyena Merry Christmas

χρόνος (ο) khronos time ; year

χρυσός/ή/ό khreesos/ee/o
  (made of) gold
  Χρυσός Οδηγός khreesos odheeghos
  Yellow Pages

χρώμα (το) khroma colour ; paint

χταπόδι (το) khtapodhee octopus

χτένα (η) khtena comb

χτες khtes yesterday

χυμός (ο) kheemos juice
  χυμός λεμονιού kheemos lemoneeoo
  lemon juice
  χυμός πορτοκαλιού kheemos
  portokaleeoo orange juice

χώρα (η) khora country

χωράφια (τα) khorafeea fields

χωριάτικο ψωμί (το) khoreeateeko
  psomee bread (round, flat loaf)

χωριό (το) khoreeo village

χωρίς khorees without

χώρος (ο) khoros area ; site
  αρχαιολογικός χώρος
  arkheologheekos khoros archaeological
  site
  ιδιωτικός χώρος eedheeoteekos
  khoros private land
  χώρος σταθμεύσεως khoros
  stathmefseos parking area

ψ Ψ

ψάρεμα (το) psarema fishing

ψαρεύω psarevo to fish

ψάρι (το) psaree fish

ψαρόβαρκα (η) psarovarka fishing
  boat

ψαροταβέρνα (η) psarotaverna
  fish tavern

ψημένος/η/ο pseemenos/ee/o roasted ;
  grilled

ψητός/ή/ό pseetos/ee/o roasted ;
  grilled

ψυγείο (το) pseegheeo fridge ;
  radiator (of car)

ψύχω pseekho to cool

ψωμάς (ο) psomas baker

ψωμί (το) psomee bread

ω Ω

ΩΘΗΣΑΤΕ otheesate PUSH

ωτοστόπ (το) otostop hitchhiking

ώρα (η) ora time ; hour
  ώρες επισκέψεως ores epeeskepseos
  visiting hours
  ώρες λειτουργίας ores leetoorgheeas
  opening hours
  ώρες συναλλαγής ores seenalaghees
  banking hours
  της ώρας tees oras freshly cooked
  (food)

ωραίος/α/ο oreos/a/o beautiful ; nice

ωράριο (το) orareeo timetable

ως os as ; while

ωστόσο ostoso however

How Greek Works

The following basic rules of Greek grammar will help you make full use of the information in this book.

Greek grammar is rather complicated by the fact that pronouns, nouns and adjectives change their ending according to their function in the sentence, according to whether they are singular or plural, or whether they are masculine, feminine or neuter (rather like German). We give a basic outline of the grammar, but for a more full explanation you should consult a Greek grammar book.

Greek Alphabet

Greek is spelt exactly as it sounds. The only difficulty may occur with letters which have the same sound, e.g. υ, η, ι or ει or even οι and with double consonants.

The names of the 24 letters of the Greek alphabet are given below:

			SOUND
α, Α	άλφα	alfa	ah
β, Β	βήτα	veeta	vee
γ, Γ	γάμα	ghama	gh
δ, Δ	δέλτα	dhelta	dh
ε, Ε	έψειλον	epseelon	eh
ζ, Ζ	ζήτα	zeeta	z
η, Η	ήτα	eeta	ee
θ, Θ	θήτα	theeta	th
ι, Ι	γιώτα	yota	ee
κ, Κ	κάπα	kapa	k
λ, Λ	λάμδα	lamdha	l
μ, Μ	μι	mee	m
ν, Ν	νι	nee	n
ξ, Ξ	ξι	ksee	ks
ο, Ο	όμικρον	omeekron	oh
π, Π	πι	pee	p
ρ, Ρ	ρο	ro	r
σ, ς, Σ	σίγμα	seeghma	s
τ, Τ	ταυ	taf	t
υ, Υ	ύψιλον	eepseelon	ee
φ, Φ	φι	fee	f
χ, Χ	χι	khee	kh
ψ, Ψ	ψι	psee	ps
ω, Ω	ωμέγα	omegha	oh

Nouns

> A **noun** is a word such as **car**, **horse** or **Mary** which is used to refer to a person or thing.

Greek nouns can be *masculine*, *feminine* or *neuter* and the words for **the** and **a** (the articles) change according to the gender of the noun.

ο *(o)*	= **the** with *masculine* nouns
η *(ee)*	= **the** with *feminine* nouns
το *(to)*	= **the** with *neuter* nouns
ένας *(enas)*	= **a** with *masculine* nouns
μία *(meea)*	= **a** with *feminine* nouns
ένα *(ena)*	= **a** with *neuter* nouns

The article is the most reliable indication of the gender of a noun, i.e. whether it is *masculine*, *feminine* or *neuter*.

In the dictionary sections you will come across examples like this: **ο/η γιατρός** *(yatros)* **doctor**. This means that the same ending is used for men as well as women doctors i.e. **ο γιατρός** is a male doctor, **η γιατρός** is a female doctor.

You will also encounter entries like **ο Άγγλος/η Αγγλίδα** indicating that an **Englishman** is referred to as **ο Άγγλος** *(anglos)* while an **Englishwoman** is **η Αγγλίδα** *(angleedha)*.

Masculine endings of nouns

The most common endings of *masculine* nouns are **-ος** *(os)*, **-ας** *(as)*, **-ης** *(ees)*, e.g.

ο καιρός *(keros)*	**weather**
ο πατέρας *(pateras)*	**father**
ο κυβερνήτης *(keeverneetees)*	**captain** *(of aeroplane)*

Feminine endings of nouns

The most common endings of *feminine* nouns are **-α** *(a)*, **-η** *(ee)*, e.g.

η μητέρα *(meetera)*	**mother**
η Κρήτη *(kreetee)*	**Crete**

Neuter endings of nouns

The most common *neuter* endings are: **-ο** *(o)*, **-ι** *(ee)*, e.g.

το κτίριο *(kteereeo)*	**building**
το πορτοκάλι *(portokalee)*	**orange** *(fruit)*

Plurals

The article **the** changes in the plural. For *masculine* (**ο**) and *feminine* (**η**) nouns it becomes **οι** *(ee)*. For *neuter* nouns (**το**) it becomes **τα** *(ta)*.

Nouns have different endings in the plural.

Masculine nouns change their endings to **-οι** *(ee)*, e.g.

ο βράχος *(vrakhos)*   οι βράχοι *(vrakhee)*

Feminine nouns change their endings to **-ες** *(es)*, e.g.

η κυρία *(kereea)*   οι κυρίες *(keree-es)*

Neuter nouns change their endings to **-α** *(a)*, e.g.

το κτίριο *(kteereeo)*   τα κτίρια *(kteereea)*

There are many exceptions to the above rules such as:

ο άντρας *(andhras)*   οι άντρες *(andhres)*

Adjectives

> An **adjective** is a word such as **small**, **pretty** or **practical** that describes a person or thing, or gives extra information about them.

Adjective endings must agree with the gender and number of the noun they describe, e.g.

ο καλός πατέρας *(kalos pateras)*	the good father
η καλή κυρία *(kalee kereea)*	the good lady
οι καλοί πατέρες *(kalee pateres)*	the good fathers
οι καλές κυρίες *(kales kereees)*	the good ladies

You will see that in the Greek-English dictionary section of this book, all adjectives are given with their endings clearly marked e.g.

κρύος/α/ο *(kree-os/a/o)*   **cold**

By far the most common adjectival ending are **-ος** *(os)* for *masculine*, **-α** *(a)* for *feminine* and **-ο** *(o)* for *neuter* nouns.

In Greek, adjectives go before the noun they describe.

Possessive Adjectives

In Greek the possessive adjective: my, your, his, etc. follow the noun. And they don't change even if the noun is *masculine, feminine, singular* or *plural*. The article will still go in front of the noun.

my	μου	*moo*
your	σου	*soo*
his	του	*too*
her	της	*tees*
its	του	*too*
our	μας	*mas*
your *(plural)*	σας	*sas**
their	τους	*toos*

*This is also the polite form

my key	το κλειδί μου	*to kleethee moo*
your room	το δωμάτιο σας	*to dhomateeo sas*

Verbs

> A **verb** is a word such as **sing**, **walk** or **cry** which is used with a subject to say what someone or something does or what happens to them. **Regular verbs** follow the same pattern or endings. **Irregular verbs** do not follow a regular pattern so you need to learn their different endings.

The most essential verbs in Greek are the verbs είμαι I am and έχω I have. Unlike verbs in English, Greek verbs have a different ending for each person and number.

to be

είμαι	I am	*eeme*
είσαι	you are	*eese*
είναι	he/she/it is	*eene*
είμαστε	we are	*eemaste*
είστε	you are	*eeste**
είστε	they are	*eene*

* This form is also used when addressing people we do not know very well; it is generally referred to as the polite plural (like the French 'vous').

NOTE: While in English it is necessary to use the personal pronoun i.e. **we**, **you** etc, in order to distinguish between **we are**, **you are** etc, in Greek this function is carried out by the different endings of the verb itself. This way in Greek, **we are** and **they are** can be simply είμαστε (*eemaste*), είναι (*eene*).

to have

έχω	I have	*ekho*
έχεις	you have	*ekhees*
έχει	he/she/it has	*ekhee*
έχουμε	we have	*ekhoome*
έχετε	you have	*ekhete*
έχουν	they have	*ekhoon*

NOTE: As above, **I have** can be expressed in Greek with simply the verb έχω; each ending is particular to a specific person.

Verbs in Greek in the active voice, end in **-ω** (*o*) or **-ώ** (*o*). This is the ending with which they generally appear in dictionaries. Please note that in everyday speech a more usual ending for **-ώ** (*o*) is **-άω** (*ao*). If a verb does not have an active voice form, in a dictionary it will appear with the ending **-μαι** (*-me*), e.g. λυπάμαι (*leepame*) **to be sad** or **sorry**, θυμάμαι (*theemame*) **to remember**.

The verb αγαπώ *aghapo* **to love** has typical endings for verbs ending in
-ώ (-*o*) while those ending in -ω (-*o*) follow the pattern of έχω (*ekho*) above.

αγαπώ/άω (*aghapo/ao*)	**I love**
αγαπάς (*aghapas*)	**you love**
αγαπά (*aghapa*)	**he/she/it loves**
αγαπούμε (*aghapoome*)	**we love**
αγαπάτε (*aghapate*)	**you love**
αγαπούν (*aghapoon*)	**they love**

In Greek, there are two ways of addressing people, depending on their
age, social or professional position, and how formal or informal the
relationship is between two people. e.g. an older person will probably
speak to a much younger one using the singular (informal way) but the
younger person will use the plural (formal) unless well acquainted.
Similarly two friends will speak to each other using the informal singular:

Τι κάνεις; (*tee kanees*)	**How are you?**
Καλά, εσύ; (*kala esee*)	**Fine, and you?**

While two acquaintances will address each other in a more formal way
using the second person plural, like this:

Τι κάνετε; (*tee kanete*)	**How are you?**
Καλά, εσείς; (*kala esees*)	**Fine, and you?**

Personal Pronouns

> A **pronoun** is a word that you use to refer to someone or something
> when you do not need to use a noun, often because the person or
> thing has been mentioned earlier. Examp/es are **it**, **she**, **something**
> and **him**.

There are times when the pronoun needs to be used as e.g. in conjunction
with the verb in order to establish the sex of the person involved, i.e. **he**
or **she**, or indeed **it**.

εγώ	**I**	*egho*
εσύ	**you**	*esee*
αυτός	**he**	*aftos*
αυτή	**she**	*aftee*
αυτό	**it**	*afto*
εμείς	**we**	*emees*
εσείς	**you**	*esees*
αυτοί	**they** (masc.)	*aftee*
αυτές	**they** (fem.)	*aftes*
αυτά	**they** (neut.)	*afta*

Thus: αυτός έχει (*aftos ekhee*)   **he has**
        αυτή έχει (*aftee ekhee*)   **she has**

Negative

To make a sentence negative, you put δεν (dhen) immediately before the verb, e.g.

I don't know	δεν ξέρω *dhen ksero*
I have no...	δεν έχω... *dhen ekho*

Future

The future tense is made by adding **θα** *tha* immediately before the verb, e.g.

θα πάο *tha pao*	**I shall go**
θα δεν πάο *tha pao*	**I shall not go**